ALSO BY THE AUTHOR

*The New American Economy: The Failure of
Reaganomics and a New Way Forward*

*Impostor: How George W. Bush Bankrupted
America and Betrayed the Reagan Legacy*

Wrong on Race: The Democratic Party's Buried Past

The Benefit
and
the Burden

Tax Reform—
Why We Need It and
What It Will Take

BRUCE BARTLETT

SIMON & SCHUSTER PAPERBACKS

NEW YORK   LONDON   TORONTO   SYDNEY   NEW DELHI

Simon & Schuster Paperbacks
A Division of Simon & Schuster, Inc.
1230 Avenue of the Americas
New York, NY 10020

First Simon & Schuster trade paperback edition January 2013

SIMON & SCHUSTER PAPERBACKS and colophon are registered trademarks of Simon & Schuster, Inc.

For information about special discounts for bulk purchases, please contact Simon & Schuster Special Sales at 1-866-506-1949 or business@simonandschuster.com.

The Simon & Schuster Speakers Bureau can bring authors to your live event. For more information or to book an event contact the Simon & Schuster Speakers Bureau at 1-866-248-3049 or visit our website at www.simonspeakers.com.

Designed by Level C

Manufactured in the United States of America

10 9 8 7 6 5 4 3 2 1

The Library of Congress has cataloged the hardcover edition as follows:

Bartlett, Bruce R., 1951-
   The benefit and the burden : tax reform—why we need it and what it will take / Bruce Bartlett.
       p. cm.
   Includes bibliographical references and index.
   1. Taxation—United States. 2. Income tax—United States. 3. Fiscal policy—United States. I. Title.
HJ2381.B375 2012
336.2'050973—dc23   2011048585

ISBN 978-1-4516-4619-1
ISBN 978-1-4516-4625-2 (pbk)
ISBN 978-1-4516-4626-9 (ebook)

For my brother and sister

Systems of taxation are not framed, nor is it possible to frame them, with perfect distribution of benefit and burden. Their authors must be satisfied with a rough and ready form of justice.

Supreme Court Justice Benjamin Cardozo
Louis K. Liggett v. Lee
288 U.S. 517 (1933)

Contents

Introduction   ix

PART I: THE BASICS

1. A Brief History of Federal Income Taxation   3
2. How a Tax Bill Is Made   13
3. The Definition of Income   21
4. How to Understand Tax Rates   31
5. The Relationship Between Tax Rates and Tax Revenues   39
6. How Taxes Affect Economic Growth   49
7. The Question of Progressivity   59
8. Taxes and the Business Cycle   67
9. How Other Countries Tax Themselves   75

PART II: SOME PROBLEMS

10. Spending Through the Tax Code   87
11. Taxes and the Health System   97
12. Tax Preferences for Housing   107
13. How Federal Taxes Affect the States   115
14. The Problem of Charitable Contributions   123
15. The Problem of Taxing Capital Gains   133

16. Some Unresolved Issues in
the Taxation of Corporations   143

17. The Problem of Tax Administration   155

PART III: THE FUTURE

18. The History of Tax Reform   167

19. The Pros and Cons of Popular
Tax Reform Proposals   175

20. The Need for More Revenue   185

21. The Case for a Value-Added Tax   197

22. The Case Against a Value-Added Tax   207

23. What Should Be Done About
the Bush Tax Cuts?   215

24. If Tax Reform Happens, It Will Be
Because Grover Norquist Permits It   225

Conclusion   235

Additional Readings   239

Appendixes

I. Federal Revenues and Outlays as a Share of GDP   245

II. Lowest and Highest Federal Income Tax Rates   247

III. The Personal Exemption   251

IV. Average and Marginal Federal Income Tax Rates   255

V. Capital Gains and Taxes Paid on Capital Gains   257

Index   259

Introduction

The tax code is like a garden. Without regular attention, it grows weeds that will soon overwhelm the plants and flowers. Unfortunately, no serious weeding had been done to the tax code since 1986. In the meantime, many new plants and flowers have been added without regard to the overall aesthetic of the garden. The result today is an overgrown mess. There is a desperate need to pull the weeds, cut away the brush, and rethink some of the plantings to restore order, beauty, and functionality to the garden.

At its core, the purpose of any tax system is to raise the revenue needed to pay the government's bills. Ideally, one would like to start with a clear philosophy of what government should do and how much it should spend, and only then decide how to raise the revenue to pay for it. The size and composition of spending are critical determinants of the nature of a proper tax system.

A small government, such as we had in the nineteenth century, could be funded almost entirely by tariffs and taxes on alcohol and tobacco. A larger government, even one as small as we had in the 1920s, required a much broader tax base. A Social Security system required a payroll tax and so on.

The problem we have today is that there has been a serious divergence between the size of government that people want and what they are willing to pay for. The idea that deficits are an irresponsible passing on of debt to future generations is no longer sufficient to support a tax system capable of raising adequate revenue to finance current spending. Nor is there the political will to cut spending to the level people are willing to pay. At the same time, no one believes this trend is sustainable.

A debate about tax reform may help clarify the role of government in the twenty-first century. The public misunderstands basic facts about the tax system. Polls show that people consistently believe the federal tax burden to be significantly higher than it actually is, and few know that close to half of all tax filers either pay no federal income taxes at all or get a refund; that is, they have a negative tax rate.

The purpose of this book is to walk readers through the fundamentals of taxation at the simplest level: What is an effective tax rate? How does that differ from the statutory rates in the 1099 form? What is a marginal tax rate? What is the tax base? Why are different forms of income taxed differently? What is a tax expenditure? Is that the same thing as a tax loophole?

To cover a vast amount of material in a small number of pages and to make the discussion comprehensible, a lot of detail has been sacrificed and many nuances have been glossed over. No one should attempt to use this book to prepare their tax returns. The questions anyone might have about how the tax system affects them personally should be directed to a tax professional.

MY BIASES

I have tried to be fair. That is, I have attempted to cover the waterfront and present all the issues and various alternatives and options accurately and without distortion. But I haven't tried too hard to hide my biases, either.

I believe that federal revenues will need to rise as a share of GDP in coming years to pay for the cost of an aging society and stabilize the nation's finances. I think it is unrealistic to try to accomplish that solely by cutting spending. I also believe that should the need for higher revenues be accepted by Congress, it would be better to raise those additional revenues by taxing consumption rather than raising tax rates. But the wealthy will also have to increase their contribution. If they don't, the rest of us will have to pay more.

I think it is irresponsible to view tax expenditures as fundamentally different from spending. Many conservatives and libertarians foolishly think every provision of the tax code that reduces revenue is per se good because it shrinks the size of government and allows people to spend their own money. This is nonsense. Any tax provision that causes economic resources to be utilized differently from their use in a free market—as all tax expenditures do by definition—cannot meaningfully be distinguished from direct spending in terms of government control over these resources. It is myopic in the extreme to view all tax cuts as good and all spending as bad, whether from a philosophical or an economic point of view.

While I do not present my own plan for tax reform, if it were up to me, I would institute a value-added tax (VAT) and use the revenue to make obvious fixes in the tax code. I would abolish the Alternative Minimum Tax and reduce the corporate tax rate, and put in place a tax that can be raised gradually over time to pay for rising entitlement spending. One idea might be to abolish the payroll tax for Medicare and earmark VAT revenues to pay for Medicare. That way, everyone will have an incentive to control Medicare costs, and at least some of the tax will be borne by its beneficiaries.

A NOTE ON FURTHER READINGS

The Further Readings appended to each chapter are not intended to be comprehensive. Their purpose is twofold: first, to give those curious about researching the topic themselves a starting point to begin; second, to document a few specific points in lieu of footnotes. Hopefully, readers will have no difficulty determining from the authors and titles which publications are relevant.

I have tried to limit myself to recent publications and emphasized those that are freely available online. Growing numbers of organizations have posted all of their publications online. These include the Congressional Budget Office (www.cbo.gov), Joint Committee on Taxation (www.jct.gov), U.S. Government Accountability Office (www.gao.gov), and National Bureau of Economic Research (www.nber.org), among others. The Treasury Department's Office of Tax Policy also makes available a number of important tax policy documents that I reference (www.treasury.gov/resource-center/tax-policy/Pages/tax-reform.aspx). And many of the nation's top law reviews now post all of their recent issues online for free. (A list is available at http://jurist.law.pitt.edu/lawreviews.)

Many of the academic articles I have listed are available with a simple search. I recommend Google Scholar (http://scholar.google.com). Type the title of an article you are interested in finding into the search engine, and often you will find a free copy. It is common for university professors to post all their work on personal websites or at the Social Science Research Network (www.ssrn.com). This is especially so for economists and law professors. Google Scholar also provides lists of articles similar to the one you have searched and those that have referenced it. If you search for a known classic in a particular field, you will often find almost everything on the topic ever published in an academic journal ranked in order of importance.

If such sources don't work, try local libraries. Almost all now have powerful databases available online that are freely accessible for anyone with a library card and an Internet connection. My personal library in Fairfax Country, Virginia, for example, provides access to a database called ProQuest that makes available hundreds of newspapers, law reviews, and academic journals. In the event that the one I am looking for isn't available, the Virginia State Library in Richmond has additional databases.

Many universities now provide limited access to their library databases for alumni. And many of the commercial publishers of academic journals now allow people to buy copies of individual articles. The price is usually excessive, but may be worth it in some cases.

HIGHLY RECOMMENDED RESOURCES

Insofar as the tax law is concerned, the resources of the Joint Committee on Taxation (JCT) are essential. It periodically publishes surveys of tax issues to inform members of the Senate Finance Committee and House Ways and Means Committee and help them prepare for hearings. Since many members of these committees are not lawyers, JCT reports tend to be relatively accessible to nonspecialists, yet are authoritative.

I would also recommend reports from the Congressional Research Service (CRS). Unfortunately, CRS distributes its publications only through congressional offices. However, most become publicly available and are often posted online through the Federation of American Scientists (www.fas.org/sgp/crs) and Open CRS (http://opencrs.com). Your representative or senator can always supply you with a CRS report if you know it exists.

On the economics of taxation, the premier research organization is the National Bureau of Economic Research. On a weekly basis, it publishes research by the top public finance economists in the United States. Its working papers are available for a modest fee, and all of its out-of-print books and journals are available free. One that I have referenced frequently is *Tax Policy and the Economy*, published annually.

Equally valuable is the Tax Policy Center (TPC, www.taxpolicy center.org). It is especially useful for those researching topical tax proposals. TPC often posts revenue estimates and distribution tables for recent tax initiatives that are equal in quality to those produced by the JCT and the Treasury. There is also a wealth of historical data on the tax system that I have relied upon heavily in writing this book. Another good source is the Tax Foundation (www .taxfoundation.org). It tilts to the right side of the political spectrum, but its numbers are solid.

Regarding international tax issues, the Organization for Economic Cooperation and Development in Paris (OECD, www.oecd .org) is a central data source. It maintains an extensive tax database with files easily downloadable into spreadsheets. The OECD covers only major market-oriented economies, however. The best source for tax data on other countries is an annual report from the World Bank called "Paying Taxes." The international accounting firm PWC compiles the data, which are available free to download (www.pwc.com/payingtaxes).

PWC also has a website with detailed information on the tax systems of virtually every country; this information is free except for a registration requirement (www.pwc.com/gx/en/worldwide-tax -summaries/index.jhtml). The international accounting firm KPMG produces an annual report called "Competitiveness Alternatives" that contains comparable tax data oriented more toward corporations. It is free to download (www.competitivealternatives.com).

Two indispensable journals in the field of tax policy are the *National Tax Journal* and *Tax Notes*. The former is published by the National Tax Association (http://ntanet.org). Recent issues are available only to members, but issues more than two years old are freely available back to 1988. The latter is a weekly magazine published by Tax Analysts (www.taxanalysts.com). It is expensive but invaluable. It is probably available online at any good university library. Another useful publication is the *Statistics of Income Bulletin*, which is published by the IRS and freely available on its website.

Part I

THE BASICS

Chapter 1

A Brief History of Federal Income Taxation

As every schoolchild knows, following the American Revolution, the Articles of Confederation governed the United States from 1781 to 1789. But the government established by the Articles proved to have a fatal weakness in the area of taxation. The federal government depended on the states to provide it with revenue, and like all taxpayers, the states didn't much enjoy paying taxes to Washington. The federal government soon had a financial crisis. It lacked the revenue to function adequately, and so a constitutional convention was assembled to write a new basic law for the nation.

The Constitution, which replaced the Articles, gave the federal government independent taxing power so that it was no longer dependent on the states for revenue. The precise terms of the government's taxing power are surprisingly vague. It is free to tax what it likes, subject to just two constraints: exports may not be taxed, and the federal government is prohibited from levying a direct tax unless it is proportionate to the population. The main purpose of the latter clause was to limit the federal government's ability to tax slaves—one of the many compromises made by the Founding Fathers to accommodate the South's "peculiar institution."

Initially there was resistance to federal taxation, especially the whiskey tax, which led to a rebellion in 1794. But after Treasury Secretary Alexander Hamilton had the federal government assume state debts from the war, state taxes fell. On balance, the tax burden declined.

THE TARIFF

From the beginning, the federal government's primary revenue source was the tariff. This led to continuing tensions between the northern states, where manufacturing was the dominant industry—manufacturers favored high, protective tariffs—and the southern states, where agriculture was the dominant industry and tariffs were thus unpopular. Interestingly, one argument for raising revenue through tariffs was that it was a progressive form of taxation, one that takes more, proportionately, from the rich than the poor. As Thomas Jefferson wrote in 1811 in a letter to Thaddeus Kościuszko, "The rich alone use imported articles, and on these alone the whole taxes of the General Government are levied. The poor man, who uses nothing but what is made in his own farm or family, or within his own country, pays not a farthing of tax to the General Government."

Until the Civil War, tariffs constituted about 90 percent of all federal revenues. The balance came mainly from sales of federal lands. On the eve of the war, total federal revenues were $53.5 million, of which $49.6 million came from customs duties. Federal revenues consumed about 1.2 percent of the gross domestic product (GDP); they have averaged 18.5 percent of GDP since World War II.

The war increased the need for revenue. By 1866 federal revenues were ten times greater than they had been before the war. An important innovation was the creation of the first federal income tax in 1861. As the war progressed, the government's revenue needs increased, and it raised the income tax. By 1866 income taxes constituted 55 percent of federal revenues. But even at the end of the war, the top rate was just 10 percent on incomes over $10,000 (equivalent to $142,000 today).

The unpopularity of the income tax led to its expiration in 1872. To replace the lost revenue, the federal government expanded the taxation of alcohol and tobacco. By 1900 these taxes constituted 43 percent of federal revenue. Customs duties raised 41 percent.

In 1894, Democrats attempted to revive the income tax in order to finance a reduction in tariffs, which fell heavily on the farmers and workers who constituted their base. A 2 percent flat-rate income tax was enacted on incomes over $4,000 (about $105,000 today). However, the following year the Supreme Court found it to be unconstitutional in the case of *Pollock v. Farmers' Loan and Trust Co.* (1895), even though the Civil War income tax had been found to be constitutional in *Springer v. United States* (1880). The Court found that the income tax was a direct tax and not apportioned uniformly.

Although it was widely believed among legal scholars that the Supreme Court erred in the *Pollock* decision, this ruling nevertheless effectively foreclosed any further legislative efforts regarding an income tax without a change in the Constitution.

Growth of the Progressive movement and continuing agitation for tariff cuts kept up the pressure for an income tax. In 1909 President William Howard Taft, a Republican, endorsed a constitutional amendment to permit one. In part it was a delaying tactic to fend off increasing support for tariff cuts, which would have angered the GOP's base among manufacturers.

SIXTEENTH AMENDMENT

The proposed Sixteenth Amendment passed both the House and the Senate surprisingly easily, but ratification by the states was slow. The last state, Delaware, didn't ratify it until 1913, just days before Woodrow Wilson became only the second Democratic president since before the Civil War.

Wilson brought with him a Democratic Congress, which quickly enacted legislation reducing tariffs and creating a permanent income tax. The 1913 act imposed a 1 percent tax rate on all those with incomes above a personal exemption of $3,000 (about $66,000 today) and a top rate of 7 percent on those with incomes above $500,000 (about $11 million today). Consequently, few people paid substantial income taxes. But that changed with the outbreak of World War I. Anticipating U.S. involvement, the government raised tax rates in 1914 and 1916. The United States' formal entry into the war in 1917 led to a further rise.

By 1918 the lowest rate of taxation was up to 6 percent on incomes over $1,000 (about $14,000 today), and the top rate was 77 percent on incomes over $1 million (about $14 million today). Although taxes were quickly reduced after the war, they were not lowered to their prewar level. By 1920 the bottom rate was down only to 4 percent, and the top rate fell to 73 percent. The thresholds were unchanged, but there was considerable inflation, which lowered the real income levels at which tax rates became effective.

The desire for significant income tax cuts helped Republican Warren Harding win the White House in 1920. He appointed the financier Andrew Mellon as his Treasury secretary, and Mellon began a decade-long effort to bring down the wartime tax rates. Kept on in his position by Calvin Coolidge, Mellon succeeded in getting the bottom tax rate down to just 0.375 percent in 1929 and the top rate down to 24 percent. However, in the process the threshold for the top rate was reduced to $100,000 (about $1.3 million today).

The Great Depression decimated federal finances. Revenues fell more than half between 1930 and 1932, while relief measures caused spending to rise 40 percent. In 1932 Herbert Hoover asked Congress to raise taxes to reduce the deficit. The bottom rate went back up to 4 percent and the top rate increased to 63 percent. In dollar terms, however, the largest increases were for excise taxes on a wide variety of goods and services, including gasoline, telephones, tires, and many others.

Franklin D. Roosevelt's first major contribution to tax policy came in 1935, when he asked Congress to raise taxes on the rich. This move was driven less by revenue needs than by fairness. In a message to Congress on June 19, he said, "People know that vast personal incomes come not only through the effort or ability or luck of those who receive them, but also because of the opportunities for advantage which government itself contributes. Therefore, the duty rests upon the government to restrict such incomes by very high taxes."

SOAKING THE RICH

Privately Roosevelt worried about the growing political support for socialist and crackpot schemes. To keep them in check, he had to increase the perception of fairness in the capitalist system. "I want to save our system, the capitalistic system," he told an emissary of the archconservative newspaper publisher William Randolph

Hearst. To do so, Roosevelt said, "it may be necessary to throw to the wolves the forty-six men who are reported to have incomes in excess of one million dollars a year."

The 1935 tax bill raised the top rate to 79 percent, but also raised the income threshold at which the top rate applied, from $1 million to $5 million (about $78 million in today's dollars). It was reported that only one person in America, John D. Rockefeller Jr., paid taxes at the top income tax rate.

The institution of Social Security that same year also had a major impact on taxation. Roosevelt insisted that it be financed conservatively to impress upon people that it was an earned benefit, not a giveaway welfare program. People had to pay into Social Security to get benefits; it was financed with a flat-rate tax of 2 percent; and revenues went into a trust fund, not unlike a private pension fund.

Social Security taxes began being collected in 1937, but the first benefits weren't paid out until 1940. The payroll tax constituted a significant tax increase on the working population, most of whom paid no federal income taxes. Many economists believe that this increase was a major contributor to the recession of 1937–38 after several years of double-digit real growth in the economy. For three years the payroll tax took money out of the economy before benefit payments started putting it back in again.

World War II led to a drastic expansion of federal taxation. With the top rate already at virtually a confiscatory level after 1935, there was limited scope for raising significant additional revenues from the rich. The tax base had to expand to include the middle and working classes previously exempt from income taxes. On the eve of war only about 3 percent of Americans paid any income taxes. By the end of the war the rate was up to 30 percent. There were fewer than 4 million taxable returns in 1939. By 1943 this figure was up to more than 40 million.

During the war the bottom tax rate rose from 4 percent to 23 percent on incomes over $500 (about $6,000 today). The top rate increased from 79 percent to 94 percent on incomes above $200,000 (about $2.4 million today). Although tax rates were reduced after the war, the reduction was modest due to growth in the national debt and fears of inflation, which prohibited a large cut in federal revenues that would have increased the budget deficit. By 1949 the bottom income tax rate was down to just 16.6 percent and the top rate fell to 82.1 percent.

Concerns about Soviet expansionism prevented the sort of demobilization and cuts in military spending that accompanied previous major wars. Moreover, by 1950 the United States was again involved in a shooting war, this time in Korea. Consequently there was little scope for tax reduction throughout the 1950s, reinforced by Dwight Eisenhower's opposition to deficit spending. The bottom tax rate stayed at 20 percent throughout the 1950s, while the top rate remained above 90 percent.

KENNEDY TAX CUT

By 1960 there was general agreement among economists that the economy needed a boost. Keynesian economists, who increasingly dominated economic discussions, wanted the federal government to increase federal spending and the budget deficit to increase aggregate demand and raise growth. While John F. Kennedy was sympathetic to the Keynesian argument, he worried about inflation and the precarious position of the dollar. He therefore resisted the recommendations of his economic advisers.

House Ways and Means Committee Chairman Wilbur Mills convinced Kennedy that a fiscal stimulus could just as well be done on the tax side as the spending side. A big cut in tax rates could serve the dual purpose of stimulating the supply and demand sides of the economy. It was also less likely to upset financial markets and was easier to enact, politically, than an equivalent increase in spending.

In 1963 Kennedy asked Congress to reduce the top income tax rate to 65 from 91 percent, and the bottom rate to 14 from 20 percent. Unfortunately he was assassinated before congressional action could be completed. Lyndon Johnson finished the job in 1964. The final bill was close to Kennedy's proposal, except that the top rate was reduced only to 70 percent.

By the end of the 1960s inflation was becoming the nation's number one economic problem. Keynesian economics recommended a tax increase to reduce aggregate demand. Reluctantly Johnson supported a surtax in 1968 that temporarily raised everyone's income taxes by 10 percent. The impact on inflation was modest and due largely to a recession that began in December 1969.

Although more and more economists concluded that the Federal Reserve's monetary policy was primarily responsible for inflation, the Keynesians had enough influence to prevent any permanent tax cuts during the 1970s. They believed that budget deficits were primarily responsible for inflation. Tax cuts would make it worse.

However, one of the most important ways that inflation harms the economy is by pushing people into higher tax brackets. This is the main reason federal revenues rose from 17.3 percent of GDP in 1971 to 19 percent in 1980. Marginal tax rates also increased for the same reason. According to the Treasury Department, for a four-person family with the median income, the marginal income tax rate—the tax on each additional dollar earned—rose from 19 to 24 percent over the same period. The marginal rate on a family with twice the median income went from 28 to 43 percent.

REAGAN TAX CUT

In the 1980 presidential campaign Ronald Reagan promised to replicate the Kennedy tax cut and reduce rates across the board. He supported the tax proposal sponsored by Rep. Jack Kemp of New York and Sen. Bill Roth of Delaware. As a member of Kemp's staff, I had a key role in developing this legislation.

Reagan's tax cut, enacted in 1981, reduced the top rate from 70 to 50 percent and the bottom rate from 14 to 11 percent. Reagan also supported the Tax Reform Act of 1986, which raised the bottom rate to 15 percent but reduced the top rate to just 28 percent. His successor, George H. W. Bush, agreed to a budget deal in 1990 that raised the top rate to 31 percent. Not only did this action undermine his conservative support in 1992, but it also poisoned the well for future tax reforms. The 1986 act was a deal in which the wealthy gave up their tax preferences in return for a lower top rate, but when the top rate was increased in 1990, the preferences were not restored.

Having broken the deal that underlay the 1986 reform, Bush made it easier for Bill Clinton to go back to the same well and raise the top rate to 39.6 percent in 1993. However, it is seldom noted that Clinton raised the threshold for the top rate from $86,500 to $250,000 ($500,000 for couples), equivalent to $375,000 ($750,000 for couples) today.

Although Republicans predicted an economic apocalypse from the 1993 tax increase, the opposite occurred, and a period of exceptionally rapid growth followed. Also, contrary to Republican predictions that the new revenue would be spent and not reduce the deficit, spending and the deficit both fell. Federal outlays fell from 22.1 percent of GDP in 1992 to 18.2 percent of GDP in Clinton's last year in office; revenues rose from 17.5 percent of GDP to 20.6 percent of GDP. The deficit went from 4.7 percent of GDP to a surplus of 2.4 percent of GDP over the same period, a remarkable improvement of 7.1 percent of GDP. Thus, ironically, a liberal Democrat turned out to be America's most fiscally conservative president since Calvin Coolidge.

In the 2000 election Republican George W. Bush campaigned on the idea that the budget surplus was dangerous because Congress might spend it. It was better, he said, to dissipate the surplus through tax cuts. True to his word, Bush supported tax cuts that caused the budget surplus to evaporate into a deficit of 3.2 percent of GDP by his last year in office, a fiscal reversal of 5.6 percent of GDP. And contrary to Republican promises that tax cuts would stimulate the economy, economic growth was sluggish throughout the early 2000s, culminating in the second worst economic slump in American history.

Barack Obama's principal contribution to tax policy was to insist that the Bush tax cuts be allowed to expire on schedule at the end of 2010—exactly as Republicans had written the legislation in the first place—for those with incomes above $250,000. At the last minute, however, he agreed to extend the Bush tax cuts for another two years without change. They are scheduled to expire at the end of 2012 and will, undoubtedly, be a major issue in the presidential campaign that year.

FURTHER READINGS

Ackerman, Bruce. "Taxation and the Constitution." *Columbia Law Review* (Jan. 1999): 1–58.

Baack, Bennett D., and Edward John Ray. "Special Interests and the Adoption of the Income Tax in the United States." *Journal of Economic History* (Sept. 1985): 607–25.

Bank, Steven A. "Origins of a Flat Tax." *Denver University Law Review* (1996): 329–402.

Bank, Steven A., Kirk J. Stark, and Joseph J. Thorndike. *War and Taxes*. Urban Institute, 2008.

Bartlett, Bruce. *The New American Economy*. Palgrave Macmillan, 2009.

Bartlett, Bruce. *Reaganomics: Supply-Side Economics in Action*. Arlington House, 1981.

Blakey, Roy G., and Gladys C. Blakey. "The Revenue Act of 1932." *American Economic Review* (Dec. 1932): 620–40.

Blakey, Roy G., and Gladys C. Blakey. "The Revenue Act of 1935." *American Economic Review* (Dec. 1935): 673–90.

Brown, Roger H. *Redeeming the Republic: Federalists, Taxation, and the Origins of the Constitution*. Johns Hopkins University Press, 1993.

Brownlee, W. Elliot. *Federal Taxation in America: A Short History*. Cambridge University Press, 1996.

Edling, Max M., and Mark D. Kaplanoff. "Alexander Hamilton's Fiscal Reform: Transforming the Structure of Taxation in the Early Republic." *William and Mary Quarterly* (Oct. 2004): 714–44.

Einhorn, Robin L. *American Taxation, American Slavery*. University of Chicago Press, 2006.

Ekirch, Arthur A. "The Sixteenth Amendment: The Historical Background." *Cato Journal* (Spring 1981): 161–82.

Evans, Michael W. "Foundations of the Tax Legislative Process: The Confederation, Constitutional Convention, and the First Revenue Law." *Tax Notes* (Jan. 21, 1991): 283–93.

Flaherty, Jane. *The Revenue Imperative*. Pickering & Chatto, 2009.

Jones, Carolyn C. "Class Tax to Mass Tax: The Role of Propaganda in the Expansion of the Income Tax during World War II." *Buffalo Law Review* (Fall 1988–89): 685–737.

Joseph, Richard J. *The Origin of the American Income Tax: The Revenue Act of 1894 and Its Aftermath*. Syracuse University Press, 2004.

Leff, Mark H. "Taxing the 'Forgotten Man': The Politics of Social Security Finance in the New Deal." *Journal of American History* (Sept. 1983): 359–81.

McMahon, Stephanie. "A Law with a Life of Its Own: The Development of the Federal Income Tax Statutes through World War I." *Pittsburgh Tax Review* (Fall 2009): 1–41.

Mehrotra, Ajay K. "Lawyers, Guns, and Public Moneys: The U.S. Treasury, World War I, and the Administration of the Modern Fiscal State." *Law and History Review* (2010): 173–225.

Mehrotra, Ajay K. "'More Mighty Than the Waves of the Sea': Toilers, Tariffs, and the Income Tax Movement, 1880–1913." *Labor History* (May 2004): 165–98.

Slaughter, Thomas P. "The Tax Man Cometh: Ideological Opposition to Internal Taxes, 1760–1790." *William and Mary Quarterly* (Oct. 1984): 566–91.

Slaughter, Thomas P. *The Whiskey Rebellion*. Oxford University Press, 1986.

Stanley, Robert. *Dimensions of Law in the Service of Order: Origins of the Federal Income Tax, 1861–1913*. Oxford University Press, 1993.

Thorndike, Joseph J. "An Army of Officials: The Civil War Bureau of Internal Revenue." *Tax Notes* (Dec. 24, 2001): 1739–60.

Thorndike, Joseph J. "Four Things That Everyone Should Know about New Deal Taxation." *Tax Notes* (Nov. 24, 2008): 973–75.

Thorndike, Joseph J. "The Limited Lessons of 1937." *Tax Notes* (Jan. 25, 2010): 429–32.

Weisman, Steven. *The Great Tax Wars: Lincoln to Wilson—The Fierce Battles over Money and Power That Transformed the Nation*. Simon & Schuster, 2002.

Witte, John F. *The Politics and Development of the Federal Income Tax*. University of Wisconsin Press, 1985.

Zelizer, Julian E. *Taxing America: Wilbur D. Mills, Congress, and the State, 1945–1975*. Cambridge University Press, 1998.

Chapter 2

How a Tax Bill Is Made

The Constitution grants the House of Representatives the exclusive right to originate revenue bills. All tax bills that pass Congress must have the letters H.R. before them. H.R. simply stands for House of Representatives. Senate bills are similarly designated by S.

Of course, this doesn't mean that a senator cannot introduce a tax bill. But the House is disinclined to consider such legislation even if it passes the Senate, although there are exceptions. The Tax Equity and Fiscal Responsibility Act of 1982 (TEFRA) essentially originated in the Senate. Some congressmen later sued in court, arguing that the Constitution had been violated. The Supreme Court responded, quite correctly, that the House had the power to enforce this provision on its own. There was no reason for the Court to intervene if the House chose to look the other way. In any case, the technical constitutional requirement was upheld. Eventually the Senate version of TEFRA was added as an amendment to an unrelated House bill, H.R. 4961.

Something similar happened when I was working for Rep. Jack Kemp in 1977. He had been trying to help one of his constituents with a tax problem that could only be fixed legislatively by enacting a private relief bill. Kemp's bill passed the House in early 1977 and was awaiting action in the Senate Finance Committee when President Jimmy Carter asked Congress to enact a big new energy bill with many tax provisions. For tactical reasons, it was decided that the Senate should act first on this legislation, but the only House-passed tax bill the Senate had at its disposal was Kemp's bill, so it added the energy bill to it as an amendment. Thus for a time Kemp was the primary sponsor of the Carter energy bill, which he strongly opposed.

TREASURY DEPARTMENT

Generally speaking, major tax bills originate with the Treasury Department, which has a division called the Office of Tax Policy staffed by a large number of economists and lawyers who have long and deep experience with the tax code. It can also draw upon the resources of the Internal Revenue Service if needed.

Historically the Treasury initiates big tax bills with a study or detailed proposal. Moreover it's a rare year when the president doesn't propose a laundry list of tax initiatives in his budget. The tax law is constantly changing even without new legislation, due to court cases and changing interpretations of existing tax provisions, which often lead to unintended consequences that require legislative fixes. Simultaneously with the budget, which is usually sent to Capitol Hill in late January or early February, the Treasury publishes what is called the Green Book, containing additional details on the administration's tax proposals.

The House Ways and Means Committee usually gets the tax legislative process going by inviting the secretary of the Treasury to present the administration's initiatives. This occasion is typically somewhat ceremonial. Afterward the committee will deal almost exclusively with the assistant secretary for tax policy. This person is a highly respected lawyer or law professor at the pinnacle of the tax profession. He or she normally has two deputy assistant secretaries, one a lawyer and the other an economist, who will also work closely with the Ways and Means Committee and Senate Finance Committee during the legislative process. Treasury's Office of Legislative Affairs will also normally have a staff person who specializes in tax legislation.

In the 1920s both congressional tax-writing committees recognized that it was highly useful to have a permanent staff of tax experts at their disposal. This need led to creation of the Joint Committee on Taxation (JCT). Like the Office of Tax Policy, it is staffed with extremely knowledgeable economists and lawyers who are experts at drafting tax legislation and calculating the impact of various provisions on federal revenues and the impact on taxpayers at particular income levels. The chief of staff of the JCT has a status equal to the assistant secretary for tax policy. They work closely together on all aspects of the tax legislative process.

CONGRESSIONAL COMMITTEES

The Ways and Means Committee holds many days of public hearings on major tax bills. A variety of experts testify. They are often drawn from Washington-based think tanks and trade associations that represent businesses, industries, and taxpayer groups affected by proposed tax changes.

After many years of observing the hearing process and having been staff director for a congressional committee, I still have no idea whether congressional testimony has any real impact on legislation. There certainly have been cases when it did, and the testimony of true experts always carries a great deal of weight. But in many cases, the main purpose of testimony is to give people their day in court, so to speak, and let them feel that they at least had the opportunity to present their views formally. A committee chairman may also use testimony for marketing purposes by stacking the witness list with advocates sympathetic to his point of view.

Of course, one problem with this theory is that it is rare that even a majority of the members of the Ways and Means Committee or the Senate Finance Committee are around to hear testimony unless it is a high-profile witness such as the secretary of the Treasury, when C-SPAN cameras will likely be present. Most of the time a witness is lucky if there is one member of each party present for her testimony. Moreover a witness is usually limited to a five-minute summary of her views, with full statements published in the official record, which in years past may not have been published for months or even years after the hearing. These days witness statements are posted on committee websites and hearings may be televised on the Internet.

Generally the only people who come to congressional hearings are committee staff, reporters from trade publications, and lobbyists. Indeed lobbyists often arrange testimony in order to give their clients a belief that they have done something meaningful to advance their interests. They may have even gone so far as to beg a few members of the committee to show up for the testimony of their client, who may be a corporate CEO, and say a few words for the record implying that they care what he has to say.

This wasn't always the case. In the past, testimony was an important part of the legislative process. The House and Senate usually would not take up a major bill or allow significant amendments unless hearings had been held on their provisions. This care was important because mistakes are easily made when legislation is made in haste. Even so, Congress almost always has to enact a technical corrections bill following every major tax bill to fix inevitable drafting errors.

Unfortunately, when Republicans took control of Congress in 1995 they dispensed with the hearing requirement. Tax bills were often brought up in committee for mark-up sessions when no member other than the chairman had seen it, making it difficult for congressmen to known and understand key provisions before the legislation reached the floor for a final vote.

LOBBYISTS

This short-circuited legislative process enhances the power of lobbyists. Such people are paid vast sums of money to be in the know about legislative provisions that affect their clients. Indeed oftentimes they are among the very few people who know what is in complex legislation. Their mastery of those details gives them far more influence than campaign contributions. And in the hothouse atmosphere in which final legislative language is worked out, just knowing the precise wording of a provision and suggesting the tiniest little tweak can be worth millions of dollars to those in the right place at the right time. For this reason tax lobbyists are the highest paid of all Washington lobbyists.

The power of lobbyists is especially pronounced in what are called conference committees. These are temporary joint committees established to work out the differences in House- and Senate-passed bills, which must be reconciled and repassed in exactly the same form before they can be sent to the president for his signature. Conference committees tend to be small and often are under intense pressure to finish their work quickly, with important decisions about whether to accept the House's or Senate's legislative language made in the blink of an eye. Although theoretically prohibited, conference bills sometimes contain provisions in neither the House nor the Senate bill, emerging through a sort of Immaculate Conception, often at the behest of a lobbyist.

Lest one think that the influence of lobbyists is entirely negative,

I often found them to be helpful when I was a congressional staffer. One reason is that members of Congress tend to be myopic, aware only of what is happening on their side of the Capitol. Lobbyists were often the best sources of information about what was happening on the other side. And oftentimes lobbyists' interests were the same as my boss's, making them a sort of temporary adjunct staff in terms of advancing some shared interest. Keep in mind that many—perhaps most—lobbyists don't work for big corporations; they work for associations such as the Farm Bureau, U.S. Chamber of Commerce, AFL-CIO, AARP, or other large groups with broad membership and legitimate interests.

In the past, Congress tried to protect itself from the influence of tax lobbyists by having a legislative process much more opaque and closed than it is today. The Ways and Means and Finance committees were much smaller and their membership was restricted to members with long seniority and safe seats, making them largely immune from the necessity of fundraising. Tax bills were often marked up behind closed doors, and amendments from the floor were discouraged. But in the 1970s congressional reformers revolted against this insular system and demanded more openness and transparency. This made the tax legislative process more democratic, but also less coherent.

INCOHERENT POLICY

Whether the tax legislative process we have today is better than what we had in the past is a matter of debate. During the George W. Bush and Obama administrations, the Treasury has been much less influential. The administration would often just signal a tax idea informally and then let the congressional meat grinder go to work. The result has been increasingly disjointed tax bills that have cluttered the tax code with a lot of ineffective incentives and giveaways for favored constituencies.

Such a process may work well enough when the administration's goals are limited and tax cutting is the order of the day. But it does not work when the goal is reform. When taxes are being reduced there are only winners and no losers. But tax reform has both winners and losers because it presupposes revenue-neutrality, neither raising nor lowering the overall level of taxes. Those that would lose tax benefits have a powerful incentive to shift the burden onto someone else. This means that the process must be much more tightly controlled.

Another reason there needs to be central control in the tax reform process is that many provisions of the tax code interact with each other. When one element changes, it can set off a domino effect that requires many additional changes, lest the legislation inadvertently create an unjustified tax loophole, unintentionally penalize some group or activity, or fail to accomplish the purpose of the original change. Given the complexity of large tax reform bills, the Treasury needs to be involved in every aspect of the process from beginning to end. The end product should be coherent and not just a random collection of tax provisions that serve no larger social or economic purpose.

Historically, major tax reform bills have been drafted by the Treasury. The three most important tax reform bills of the past fifty years—enacted in 1969, 1976, and 1986—were all developed and shepherded through Congress this way. If the Obama administration wants to have real tax reform, it will need to return to this system and put Treasury back in charge of tax policy.

FURTHER READINGS

Birnbaum, Jeffrey H., and Alan S. Murray. *Showdown at Gucci Gulch.* Random House, 1987.

Coder, Jeremiah. "Treasury Takes Low Profile on Tax Reform." *Tax Notes* (June 13, 2011): 1116–19.

Doernberg, Richard L., and Fred S. McChesney. "On the Accelerating Rate and Decreasing Durability of Tax Reform." *Minnesota Law Review* (April 1987): 913–62.

Graetz, Michael J. "Reflections on the Tax Legislative Process: Prelude to Reform." *Virginia Law Review* (Nov. 1972): 1389–1450. Graetz held high-level positions at the Treasury Department during both the Nixon and the George H. W. Bush administrations.

Inman, Robert P. "Presidential Leadership and the Reform of Fiscal Policy: Learning from Reagan's Role in TRA 86." National Bureau of Economic Research Working Paper No. 4395 (July 1993).

Manley, John F. "Congressional Staff and Public Policy-Making: The Joint Committee on Internal Revenue Taxation." *Journal of Politics* (Nov. 1968): 1046–67.

Shaviro, Daniel. "Beyond Public Choice and Public Interest: A Study of the Legislative Process as Illustrated by Tax Legislation in the 1980s." *University of Pennsylvania Law Review* (Nov. 1990): 1–123. Shaviro served on the staff of the Joint Committee on Taxation in the 1980s.

Surrey, Stanley S. "The Congress and the Tax Lobbyist—How Special Tax Provisions Get Enacted." *Harvard Law Review* (May 1957): 1145–82. Surrey served as assistant secretary of the Treasury for tax policy during both the Kennedy and the Johnson administrations.

Yin, George K. "The Evolving Legislative Process: Implications for Tax Reform." *Tax Notes* (Jan. 22, 2007): 313–25. Yin was chief of staff of the Joint Committee on Taxation from 2003 to 2005.

Chapter 3

The Definition of Income

To tax income, one has to know what income is. That may seem obvious, but it becomes complicated the more one thinks about it. That is a key reason the term "income" is nowhere defined in law. Section 61 of the tax code is a tautology; it says that gross income "means all income from whatever source derived" and then lists a few examples. The leading Supreme Court case on the subject, *Commissioner v. Glenshaw Glass* (1955), adds little clarification, saying only that income consists of "undeniable accessions to wealth, clearly realized, and over which the taxpayers have complete dominion." In practice "income" is whatever the Internal Revenue Service says it is.

Historically, governments did not tax incomes. The main reason is that until the Industrial Revolution, incomes were too low to tax. The vast majority of people made barely enough to survive. They had no significant surplus from which to pay more than a small amount of taxes. Governments got most of their revenue from taxes on trade, mainly because there were few major ports and imports could be tracked relatively easily. Also, imported goods tended to benefit the well-to-do, making tariffs a fairly progressive form of taxation. Taxes on real property were another mainstay of taxation because land and buildings were fixed.

But governments have always been creative in finding ways to tax. In medieval England, taxes were assessed on windows, the theory being that the more windows in a house, the more well-to-do the owner. Also, tax collectors could easily observe whether a house had windows and assess taxes without having to dig into a taxpayer's finances. Only in the nineteenth century did income taxes become widespread.

Although in England, one of the first countries to adopt a permanent income tax, there was a lively debate about the precise definition of income, no such debate ever really took place in the United States. That is because in the case of the Civil War income tax and the 1913 income tax, war and the government's desperate need for revenue precluded much discussion of basic principles. The government needed too much money too quickly to have the luxury of weighing all the options for constructing a logically consistent tax system.

ARE CAPITAL GAINS AND INTEREST INCOME?

An early problem was whether capital gains are income. In the case of *Gray v. Darlington* (1872), relating to the Civil War income tax, the Supreme Court originally held that they aren't. The Court held that income necessarily implies a regular flow of consumable resources. But capital gains are irregular and often represent only inflation, giving owners of assets that have risen in monetary value no increased ability to consume. Moreover a capital gain realized in one year may represent small gains that arose over many years. Taxing such accumulated gains as if they were all earned in one year often made those with modest incomes appear to be rich in that one year. This is still a big problem.

The British took the view for many years that capital gains are not income except to professional traders. Occasional capital gains were excluded from taxation. Many American scholars in the early twentieth century took the same view. Perhaps if the government's revenue needs hadn't become so great after enactment of the income tax, with the onset of World War I, tax policy might have evolved differently. As it was, the government needed the revenue too badly to exclude anything from taxation. It was only because of a Supreme Court case, *Eisner v. Macomber* (1920), in which the Court ruled that capital gains had to be realized to be taxed, that the government didn't tax unrealized gains.

Another important issue glossed over in the early development of the income tax was the issue of taxing saving. For centuries a long line of tax theorists, including Alexander Hamilton, argued that governments ought to tax only what people took out of the economy: what they consumed, in other words. Since saving added to society's wealth, it should be exempt. Moreover, as a matter of fairness, it didn't seem right to tax the frugal at the same rate as spendthrifts.

In the nineteenth century the great British economist John Stuart Mill took this argument a step further. He said that if saving is justly exempted from taxation, it follows that the return to saving—rent, dividends, and interest—should be free of taxation. He argued that taxing the income from capital is essentially a double tax if people are also taxed on the income from which they acquired their saving in the first place.

In the twentieth century the American economist Irving Fisher developed a more sophisticated version of Mill's argument. He believed that interest can never be considered income, because it is simply the discount between present and future consumption. People will always prefer consumption today to consumption in the future, Fisher reasoned, and interest compensates them for the loss they suffer when they wait to consume income. Thus we shouldn't tax interest for the same reason we don't tax insurance settlements.

HAIG-SIMONS

In the 1920s and 1930s, however, most economists came around to the idea that the proper definition of income consists of consumption during the course of a calendar year plus the change in net worth. In short, it went beyond defining income as what people took out of the economy to include what they theoretically could take out if they wanted to. The primary purpose was to achieve fairness by taxing those with substantial assets, even if those assets were never spent or consumed in any way.

The two economists identified with this broader definition of income were Robert M. Haig and Henry C. Simons. They strongly influenced generations of tax administrators and theorists. Legislators have been less enamored with the Haig-Simons definition of income. In principle, it would require the taxation of unrealized capital gains, the abolition of all savings incentives such as Individual Retirement Accounts and 401(k) plans, and the taxation of many forms of income people may not even realize they have, such as the imputed rent homeowners pay to themselves by virtue of simultaneously being both landlord and renter.

In practice Congress and the Internal Revenue Service have never attempted to achieve a consistent approach to defining income, rejecting both a pure consumption tax that would exempt all saving and capital gains, and a comprehensive income tax based on Haig-Simons. We have always had a hybrid tax system that taxes some things that neither definition of income would tax at all, such as capital gains resulting only from inflation, while exempting other forms of income that would be taxed under either definition, such as employer-provided health insurance.

THE TAX UNIT

Another fundamental tax question that has never been resolved properly is the appropriate tax unit. Is the individual or the family the right unit of income taxation? At first the tax code treated everyone the same and taxed them all as individuals. However, a Supreme Court case, *Poe v. Seaborn* (1930), threw a monkey wrench into this system by ruling that married couples in community property states such as California could be taxed as if a husband and wife each earned half the couple's total income.

This decision mattered because in those days there were few two-earner couples. Generally speaking, the husband earned all the income and the wife stayed home and raised the children. But if the wife was assumed to earn half her husband's income, then because of progressive tax rates the couple would pay less in total taxes than if all the income was attributed to the husband.

Consequently married couples in some states paid less in federal income taxes than those with the same income living in other states. Not surprisingly, states moved to give their citizens a tax cut by adopting community property laws. To deal with this problem, Congress changed the tax code to tax individuals and families differently. But this "fix" just led to a new unfairness: two-earner couples would often pay more in combined taxes than they would if each were taxed separately, leading to further legislative fixes. As long as there are progressive tax rates, it's not possible to resolve this problem so that everyone is happy.

APPROPRIATE TIME PERIOD

Finally, there is the question of the appropriate time period over which to tax people. It may seem obvious that a calendar year is the right one, but there's no real reason why this should be the case. One unfairness that arises is that people with roughly the same income annually will be taxed less than others who have the same income over the same period of years, but who earned that income erratically, making a lot in some years, little in others. This system tends to put entrepreneurs and business owners at a disadvantage compared with steady wage earners.

Using a calendar year to measure taxable income also leads people and businesses to do a lot of income shifting and game playing with tax deductions. At the end of every year personal finance publications list tips on how people can save taxes by moving income forward and advancing payments for deductible expenses such as property taxes and mortgage interest. But of course that just makes one's taxes higher the following year. It's economically wasteful and doesn't save taxes in the long run.

In principle, two people with the same lifetime incomes ought to pay roughly the same lifetime taxes. This could be accomplished relatively easily by taxing people on their average income over a period of years, rather than on just what they earned in a single year. The problem, of course, is that although they would pay less in good years, they would pay more in bad years, when they might otherwise pay nothing. This would tend to make the tax code procyclical, increasing both the highs and the lows of the business cycle.

DISTRIBUTION TABLES

Aside from the issue of fairness, there are practical problems with making tax policy that the definition of income imposes. These are embodied in the distribution tables produced for every major tax bill by the Treasury Department and the Joint Committee on Taxation. These tables put all taxpayers into different income classes and show how a tax bill will affect them. They will also often show how tax changes will affect groups of taxpayers depending on whether they are married or have children.

One problem with these tables is that they are not based on cash income or the definition used by the IRS for tax purposes. They are essentially based on a Haig-Simons definition of income, which tends to make people look richer than they are due to the inclusion of income they may not be aware they had. The Treasury Department's distribution tables, for example, add to gross income unreported and underreported income, contributions to pension plans, nontaxable transfer payments, employer-provided fringe benefits, and many other forms of income for which there are no lines on tax returns.

The success or failure of a piece of tax legislation will often depend on how the distribution tables look. Congress almost always strives to make sure that every income group benefits or suffers proportionately in percentage terms. Much of the complexity of the tax code results because a tax bill was being tweaked to make the distribution tables come out right. This often means phasing out tax benefits for the wealthy, which creates a crazy quilt of effective tax rates at different income levels. People may see a sharp increase in taxes once they are over some income threshold, and then a sharp cut in taxes once they pass some other threshold.

This problem doesn't affect just the wealthy. The working poor face high implicit tax rates when the Earned Income Tax Credit (EITC), a refundable credit for the working poor, is withdrawn as their income rises. They may also suffer by losing certain welfare benefits, such as housing subsidies, when they earn more than a relatively small amount of money. It's not uncommon for poor people to lose more than a dollar of benefits when they earn an additional dollar over a modest threshold. They are paying a 100 percent tax rate on each additional dollar earned—a powerful barrier to self-improvement.

In recent years a big problem has been that because of the EITC and various other tax credits, close to half of all people filing federal income tax returns pay no income taxes at all (Table 3.1). Indeed because some credits are refundable, they may even get a government refund despite paying no income taxes. In other words, they have a negative tax rate.

Table 3.1 Tax Units Paying No Federal Income Tax, 2011

Cash Income Class	Income Above	Number of Non-paying Tax Filers	Percentage of Total Nonpaying Tax Filers	Percentage of Nonpayers Within Class
Lowest 20%		40,739,000	53.6	93.3
Second 20%	$16,812	22,200,000	29.2	60.3
Middle 20%	$33,542	9,705,000	12.8	30.0
Fourth 20%	$59,486	1,956,000	2.6	7.3
Top 20%	$103,465	443,000	0.6	1.9
Total		**76,069,000**	**100.0**	**46.4**
90th to 95th percentile	$163,173	57,000	0.1	1.0
95th to 99th percentile	$210,998	78,000	0.1	1.7
Top 1%	$532,613	24,000	0.0	2.1
Top 0.1%	$2,178,886	3,000	0.0	2.3

Source: Tax Policy Center.

Consequently it is difficult for Congress to cut income taxes in any way without appearing to favor the relatively well-to-do. The only way to cut taxes for those who don't pay any is to increase refundable credits, which is exactly the same thing as sending people a government check. But because it is being done via the tax system, it's called a tax cut rather than a government handout.

Curiously, the government never calculates distribution tables for spending. It has little idea who benefits from the vast bulk of spending programs or how they interact with each other. This makes it hard for Congress to offset the effect of some tax change by increasing spending. Unless it is done in the form of a refundable tax credit, it won't show up in distribution tables. This opacity encourages Congress to do more and more de facto spending through the tax code, where it may lack the transparency of direct spending.

One goal of tax reform ought to be to rationalize our basic concept of taxable income. Many economists believe that the confusion over income strengthens the case for a pure consumption tax. Consumption can be more easily defined. A direct consumption tax could easily raise as much money as the federal income tax and relieve everyone from even having to file a tax return. But it would also mean that those now paying no federal income taxes would face a significant increase in taxation.

FURTHER READINGS

Abreu, Alice G., and Richard K. Greenstein. "Defining Income." *Florida Tax Review* (July 2011): 295–348.

Bartlett, Bruce. "The Marriage Penalty: Origins, Effects, Solutions." *Tax Notes* (Sept. 14, 1998): 1341–57.

Bartlett, Bruce. "Recent Proposals Relating to Family Taxation." *Tax Notes* (Apr. 2, 2001): 153–57.

Bartlett, Bruce. "Why the Correct Capital Gains Tax Rate Is Zero." *Tax Notes* (Sept. 6, 1999): 1411–18.

Bittker, Boris. "Federal Income Taxation and the Family." *Stanford Law Review* (July 1975): 1389–463.

Buchanan, Neil H. "The Case against Income Averaging." *Virginia Tax Review* (Spring 2006): 1151–217.

Congressional Budget Office. *For Better or for Worse: Marriage and the Federal Income Tax.* June 1997.

Cronin, Julie-Ann. "U.S. Treasury Distributional Analysis Methodology." U.S. Treasury Department, Office of Tax Analysis Working Paper No. 85 (Sept. 1999).

Gann, Pamela. "Abandoning Marital Status as a Factor in Allocating Income Tax Burdens." *Texas Law Review* (Dec. 1980): 1–69.

Graetz, Michael. "Paint-by-Numbers Lawmaking." *Columbia Law Review* (Apr. 1995): 609–82.

Groves, Harold M. *Federal Tax Treatment of the Family.* Brookings Institution, 1963.

Hubbard, R. Glenn. "On the Use of 'Distribution Tables' in the Tax Policy Process." *National Tax Journal* (Dec. 1993): 527–37.

Joint Committee on Taxation. *Methodology and Issues in Measuring Changes in the Tax Burdens.* Report No. JCS-7-93 (June 14, 1993).

McCaffery, Edward J. *Taxing Women.* University of Chicago Press, 1997.

McMahon, Stephanie H. "To Save State Residents: States' Use of Community Property for Federal Tax Reduction." *Law and History Review* (Fall 2009): 585–625.

Mill, John Stuart. *Principles of Political Economy.* Longmans, Green, 1909.

Phillips, William. "Living in Glasshouses." *British Tax Review* (Mar.–Apr. 1966): 104–14.

Surrey, Stanley S. "The Personal Income Tax Base for Individuals." *Columbia Law Review* (June 1958): 815–30.

Thuronyi, Victor. "The Concept of Income." *Tax Law Review* (Fall 1990): 45–105.

Vickrey, William. "Averaging of Income for Income Tax Purposes." *Journal of Political Economy* (June 1939): 379–97.

Vickrey, William. "Tax Simplification through Cumulative Averaging." *Law and Contemporary Problems* (Autumn 1969): 736–50.

Zelenak, Lawrence. "Marriage and the Income Tax." *Southern California Law Review* (Jan. 1994): 339–405.

Chapter 4

How to Understand Tax Rates

The concept of a "tax rate" is confusing because there are many different tax rates. Knowing which one to use is a matter of what sort of analysis one is doing. Table 4.1 shows the basic rate schedule that taxpayers used to calculate their federal income tax liability for 2011. There are also schedules for married people filing separately and heads of households.

Table 4.1 Federal Income Tax Rate Schedule, 2011

Single Individuals				
Taxable Income		**Tax Payment**		
Over	But Not Over	Pay	Percent on Excess	Of the Amount Over
$0	$8,500	$0	10	$0
$8,375	$34,500	$850.00	15	$8,500
$34,500	$83,600	$4,750.00	25	$34,500
$83,600	$174,400	$17,025.00	28	$83,600
$174,400	$379,150	$42,449.00	33	$174,400
$379,150		$110,016.50	35	$379,150
Married Filing Jointly and Surviving Spouses				
$0	$17,000	$0	10	$0
$17,000	$69,000	$1,700.00	15	$17,000
$69,000	$139,350	$9,500.00	25	$69,000
$139,350	$212,300	$27,087.50	28	$139,350
$212,300	$379,150	$47,513.50	33	$212,300
$379,150		$102,574.00	35	$379,150

Source: Joint Committee on Taxation.

WHAT RATE MATTERS?

Generally speaking, economists are primarily concerned with the average or effective tax rate, which is simply taxes paid divided by income. That is the most meaningful measure of the burden of taxation. It also tells us how taxation affects disposable income, which is significant analytically for factors such as consumer spending, a key determinant of short-run economic growth. The broadest measure of the effective tax rate would be all federal taxes as a share of the gross domestic product, which measures the economy's total income.

The marginal tax rate is also important. That is the tax rate that applies to the last dollar earned. It is essentially the statutory tax rate and can be seen in Table 4.1 as the percent on excess. It is critical for determining many investment decisions, such as whether to buy taxable bonds or tax-free municipal bonds. For example, if the interest spread between a taxable bond and an equivalent municipal bond is, say, 30 percent, then those in marginal tax brackets below that percent would come out ahead by buying taxable bonds and paying the tax. Those in higher brackets would be better off buying tax-free municipal bonds. Consequently many economists look at the spread between interest on taxable and tax-free bonds as a good measure of the average marginal tax rate in the economy. As one can see in Table 4.2, the vast bulk of taxpayers pay at most 15 percent on their last dollar earned. Only a very small number pay more than that.

Table 4.2 Distribution of Marginal Tax Rates, 2011

Marginal Tax Bracket	Number of Taxpayers	Percent Distribution
0%	58,935,000	35.4
10%	26,292,000	15.8
15%	49,945,000	30.0
25%	24,380,000	14.6
28%	4,628,000	2.8
33%	1,537,000	0.9
35%	869,000	0.5

Source: Joint Committee on Taxation.

Keep in mind that Table 4.2 looks only at federal income taxes. The payroll tax and state and local income taxes would also apply to many taxpayers.

A curious phenomenon is that a great many people grossly overestimate their average tax rate (Table 4.3). An April 2010 poll asked people what they thought it was. The vast majority of respondents said it was much, much higher than it actually is. A goodly number believed that their federal income tax payment as a share of their income was well above the highest marginal tax rate of 35 percent.

Table 4.3 Tax Rate Perceptions and Reality, 2010

On average, about what percentage of their household incomes would you guess most Americans pay in federal income taxes each year: less than 10 percent, between 10 and 20 percent, between 20 and 30 percent, between 30 and 40 percent, between 40 percent and 50 percent, or more than 50 percent, or don't you know enough to say?			
Tax Percentage/Income	All	Tea Party Members	Actual
Less than 10%	5%	11%	86.5%
10–20%	26%	25%	12.9%
20–30%	25%	26%	0.6%
30–40%	10%	14%	
40–50%	2%	3%	
More than 50%	1%	1%	
Don't know	31%	15%	n/a

Sources: CBS News/New York Times poll (April 14, 2010); Joint Committee on Taxation.

TAXES ON THE RICH

Even among the wealthiest people in America, tax rates are not nearly as high as many people imagine. The Internal Revenue Service annually publishes data on the sources of income and taxes paid by the 400 Americans with the largest incomes. In 2008 only 60 percent of them paid any income taxes at the top rate of 35 percent; 40 percent paid at most 28 percent, and seventeen members of the top 400 (4.25 percent) were in a marginal tax bracket below 26 percent.

As Table 4.4 illustrates, effective tax rates on those with the 400 largest incomes have fallen sharply over the years since data first began being published. The average tax rate on the entire group—their total income divided by their total federal income taxes—fell from almost 30 percent in 1993 to less than 20 percent after 2002. And whereas the bulk of the top 400 paid at least 25 percent of their income in taxes in the early 1990s, in the 2000s 66 percent paid less than 20 percent, with some paying less than 10 percent.

Table 4.4 Average Tax Rates for the 400 Taxpayers with the Largest Incomes

Tax Year	Distribution of Top 400 by Average Tax Rate							Average Tax Rate
	0–9	10–14	15–19	20–24	25–30	30–34	35+	
1992	6	10	17	62	234	71	—	26.38
1993	9	5	15	50	147	77	97	29.35
1994	9	4	16	55	156	64	96	28.57
1995	7	5	13	32	148	85	110	29.93
1996	3	7	24	61	180	57	68	27.81
1997	7	10	70	141	67	42	63	24.16
1998	7	31	109	146	28	27	52	22.02
1999	7	31	104	133	27	34	64	22.23
2000	11	29	96	141	36	35	52	22.29
2001	19	30	108	94	22	44	83	22.85
2002	10	34	86	110	38	60	62	22.88
2003	24	75	116	53	52	80	—	19.53
2004	27	112	103	34	51	73	—	18.16
2005	23	121	111	39	47	59	—	18.23
2006	31	113	125	34	50	47	—	17.17
2007	25	127	137	40	38	33	—	16.62
2008	30	101	112	52	46	59	—	18.11

Source: Internal Revenue Service.

TAXABLE INCOME

One reason many people are confused about how much federal income tax they pay is that there are many adjustments to their nominal income, different rates applying to different forms of income, and adjustments to their tax liability.

First, certain types of income are excluded from taxable

income altogether. These include employer-provided health insurance and interest on municipal bonds. Also, certain expenses are allowed to be deducted from gross income before adjusted gross income (AGI) is determined. These include trade or business expenses for the self-employed, contributions to pension and retirement plans, and alimony payments, among others. AGI is the basic measure of income from which taxable income is calculated.

Second, people get a personal exemption, which was $3,800 in 2011. This amount is increased annually by the rate of inflation. In addition, people are allowed to take a standard deduction if they choose not to itemize their deductions. In 2011 the standard deduction was $5,800 for single persons and $11,600 for married couples filing jointly. For those who itemize, common deductions are those for mortgage interest, state and local taxes, and charitable contributions. Once all deductions have been taken, taxable income is determined and statutory tax rates are applied to calculate one's tax liability. In general the rates in Table 4.1 apply, but there is a maximum tax rate of 15 percent on capital gains and dividends on corporate stock.

Third, some people reduce their taxes with tax credits, which are subtracted directly from their tax liability. These include a credit for each child of $1,000, the Earned Income Tax Credit (EITC) for people with low wages, various education credits, and many others. These credits apply regardless of whether someone itemizes or takes the standard deduction.

Finally, the law takes back many benefits as people's incomes rise. Among them are the EITC and various tax credits. Until 2010 there was also a phaseout of the personal exemption and an overall limit on itemized deductions for those with high incomes. (Both of these provisions were temporarily repealed in 2010, but are scheduled to come back in 2013 without further congressional action.) These phaseouts have economic effects identical to marginal tax rates. If you lose a $100 tax credit once your income passes a certain point, that is no different from paying $100 more in taxes. Table 4.5 illustrates the marginal rate effect of some selected tax benefits that are phased out above certain income levels.

Table 4.5 Marginal Rate Effects of Selected Tax Provisions, 2010

Provision	Effect on Marginal Tax Rate
Alternative Minimum Tax	Exemption is reduced by 25 percent of income above phaseout threshold, raising effective marginal rate by 25 percent of Alternative Minimum Tax rate. Thresholds are $112,500 for singles and $150,000 for married couples.
Child Tax Credit	Credit is reduced $50 for each $1,000 above phaseout, in effect adding 5 percent to the tax rate for single parents with incomes above $75,000, and $110,000 for married couples.
Earned Income Tax Credit	For single persons, credit decreases during phaseout are 7.65 percent above $7,800 for those with no children; 34 percent above $16,450 for those with one child; 40 percent above $16,450 for those with two children; and 45 percent above $16,450 for those with three or more children.
Lifetime Learning Credit	Provides a tax credit of up to $10,000 for eligible education expenses and is phased out at a 20 percent rate on incomes above $50,000 for singles and $100,000 for married couples.
Taxation of Social Security Benefits	Up to 85 percent of benefits may be taxable above threshold, thus raising effective marginal tax rate by 85 percent of one's statutory tax rate in phase-out range.

Source: Tax Policy Center.

The phaseout of the EITC has especially pernicious effects on those with low incomes. The effective marginal tax rate on families with half the median income is actually well above that for families with incomes four times higher. In 2010 a four-person family with half the median income (for four-person families) faced a marginal tax rate of 31 percent on each additional dollar they earned due to the combined effect of federal income taxes plus the loss of EITC benefits, which phased out at a 40 percent rate on incomes above $16,450. By contrast, a four-person family with twice the median income made $153,000 but paid only 27 percent on each additional dollar earned. These anomalies exist throughout the tax code.

LABOR SUPPLY

While it may seem obvious that any increase in tax rates will reduce labor supply and economic output, this is not necessarily the case. Changes in average and marginal tax rates have different effects. If the average tax rate rises without any change in the marginal tax rate, this will more than likely increase work effort because of what economists call the "income effect." Workers usually have a certain target level of income or need a certain amount of after-tax income on which to live. When that amount is reduced by a higher tax, workers tend to respond by trying to work more hours or perhaps getting a second job to raise their income back up to where they need it to be.

On the other hand, if one's marginal tax rate rises and the average rate remains unchanged, then another effect, which economists call the "substitution effect," takes precedence. In terms of labor supply, people always have the choice of working or taking leisure. They will work an additional day or hour only if their after-tax income increases by an amount that makes it worthwhile to do so. If the marginal tax rate on that additional income reduces the after-tax reward too much, workers will take leisure instead.

Thus one can see that if the average tax rate increases and the marginal tax rate goes down, then both the income effect and the substitution effect will push workers in the same direction: toward additional labor supply. Conversely, if the average tax rate is reduced and the marginal tax rate is increased, then once again both effects are pushing in the same direction: against additional labor supply.

The situation becomes ambiguous if average and marginal tax rates go in opposite directions. If average and marginal tax rates are raised simultaneously it's unclear whether the income effect or the substitution effect will dominate. People will be encouraged to work more because of the former, but less because of the latter. As a matter of theory, one cannot say how people will react. The same problem would result if both average and marginal rates are cut at the same time.

The impact becomes less ambiguous when income transfers, which are financed by taxes, enter the calculation. These also have income and substitution effects. If a transfer such as unemployment compensation increases, it will reduce work effort; if it is withdrawn, it will increase labor supply. Thus an increase in the average tax rate used to finance income transfers will have equal and opposite income effects. Workers will work more to replace the lost income from the higher taxes, while those receiving transfers funded by the higher taxes will work less by about the same amount. Thus the income effect is canceled out in the aggregate.

This leaves only the substitution effect, which can be created directly by a higher marginal tax rate or effectively by withdrawing a transfer or tax benefit above a certain income level. For this reason there is a consensus view that marginal tax rates should be kept as low as possible and that taxes should be raised, when necessary, by raising the average tax rate. This can be done by closing tax loopholes, taking away tax preferences, and broadening the tax base. This is the essence of tax reform.

FURTHER READINGS

Boes, Richard, and Gary R. Wells. "Stealth Taxes." *Journal of Accountancy* (Mar. 2001): 73–80.

Congressional Budget Office. *Labor Supply and Taxes*. Jan. 1996.

Enis, Charles R., and Leroy F. Christ. "Implications of Phase-outs on Individual Marginal Tax Rates." *Journal of the American Taxation Association* (Spring 1999): 45–72.

Feenberg, Daniel R., and James M. Poterba. "The Alternative Minimum Tax and Effective Marginal Tax Rates." *National Tax Journal* (June 2004): 407–27.

Gwartney, James, and Richard Stroup. "Labor Supply and Taxes: A Correction of the Record." *American Economic Review* (June 1983): 446–51.

Joint Committee on Taxation. "Federal Tax Treatment of Individuals." Report No. JCX-43–11 (Sept. 12, 2011).

Joint Committee on Taxation. "Present Law and Analysis Relating to Individual Effective Marginal Tax Rates." Report No. JCS-3–98 (Feb. 3, 1998).

Musgrave, Richard A. *The Theory of Public Finance*. McGraw-Hill, 1959.

Musgrave, Richard A., and Carl S. Shoup. *Readings in the Economics of Taxation*. Richard D. Irwin, 1959.

Rupert, Timothy J., Louise E. Single, and Arnold M. Wright. "The Impact of Floors and Phase-outs on Taxpayers' Decisions and Understanding of Marginal Tax Rates." *Journal of the American Taxation Association* (Spring 2003): 72–86.

Tax Foundation. "PEP and Pease: Repealed for 2010 but Preparing a Comeback." Special Report No. 178 (Apr. 2010).

Chapter 5

The Relationship Between Tax Rates and Tax Revenues

O ne of the issues that undoubtedly will arise during the tax reform debate is its impact on revenues. Historically, tax reforms have striven to be revenue-neutral, neither raising nor lowering revenues in the medium to long run. This means enacting revenue-raising measures, such as closing loopholes and broadening the tax base, along with the tax rate reductions that everyone agrees are the ultimate goal of tax reform. Virtually all economists agree in principle that it is best to have the lowest possible rates on the broadest possible base.

Calculating the revenue impact of tax reform, however, will be contentious for two reasons. First, conservatives will assert that rate reductions will have an exceptionally powerful impact on economic growth that may lead revenues to rise, and that revenue-raising measures will have such a depressing effect on growth that revenues may fall. In the end the only real reform that conservatives favor is cutting rates. It will take enormous effort to get them to accept loophole closing and base broadening except in principle. The revenue estimate of various tax provisions that constitute a tax reform package will be essential to its composition and chances of enactment.

The second problem is more technical. Different provisions of the tax code interact with each other. If you change one, it affects others. For example, in 1986 Congress got rid of the deduction for interest on consumer loans, thinking that it would raise revenue and discourage borrowing. This change led banks to create home equity loans, for which the interest remained deductible because mortgage interest was still deductible. By and large, people just borrowed against their home to fund the same consumption that they had previously paid for with credit lines and credit cards. Similarly if the mortgage interest deduction is eliminated, then fewer people will itemize, thus affecting the revenue consequences of many other tax deductions.

If Congress decides to plug one loophole, it may find that it is also necessary to plug others lest one simply become a substitute for the other, substantially reducing the revenue yield. It also matters to the revenue estimates in what order various reforms are implemented. If a rate reduction is assumed to come first, it will reduce the revenue yield from closing loopholes. A $1 deduction by someone in the top bracket costs the government 35 cents; but if the top rate is reduced to 30 percent, then that same deduction costs only 30 cents in revenue. So whether rate reductions are assumed to come first or last makes an enormous difference for calculating the impact on revenues of the entire tax reform package.

A recent study by the Syracuse University economist Len Burman concluded that the aggregate size of all tax expenditures added together is actually 6 percent larger than their nominal total. A key reason is that eliminating tax exclusions—income that need not be reported—raises taxable income, thus pushing people into higher tax brackets and raising the revenue loss associated with various deductions from adjusted gross income.

REVENUE ESTIMATING

Congress has always needed to know the revenue effects of tax bills. In the era before computers, such calculations were usually done by accountants who made no effort to incorporate economic effects. They just assumed that a 10 percent tax rate increase would raise revenues 10 percent over the previous year. And they seldom calculated revenue effects for more than the first year that a tax change was in effect.

Usually the Treasury Department would supply Congress with revenue estimates. But since the 1920s the Joint Committee on Taxation (JCT) has produced them as well, often relying heavily on Treasury's Office of Tax Analysis for assistance. Other agencies may also make vital contributions in terms of data and analysis. The Congressional Budget Office provides the JCT with the underlying economic forecast and macroeconomic data upon which it scores tax bills. Treasury always uses the same economic forecast published in the budget, which is developed by a "troika" consisting of Treasury, the Office of Management and Budget, and the Council of Economic Advisers.

While policymakers often treat revenue estimates as written in stone, those familiar with how they are constructed know that the process often resembles sausage making. I learned this early in my career as a congressional staffer, when Congress was considering a windfall profits tax on oil production.

Curious about the revenue estimate, I called the JCT and was told that on this occasion it had simply used the estimate given to it by Treasury. So I called Treasury and was told that it had simply taken the Department of Energy's forecast for oil production and multiplied it by the tax. In other words, Treasury assumed that a heavy new tax on oil production would have no effect on either supply or demand. I then called DOE to see where its oil production forecast came from and whether this forecast would be affected by the new tax. The person I spoke with said that the forecast came from a private consultant. I called him next. It turned out that the consultant's estimate was a back-of-the-envelope calculation that he gave to DOE over the phone. He was horrified to learn that Congress was about to enact a major tax bill based on his computation.

For many years conservatives have complained that the traditional static revenue-estimating process, which ignores the behavioral and macroeconomic effects of tax changes, created a bias in favor of tax increases and against tax cuts. If revenue estimators took account of how taxes change behavior, economic growth, and other factors, the benefits of tax increases and the cost of tax cuts would not appear so large. This was particularly problematic during the 1990s, when Congress imposed a PAYGO (pay-as-you-go) requirement on itself such that increases in spending or tax cuts had to be offset with spending cuts or tax increases in order to keep the deficit from rising. Thus a tax cut scored on a static basis would require bigger spending cuts to be deficit-neutral, and a tax increase would finance a bigger increase in spending than was justified by a dynamic revenue score.

DYNAMIC SCORING

Over the years economists have become more sophisticated about measuring the revenue effects of tax changes. They now generally accept that a 10 percent increase in income tax rates will not raise income tax revenues 10 percent due to behavioral and macroeconomic effects; nor will a 10 percent tax rate reduction reduce revenues 10 percent.

That is, people and businesses will respond to a tax increase by reducing output and rearranging their finances to reduce the burden of the tax, and this response will lower the revenue yield. Conversely, a tax cut may lead to increased output, a reduction in the use of tax shelters, and other effects that will offset some of the revenue loss. Economists call these "feedback" or "dynamic" effects. A revenue score that did not incorporate such effects would be called a "static estimate."

Unfortunately there is still no consensus on measuring the precise effects of tax changes, thus ensuring that how to score the revenue effects of tax reform will be highly contentious. Moreover there are lots of tax changes for which there is insufficient research or data upon which to calculate a dynamic revenue effect.

The Treasury and JCT now accept the principle that revenue scores ought to incorporate dynamic factors to improve their accuracy. But there are practical problems with doing so that prevent the routine use of dynamic scoring. Many proposed tax changes have no dynamic effects or de minimis effects too small to measure. A refundable tax credit for children, for example, is going to lose revenue dollar-for-dollar because it is essentially a spending program that runs through the tax code.

Another problem is that while revenue estimators could try calculating the behavioral effects of tax changes, it is much harder to calculate the effect of any tax change on the economy as a whole. It is also time-consuming. Because the JCT uses the baseline economic forecast from the Congressional Budget Office (CBO) to score tax bills, to incorporate macroeconomic effects CBO would have to prepare a new economic forecast taking account of the tax change, and then the JCT would have to prepare a new revenue estimate based on the new forecast.

This is less of a problem for Treasury, as the troika forecast assumes the economic effects of the administration's tax proposals, which are assumed to be enacted as proposed. However, I know from personal experience that this is not necessarily true; at least it wasn't true in the past. I worked in the office that developed the economic forecast. Oftentimes we had no idea what tax initiatives would be in the budget. Nor did we have access to the sorts of econometric models that would allow us to incorporate their effects.

Finally, there are important assumptions that have to be made about subsequent policy changes that can have major effects on the revenue score. For example, if a tax cut is expected to be temporary, it may have much less impact than if it is thought to be permanent. If people believe taxes will be increased in the future to offset the revenue loss of a tax cut, this will have a different effect from a revenue loss that is assumed to be permanent. Consequently revenue estimators must make assumptions about the extent to which people have foresight regarding future tax changes because it will affect the response to near-term or temporary changes.

For these reasons it is hard to generalize about the revenue effect of any tax change. In general, economists find that the behavioral and macroeconomic effects of a tax rate reduction will not recoup more than about a third of the static revenue loss. And Republican economists share this view as well.

- A 2005 Congressional Budget Office study during the time that the Republican economist Doug Holtz-Eakin was director concluded that a 10 percent cut in federal income tax rates would recoup at most 28 percent of the static revenue loss over ten years. And this estimate assumes that taxpayers have unlimited foresight and know that taxes will be raised after ten years to stabilize the debt/GDP ratio. Without foresight and with no compensating tax increases or spending cuts—a situation leading to an increase in the debt—feedback would be negative. In other words, the actual revenue loss would be larger than the static revenue loss.

- In a 2006 article published in the *Journal of Public Economics,* the Harvard economist Greg Mankiw, who chaired the Council of Economic Advisers during Bush II's first term, estimated the long-run revenue feedback at 32.4 percent from a cut in taxes on capital and at 14.7 percent from a cut in labor taxes.

- A 2006 analysis of extending the 2001 and 2003 Bush tax cuts by the Republican-leaning Heritage Foundation estimated that only 30 percent of the gross revenue loss would be recouped through behavioral effects and macroeconomic stimulus.

DID THE REAGAN AND BUSH TAX CUTS PAY FOR THEMSELVES?

Tax cuts that don't affect behavior will not recoup any of the revenue loss. Nevertheless many Republican politicians talk about all tax cuts as if they always pay for themselves. On July 13, 2010, Sen. Mitch McConnell (R-KY) said, "There's no evidence whatsoever that the Bush tax cuts actually diminished revenue. They increased revenue, because of the vibrancy of these tax cuts in the economy." On June 13, 2011, Tim Pawlenty, a former governor of Minnesota and then a candidate for the Republican presidential nomination, said, "When Ronald Reagan cut taxes in a significant way, revenues actually increased by almost 100 percent during his eight years as president. So this idea that significant, big tax cuts necessarily result in lower revenues—history does not [bear] that out."

In point of fact, Pawlenty's assertion is completely untrue. Federal revenues were $599.3 billion in fiscal year 1981 and were $991.1 billion in fiscal year 1989. That's an increase of just 65 percent. But of course a lot of that represented simple inflation. If 1981 revenues had risen only by the rate of inflation, they would have been $798 billion by 1989. Thus the real revenue increase was just 24 percent. However, the population also grew. Looking at real revenues per capita, we see that they rose from $3,470 in 1981 to $4,006 in 1989, an increase of just 15 percent. Finally, it is important to remember that Ronald Reagan raised taxes eleven times, increasing revenues by $133 billion per year as of 1988, about a third of the nominal revenue increase during his presidency (see Table 5.1).

Table 5.1 Eleven Major Tax Increases, 1982–88: Impact as of 1988

Legislation	Billions of Dollars
Tax Equity and Fiscal Responsibility Act	57.3
Highway Revenue Act of 1982	4.9
Social Security Amendments of 1983	24.6
Railroad Retirement Revenue Act of 1983	1.2
Deficit Reduction Act of 1984	25.4
Consolidated Omnibus Budget Reconciliation Act of 1985	2.9
Omnibus Budget Reconciliation Act of 1986	2.4
Superfund Amendments and Reauthorization Act of 1986	0.6
Continuing Resolution for 1987	2.8
Omnibus Budget Reconciliation Act of 1987	8.6
Continuing Resolution for 1988	2.0
Total tax increase	**132.7**

Source: *Budget of the U.S. Government, Fiscal Year 1990.*

The only metric that really matters is revenues as a share of the gross domestic product. By this measure, total federal revenues fell from 19.6 percent of GDP in 1981 to 18.4 percent of GDP by 1989. This suggests that revenues were $66 billion lower in 1989 as a result of Reagan's policies.

This is not surprising given that no one in the Reagan administration ever claimed that his 1981 tax cut would pay for itself or that it did. Reagan economists Bill Niskanen and Martin Anderson have written extensively on this oft-repeated myth. The conservative economist Lawrence Lindsey made a thorough effort to calculate the feedback effect in his 1990 book, *The Growth Experiment.* He concluded that the behavioral and macroeconomic effects of the 1981 tax cut, resulting from both supply-side and demand-side effects, recouped about a third of the static revenue loss.

BUSH TAX CUTS

Insofar as the Bush tax cuts are concerned, the economists behind them also never claimed that they paid for themselves. For example, Alan Viard, senior economist at the Council of Economic

Advisers (CEA) during Bush's first term, told the *Washington Post* in 2006, "Federal revenue is lower today than it would have been without the tax cuts. There's really no dispute among economists about that." Robert Carroll, deputy assistant secretary for tax analysis at the U.S. Treasury Department during Bush's second term, also told the *Post,* "As a matter of principle, we do not think tax cuts pay for themselves." On September 28, 2006, the Stanford economist Edward Lazear, chairman of the CEA in Bush's second term, testified before the Senate Budget Committee:

> Will the tax cuts pay for themselves? As a general rule, we do not think tax cuts pay for themselves. Certainly, the data . . . do not support this claim. Tax revenues in 2006 appear to have recovered to the level seen at this point in previous business cycles, but this does not make up for the lost revenue during 2003, 2004, and 2005. The tax cuts were a positive step and have contributed to the enhanced economic growth, additional jobs, higher real disposable income, and the low unemployment rates that we currently see today.

A 2011 calculation by the CBO concluded that the Bush tax cuts reduced federal revenues by $2.8 trillion between 2002 and 2011. (Technical factors and slow economic growth added another $3.4 trillion to the loss of revenue over what CBO expected in January 2001.)

It may be that in the end Congress will not attempt to enact a revenue-neutral tax reform. It may decide to make the package a net revenue loser, which would aid passage by increasing the number of winners and reducing the number of losers. But a tax package that reduces revenue is not tax reform. It's just another tax cut.

FURTHER READINGS

Altshuler, Rosanne, et al. "The Role of Dynamic Scoring in the Federal Budget Process: Closing the Gap between Theory and Practice." *American Economic Review* (May 2005): 432–36.

Anderson, Martin. *Revolution.* Harcourt Brace Jovanovich, 1988.

Auerbach, Alan J. "Dynamic Revenue Estimation." *Journal of Economic Perspectives* (Winter 1996): 141–57.

Auerbach, Alan J. "Dynamic Scoring: An Introduction to the Issues." *American Economic Review* (May 2005): 421–25.

Bartlett, Bruce. "Reagan's Forgotten Tax Record." *Tax Notes* (Feb. 21, 2011): 965–66.

Burman, Leonard E., et al. "How Big Are Total Individual Income Tax Expenditures, and Who Benefits from Them?" *American Economic Review* (May 2008): 79–83.

Carroll, Robert, and Warren Hrung. "What Does the Taxable Income Elasticity Say about Dynamic Responses to Tax Changes?" *American Economic Review* (May 2005): 426–31.

Congressional Budget Office. *Analyzing the Economic and Budgetary Effects of a 10 Percent Cut in Income Tax Rates.* Dec. 1, 2005.

Congressional Budget Office. *Changes in CBO's Baseline Projections Since January 2001.* May 12, 2011.

Council of Economic Advisers. "Dynamic Revenue and Budget Estimation." *Economic Report of the President, 2004.*

Feldstein, Martin. "Effects of Taxes on Economic Behavior." *National Tax Journal* (Mar. 2008): 131–39.

Feldstein, Martin. "How Big Should Government Be?" *National Tax Journal* (June 1997): 197–213.

Foertsch, Tracy L., and Ralph A. Rector. "A Dynamic Analysis of the 2001 and 2003 Bush Tax Cuts: Applying an Alternative Technique for Calibrating Macroeconomic and Microeconomic Models." Heritage Foundation, Center for Data Analysis (Nov. 22, 2006).

Joint Committee on Taxation. "Summary of Economic Models and Estimating Practices of the Staff of the Joint Committee on Taxation." Report No. JCX-46–11 (Sept. 19, 2011).

Lindsey, Lawrence B. *The Growth Experiment.* Basic Books, 1990.

Maki, Dean M. "Household Debt and the Tax Reform Act of 1986." *American Economic Review* (Mar. 2001): 305–19.

Mankiw, N. Gregory, and Matthew Weinzierl. "Dynamic Scoring: A Back-of-the-Envelope Guide." *Journal of Public Economics* (Sept. 2006): 1415–33.

Montgomery, Lori. "Lower Deficit Sparks Debate over Tax Cuts' Role." *Washington Post* (Oct. 17, 2006).

Neubig, Thomas S., and David Joulfaian. "The Tax Expenditure Budget before and after the Tax Reform Act of 1986." U.S. Treasury Department, Office of Tax Analysis (Oct. 1988).

Niskanen, William A. *Reaganomics: An Insider's Account of the Policies and the People.* Oxford University Press, 1988.

Page, Benjamin R. "CBO's Analysis of the Macroeconomic Effects of the President's Budget." *American Economic Review* (May 2005): 437–40.

Sunley, Emil M., and Randall D. Weiss. "The Revenue Estimating Process." *American Journal of Tax Policy* (Fall 1992): 261–98. Sunley was deputy assistant secretary of the Treasury for tax analysis during the Carter administration.

U.S. Treasury Department. "A Dynamic Analysis of Permanent Extension of the President's Tax Relief." Office of Tax Analysis (July 25, 2006).

Chapter 6

How Taxes Affect Economic Growth

lthough political discussion tends to frame the issue simply as "high taxes—bad for growth," "low taxes—good for growth," the truth is much more complex. It's not just the level of taxation that is important for growth, but its composition, structure, and distribution. Also, the issue of taxation cannot be viewed in isolation from how the revenues are used. Some kinds of spending stimulate growth; some kinds retard it. Insofar as good taxes finance good spending, that will be good for growth. And tax cuts that increase the deficit may be bad for growth, while tax increases that reduce deficits may stimulate growth.

Conservatives often talk about taxation as if the optimal rate implicitly is zero. During a presidential debate in September 2011, Rep. Michele Bachmann (R-MN) said so: "I think you earned every dollar. You should get to keep every dollar you earn. That's your money. That's not the government's money." Tellingly, none of the other candidates for the Republican presidential nomination disagreed.

I have never once heard a conservative admit that there is a level of taxation below which it would be unwise to go. But of course there is a limit, unless one believes anarchy is the preferred state in which people should live. Insofar as government is legitimate, then the taxation necessary to fund it is also legitimate. That is the benefit of the burden.

Even ideological libertarians admit that some basic government functions are necessary to maximize growth. The market cannot defend itself; it requires, at a minimum, a military, a police force, and courts to protect against foreign invasion and crime and enforce contracts. And all economists recognize that there are public goods that enhance growth, which the market is incapable of producing on its own because, among other reasons, all the benefits cannot be monetized and free riders can't be excluded. The national highway system is perhaps the best example of a pure public good that continues to be an enormous stimulus to growth.

INVESTMENT

Investment is clearly the most important factor in economic growth. Historically, investment has meant building factories and filling them with machines to produce goods. But economists now understand that investments in research and development, which produce new technology, and human capital are equally if not more important. A labor force without education, training, and skills is worth less than a labor force with those elements.

The ultimate purpose of all investment is to raise productivity: output per worker. In the long run, the growth rate of the economy—the gross domestic product, or GDP—is simply the rate of productivity growth plus growth of the labor force. Highly skilled workers with the proper tools and equipment produce far more than those without. That is why businesses don't locate all their factories in developing countries, despite those countries' minuscule taxes and wages. Whatever might be saved in terms of lower taxes and wages will be lost from increased costs for training, inferior quality, poor infrastructure, risks resulting from arbitrary assessments, insecure property rights, corruption, and other factors.

The most important determinant of investment is national saving. People often talk about saving and investment as if they were the same thing, but they are not. Saving comes from forgoing consumption: that is, goods and services that are produced today, but not consumed today. It is this surplus over and above current consumption that provides the resources that investors use to create capital in the form of plants, equipment, and research and development, or just to cover operating losses while a business is getting off the ground.

Generally speaking, people will accept a fairly low yield on saving in return for the security of knowing that it is unlikely to be lost. The reward on investment is always higher, as it carries risk. The job of the entrepreneur is to take saving and turn it into investment, making his profit on the spread between the lower rate of return on saving and the higher rate of return on investment.

The financial industry exists as an intermediary between savers and investors. Some of these intermediaries, such as banks, will be conservative, lending money only to safe and sound investments with low risk. Other intermediaries, such as hedge funds and venture capital funds, and individuals investing their own saving are much more willing to take on risk in return for the chance at a high reward.

TAXES AND SAVING

Taxation will affect savers and investors differently, and also affect different classes of investors differently. Research shows that taxation has little effect on the personal savings rate, that is, saving by individuals and households. This is because their two primary motives for saving are precautionary: having resources they can fall back on in the event of an emergency, and retirement. Of course, people save for other reasons as well, such as their children's higher education or to get the down payment on a house, but these are also insensitive to the after-tax rate of return. People have to save for such things even if they get no return at all.

There's a lot of debate among economists as to whether or to what extent various savings incentives in the tax code—such as Individual Retirement Accounts and 401(k) plans, which exclude contributions from taxable income and defer the return on such saving until withdrawal—stimulate net additional saving or merely cause people to shift saving from taxable to tax-deferred accounts. Undoubtedly people do save more to some extent, but probably not by much. What is less in dispute is that people tend to invest their funds in such accounts conservatively, in part because capital losses cannot be deducted from ordinary income, since contributions were already deducted in the first place.

The ability to deduct capital losses is a powerful incentive for risk-taking. Since the government takes a share of profits, it's appropriate that it should share in losses as well. Unfortunately it does not. Individuals may take capital losses only against capital gains and can deduct just $3,000 of net losses against ordinary income per year, although unused losses may be carried forward.

From a macroeconomic point of view, the personal savings rate is generally not that important. The main contributor to gross national saving, which is all that matters for investment, is saving by businesses and governments. Businesses do the bulk of saving through depreciation allowances, deductions for the wearing out of plant and equipment so they can be replaced when the time comes, and retained earnings. They also contribute to saving through pensions provided to their employees.

Governments, on the other hand, have an ambiguous effect on saving. State and local governments add to savings because they must make contributions to pension plans for their employees and otherwise balance their operating budgets. But the federal government almost always runs a deficit. And when governments run a deficit, that is essentially negative saving, subtracting from the pool of saving available for private investment.

Gross national saving is the sum of household saving, plus business saving, plus government saving in the case of a surplus or negative saving in the case of a deficit. Thus it stands to reason that in some cases a tax increase that reduces the deficit will reduce negative saving and thereby add to national saving, which may increase investment, productivity, and growth. If a tax increase lowers the deficit by $100 billion, then in effect $100 billion has been added to national saving.

Whether a tax increase adds to national saving depends on whether the additional funds are used to reduce the deficit and not to fund additional consumption spending. Also, taxes must not be raised in a way that reduces private saving more than the additional revenue that is raised.

Nations would prefer to finance domestic investment from domestic saving. Generally speaking, more saving will encourage more investment, which will raise living standards in the long run due to increased productivity. In cases where a nation has insufficient domestic saving to finance domestic investment, saving can be imported from abroad. Conversely, an excess of domestic saving over domestic investment can be exported to other countries where there are more investment opportunities and a higher rate of return.

The United States has tended to have more investment opportunities in recent years than domestic saving to finance them. Other countries, such as China, have had more saving than they needed to finance domestic investment. Thus world saving has flowed to the United States, allowing investment to rise despite low domestic saving. As long as the rate of return on investment exceeds the rate of return on saving, this benefits everyone. But as time goes by, an increasing portion of national output will necessarily flow abroad to repay foreigners for their lending.

Taxation can affect these movements of capital to some extent. The impact is greatest in terms of foreign direct investment—investments in tangible assets such as factories and land. Portfolio investment in stocks and bonds is less sensitive to taxes and often thought of as "hot money" that responds more to interest rates, exchange rates, perceptions of national risk, and so on.

LABOR SUPPLY AND CAPITAL GAINS

Another key determinant of growth is labor supply. Economists disagree on how and to what extent taxation affects hours of work, the incentive to obtain education to increase one's earning power, and the decision to work full-time or part-time or to enter and leave the labor force. Prime-age males are much less sensitive to taxes on labor than secondary workers such as working wives, who often leave the labor force for extended periods to care for children and tend to have a preference for part-time or temporary work. Furthermore because couples' earnings are aggregated for tax purposes, the secondary earner is in effect taxed on his or her first dollar at the tax rate that applies to the primary earner's last dollar earned. Thus secondary workers generally face much higher marginal tax rates than those on primary workers.

Although the impact of taxation often focuses on the rich, they are probably among the least sensitive to the impact of taxes on their labor supply. We all know of actors, singers, and business-people who work till they drop without showing the slightest sensitivity to the marginal tax rate they face. That's not to say they pay no attention to taxes. They may work less than they could; they may move to low-tax states like Florida; and almost certainly they will arrange their finances to minimize their taxes. But labor supply is not as affected by taxes as commonly believed.

International evidence shows that corporate tax rates are especially important for economic growth, but taxes on real property, such as land and buildings, and consumption don't have much impact. The overall level of taxation and the size of government generally correlate negatively with economic growth, but there are important exceptions, discussed in the chapter on foreign taxes.

Investment is where taxes make a difference. And experience shows that the tax rate on capital gains is the one that matters most. The reason is that success can become capitalized very quickly into asset values. Since entrepreneurs typically get most of their return in the form of capital gains, the tax on this form of income is critical for investment, business start-ups, innovation, inventing, and other factors essential for growth.

A case can be made that capital gains should not be taxed at all. Since they represent only the capitalized value of future taxable income streams—interest, rent, profits, or dividends—the capital gains tax can be viewed as a double tax. However, it doesn't follow that selectively eliminating capital gains taxes is a good idea. In 1997 capital gains taxes on owner-occupied residences were effectively eliminated. Many economists now believe that this was a key factor contributing to the housing bubble of the 2000s.

On the other hand, the lower tax rate on capital gains, which has existed throughout most of the history of the income tax, may be the main reason high income tax rates didn't stifle growth during the era when the top income tax rate was more than 90 percent, in the 1940s and 1950s. Throughout that period the top tax rate on long-term capital gains was just 25 percent. Thus entrepreneurial income was taxed at a much lower rate than ordinary income.

In addition to affecting the amount of investment, taxation affects its composition. Many provisions of the tax code encourage businesses and individuals to invest in particular ways. For example, in recent years Congress has enacted numerous tax subsidies for energy production. Almost by definition such tax preferences reduce the efficiency of investment because they confer a de facto subsidy designed to compensate for a lower market return. A key goal of tax reform should be to provide as much neutrality as possible so that investments are made on the basis of supply and demand rather than government subsidies.

RESEARCH AND DEVELOPMENT

One exception is research and development, the wellspring of growth. The reason special treatment of this form of investment may be justified is the same reason true public goods must be provided by government. The social return to R&D is far greater than that which can be captured by private businesses. Therefore the economy will have less R&D than is socially optimal. This is why presidents of both parties have consistently supported the R&D tax credit.

The big problem with the R&D credit is that it has never been made permanent; it expires every few years, and getting it renewed is often a struggle. Its impermanence has greatly reduced its effectiveness. Firms are reluctant to undertake R&D projects, which may take many years to plan and organize, on the assumption that they will get the R&D credit for their qualified investments. Thus it tends to be a windfall for what businesses would do anyway, rather than a stimulus to additional investment in R&D.

I have long suspected that Congress's on-and-off treatment of the R&D credit results from a sort of conspiracy. When it gets renewed, corporate lobbyists can take credit for adding to their clients' bottom line. It also justifies political contributions to members of Congress to get the R&D credit renewed. Thus it is a sort of win-win for everyone, except that it doesn't work the way it is supposed to. Although theoretically justified, the R&D credit should be abolished unless it is made permanent.

This raises another issue about the effect of taxation on growth: the lack of permanence in the tax code. Since 2001 Congress has been unwilling or unable to enact any major tax changes permanently. The 2001 and 2003 tax cuts all expired at the end of 2010 but were renewed at the last minute and for just two years. They expire again at the end of 2012. While it goes without saying that any provision of statutory law can be changed at any time, having laws with expiration dates stamped on them discourages people and businesses from changing their behavior in response to them. As in the case of the R&D credit, it undermines their effectiveness in stimulating growth.

FURTHER READINGS

Arnold, Jens. "Do Tax Structures Affect Aggregate Economic Growth? Empirical Evidence from a Panel of OECD Countries." Organization for Economic Cooperation and Development Economics Department Working Paper No. 643 (Oct. 14, 2008).

Bajaj, Vikas, and David Leonhardt. "1997 Tax Break on Home Sales May Have Helped Inflate Bubble." *New York Times* (Dec. 19, 2008).

Bernheim, B. Douglas. *The Vanishing Nest Egg: Reflections on Saving in America.* Twentieth Century Fund, 1991.

Bernheim, B. Douglas, and John B. Shoven. *National Saving and Economic Performance.* University of Chicago Press, 1991.

Congressional Budget Office. *Assessing the Decline in the National Saving Rate.* Apr. 1993.

Congressional Budget Office. *Long-Term Economic Effects of Chronically Large Federal Deficits.* Oct. 13, 2005.

Congressional Budget Office. *R&D and Productivity Growth.* June 2005.

Congressional Research Service. "The Economic Effects of Capital Gains Taxation." Report No. R40411 (Mar. 4, 2009).

Congressional Research Service. "The Economic Implications of the Long-Term Federal Budget Outlook." Report No. RL32747 (Aug. 16, 2011).

Congressional Research Service. "Federal Tax Reform and Its Potential Effects on Saving." Report No. RS22367 (Jan. 26, 2006).

Congressional Research Service. "Saving Incentives: What May Work, What May Not." Report No. RL33482 (June 20, 2006).

Cullen, Julie Berry, and Roger H. Gordon. "Taxes and Entrepreneurial Risk-Taking: Theory and Evidence for the U.S." *Journal of Public Economics* (Aug. 2007): 1479–505.

Engen, Eric, and Jonathan Skinner. "Taxation and Economic Growth." *National Tax Journal* (Dec. 1996): 617–42.

Feldstein, Martin. "The Effect of Taxes on Efficiency and Growth." *Tax Notes* (May 8, 2006): 679–84.

Feldstein, Martin, James R. Hines Jr., and R. Glenn Hubbard. *The Effects of Taxation on Multinational Corporations.* University of Chicago Press, 1995.

King, Robert G., and Sergio Rebelo. "Public Policy and Economic Growth: Developing Neoclassical Implications." *Journal of Political Economy* (Oct. 1990): S126—S150.

Kneller, Richard, Michael F. Bleaney, and Norman Gemmell. "Fiscal Policy and Growth: Evidence from OECD Countries." *Journal of Public Economics* (Nov. 1999): 171–90.

Kosters, Marvin H. *Personal Saving, Consumption, and Tax Policy.* American Enterprise Institute, 1992.

Johansson, Åsa, et al. "Tax and Economic Growth." Organization for Economic Cooperation and Development Economics Department Working Paper No. 620 (July 11, 2008).

Joint Committee on Taxation. "Tax Incentives for Research, Experimentation, and Innovation." Report No. JCX-45–11 (Sept. 16, 2011).

Lee, Young, and Roger H. Gordon. "Tax Structure and Economic Growth." *Journal of Public Economics* (June 2005): 1027–43.

Organization for Economic Cooperation and Development. *The Sources of Economic Growth in OECD Countries.* 2003.

Organization for Economic Cooperation and Development. "Taxation and Economic Growth." *Going for Growth.* 2009.

Poterba, James M. *International Comparisons of Household Saving.* University of Chicago Press, 1994.

Poterba, James M. *Public Policies and Household Saving.* University of Chicago Press, 1994.

Widmalm, Frida. "Tax Structure and Growth: Are Some Taxes Better Than Others?" *Public Choice* (June 2001): 199–219.

Yoo, Kwang-Yeol. "Corporate Taxation of Foreign Direct Investment Income, 1991–2001." Organization for Economic Cooperation and Development Economics Department Working Paper No. 365 (Aug. 26, 2003).

Chapter 7

The Question of Progressivity

There are two basic ways that income can be taxed: proportionately or progressively. The former means that if your income goes up 10 percent, then your taxes also go up 10 percent, but that's all. The latter means that if your income goes up 10 percent, then your taxes go up more than 10 percent; how much depends on the degree of progressivity.

Progressive taxation has always been controversial. In the *Communist Manifesto* (1848) Karl Marx said that "a heavy progressive or graduated income tax" is one of the key steps on the road to communism. A few years later the economist J. R. McCulloch voiced what has long been a standard conservative critique: "The moment you abandon, in the framing of such taxes, the cardinal principle of exacting from all individuals the same proportion of their income or of their property, you are at sea without rudder or compass, and there is no amount of injustice and folly you may not commit." In other words, the problem with progressivity is the slippery slope argument. Acceptance of the principle of progressivity eventually leads to the confiscation of the wealth and income of the rich, so conservatives say.

In practice no one really believes this, although one hears echoes of it in extreme right-wing attacks on the tax system. But their real objection isn't so much to progressivity as to taxation itself. For many conservatives, no system of taxation is more or less immoral than any other. Implicitly for them, it is all theft.

The real justification for progressivity is simply that the poor don't have much income to tax. Moreover most people understand that taking a dollar out of the pocket of someone with barely enough to live on is going to cost him or her far more than taking an extra dollar from a millionaire.

DE FACTO PROGRESSIVITY

Acceptance of the principle that the poor should be exempted from income taxes and that all taxpayers deserve a personal exemption creates de facto progressivity regardless of the rate structure. Consider a single statutory rate of 10 percent and a $10,000 personal exemption. Someone earning $30,000 would pay tax on only $20,000 of income, or $2,000. Thus for this person the effective rate is $2,000 divided by $30,000, or 6.67 percent. Someone with an income of $100,000 would be taxed on $90,000 of that income, or $9,000, yielding an effective rate of 9 percent.

Thus effective progressivity has nothing to do with the rate structure. Even flat-rate tax systems have some degree of progressivity by having a personal exemption. To eliminate progressivity, it would also be necessary to eliminate the personal exemption and tax everyone on every single dollar of income. To my knowledge, no supporter of the flat tax has ever advocated such a system. On the contrary, all advocate a high personal exemption that would exempt the bulk of people from paying any taxes at all on cash wages.

Nevertheless many people object to the existence of progressive tax rates in the tax schedule. At present the lowest federal income tax rate is 10 percent, rising to 15, 25, 28, 33, and 35 percent. The income thresholds are adjusted yearly for inflation.

Over the years the degree of progressivity in the rate schedule has fallen dramatically. In the 1950s the top rate was more than 90 percent. As recently as 1980 the top rate was 70 percent. Over the past thirty years every major country has flattened its rate schedule and reduced the degree of nominal progressivity in its income tax system.

Whether actual progressivity has declined, however, depends on the various tax exemptions, deductions, and exclusions in the income tax. Tax rates apply to taxable income, which can be considerably less than one's gross income. Some income, such as that on tax-exempt municipal bonds or that earned in Individual Retirement Accounts, doesn't even have to be reported. And of course those who have mortgages can deduct the interest, and so on.

Changing various tax preferences can achieve almost any degree of progressivity even if there is one statutory rate that applies to everyone. We already raise effective progressivity on those with high incomes by phasing out their ability to claim the personal exemption. Another way to increase effective progressivity is by taxing income from capital multiple times by the corporate income tax, personal income tax, capital gains tax, and estate tax.

Think about a single rate of 10 percent. A corporation has one shareholder and one share of stock outstanding, earns $100, and pays $10 in taxes. It pays out the remaining $90 as a dividend to its shareholder, who pays $9 in taxes. But because of the dividend, the company's stock goes up by $81. If the shareholder sells the stock there will be an $8 tax on the capital gain. The shareholder now has $72 left and dies, and the estate pays another $7 in tax. Thus of the original $100 of income there is now $65 left, for an effective rate of 35 percent even though the statutory rate is just 10 percent.

Obviously this example is simplified. One could even argue that the effective rate is understated because the original income from which the shareholder bought the stock was taxed. The simple point is that progressivity involves the definition of income, adjustments to income, and so on, not just the statutory rate schedule.

Since just about everyone accepts the idea of a personal exemption, we can assume that everyone accepts the principle of progressivity, even those who say they support a flat tax. The question is, How much progressivity is too much, and what are its costs?

TAXING THE RICH

Of course the core rationale for progressivity is the government's need for revenue. Income in the United States is highly unequal. According to the Census Bureau, in 2009 the top 20 percent of households received more than half of all the income earned in the country. And according to the Tax Policy Center, 47 percent of those filing income tax returns that year owed nothing; that is, they had a zero or negative income tax liability. Therefore taxing the rich at higher rates is just a matter of practical necessity. If they didn't pay more, everyone else would have to pay more than is the case now.

Philosophically one can argue that the last dollar earned by a millionaire isn't worth as much to him or her as the first dollar. Economists call this principle "declining marginal utility." It's the reason the first donut tastes better than the second, the second tastes better than the third, and so on. So if a rich person's last dollar isn't worth that much to her, it's reasonable to tax that dollar more, so that those with lower incomes, who presumably value their last dollar more highly, can pay less.

It has also been argued that the wealthy benefit from government disproportionately and therefore ought to contribute a disproportionate share of revenue. The economist Earl Thompson has argued that the Defense Department exists primarily to protect capital, most of which is owned by the wealthy. And the same point would apply as well to the police and justice system. Moreover much recent economic research emphasizes the importance to growth of institutional factors such as having adequate enforcement of contracts and property rights, a regulatory environment that prevents fraud and corruption, and other institutions from which the wealthy benefit.

Conservatives often talk about how the rich will go on strike and stop working if taxes are too high, as they did in Ayn Rand's famous novel *Atlas Shrugged*. But the real constraint on soaking the rich is the existence of tax shelters. If you tax them too much, they will spend more of their time and effort figuring out ways to save taxes rather than earn income. And it's a simple fact of life that those with large wealth and incomes have more opportunities for tax avoidance than those whose primary income comes from wages and salaries.

One reason this is the case is that rich people often own the businesses that generate their income, or they have a great deal of control over the timing and nature of their income. Rather than paying themselves a high salary that may be taxed as much as 35 percent, they can pay themselves in the form of dividends that are now taxed at a rate of just 15 percent.

The same problem exists for corporate executives, as Congress discovered when it restricted the deductibility of salaries over $1 million in 1993. This led corporate boards to pay their CEOs more in the form of stock options, which increased their compensation. It also created problems such as managers manipulating corporate profits to meet stock option targets. This is a classic example of the law of unintended consequences at work, and of how hard it is to tax the rich as a practical matter.

The opportunities for tax avoidance by those with large wealth and income are unlimited, but they are not costless. Lawyers and accountants are expensive. Many methods of tax avoidance require acceptance of a lower rate of return or giving up control of assets. One can avoid taxes on interest income, for example, by investing in municipal bonds, but such bonds carry a much lower interest rate than taxable bonds. The higher tax rates go, the more attractive such investments become.

At the extreme, rich people can simply leave the country and go live somewhere with lower taxes. The tax code tries to make this as difficult as possible by taxing American citizens even when they live abroad. By contrast, most foreign countries don't tax their citizens on income earned abroad. Thus to really escape the U.S. tax collector, one has to renounce one's citizenship, an action no one should take lightly. In 2010 about 1,500 people renounced their U.S. citizenship or gave up permanent resident status, many for tax reasons.

Of course, rich people also have options for tax evasion as well as avoidance. (The difference is that avoidance is legal, while evasion is illegal.) Hiding one's assets in tax havens is a time-honored technique, although not as easy as it used to be. Major countries have been working together for years to crack down on tax havens and making tax evasion more difficult and costly.

PRACTICAL NECESSITY

In the end the question of progressivity is not so much a moral question as a practical one. The issue is not whether rich people should pay more than those with lower- or middle-class incomes— they will—but how much more they will pay before the opportunities for tax evasion and avoidance become too attractive and it begins to erode the tax base.

Much of the ideological opposition to progressivity stems from the view that it is less a practical means of raising the government's revenue than an effort to redistribute income and to punish the rich simply because they are rich. In other words, it is a manifestation of envy. But others argue that conservative and biblical principles both justify progressivity.

Insofar as progressivity is intended to equalize incomes, it does a poor job of doing so. One simple reason is that the main measures of income inequality compiled by the Census Bureau are based on before-tax income and also exclude noncash government benefits such as housing subsidies and food stamps. Theoretically we could tax the rich at a rate of 99 percent and give all the money to the poor in the form of free food, clothing, and housing, and it would have no effect on either the distribution of income or the poverty rate. Neither the taxes nor the benefits count in the census income data.

The main way taxation affects the distribution of income is that high rates discourage rich people from realizing taxable income. The economist Paul Craig Roberts once noted that in countries with high tax rates on the rich, the rich tended to consume more luxuries such as Rolls Royce automobiles. The "psychic" income they got from driving a fine car was one that the government couldn't tax. I think most economists would agree that it would be better if rich people use their assets to make investments that create jobs and wealth for society rather than wasting assets on conspicuous consumption. But the former will tend to raise income inequality, while the latter will reduce it.

It's worth remembering that income inequality tends to fall sharply during economic recessions and rises during economic expansions. As John F. Kennedy put it in a 1963 speech, "A rising tide lifts all the boats." The great economist Simon Kuznets theorized that income distribution necessarily worsens as an economy expands. Some people are just quicker than others to capitalize on growth, but eventually income distribution improves as the benefits become more widely dispersed.

In the end there is nothing especially pernicious about progressivity. It's inherent in the nature of any income tax with a personal exemption. Insofar as there are economic problems with progressive tax systems, it is because the rates are too high, not because they are progressive.

Perhaps the best argument against progressivity is the one articulated by the conservative economist F. A. Hayek. He feared that increasing tax rates on the rich would lead to higher rates on everyone else. This was certainly the case during the 1930s and 1940s. Confiscatory tax rates on the wealthy paved the way for higher rates on the middle class.

FURTHER READINGS

Bankman, Joseph, and Thomas Griffith. "Social Welfare and the Rate Structure: A New Look at Progressive Taxation." *California Law Review* (Dec. 1987): 1905–67.

Blum, Walter J. "Revisiting the Uneasy Case for Progressive Taxation." *Taxes—The Tax Magazine* (Jan. 1982): 16–21.

Blum, Walter J., and Harry Kalven Jr. *The Uneasy Case for Progressive Taxation.* University of Chicago Press, 1953.

Bordoff, Jason, and Jason Furman. "Progressive Tax Reform in the Era of Globalization: Building Consensus for More Broadly Shared Prosperity." *Harvard Law and Policy Review* (Summer 2008): 327–60.

Congressional Research Service. "The Economics of Corporate Executive Pay." Report No. RL33935 (Mar. 22, 2007).

Congressional Research Service. "Income Inequality and the U.S. Tax System." Report No. RL34155 (Sept. 4, 2007).

Congressional Research Service. "Redistributive Effects of Federal Taxes and Selected Tax Provisions." Report No. R40671 (June 25, 2009).

Ferris, Kenneth R., and James S. Wallace. "IRC Section 162(m) and the Law of Unintended Consequences." *Advances in Accounting* (Dec. 2009): 147–55.

Fried, Barbara H. "The Puzzling Case for Proportionate Taxation." *Chapman Law Review* (Spring 1999): 157–95.

Hamill, Susan Pace. "An Evaluation of Federal Tax Policy Based on Judeo-Christian Ethics." *Virginia Tax Review* (Winter 2006): 671–764.

Hayek, F. A. *The Constitution of Liberty.* University of Chicago Press, 1960.

Hoose, Mark S. "The Conservative Case for Progressive Taxation." *New England Law Review* (Fall 2005): 69–111.

Howard, Jay M. "When Two Tax Theories Collide: A Look at the History and Future of Progressive and Proportionate Personal Income Taxation." *Washburn Law Journal* (Fall 1992): 43–76.

Joint Committee on Taxation. "Present Law and Background Relating to Executive Compensation." Report No. JCX-39–06 (Sept. 5, 2006).

Kahn, C. Harry. *Personal Deductions in the Federal Income Tax.* Princeton University Press, 1960.

Kornhauser, Marjorie E. "Choosing a Tax Rate Structure in the Face of Disagreement." *UCLA Law Review* (Aug. 2005): 1697–744.

Kornhauser, Marjorie E. "The Rhetoric of the Anti–Progressive Income Tax Movement: A Typical Male Reaction." *Michigan Law Review* (Dec. 1987): 465–523.

Kuznets, Simon. "Economic Growth and Income Inequality." *American Economic Review* (Mar. 1955): 1–28.

Lawsky, Sarah B. "On the Edge: Declining Marginal Utility and Tax Policy." *Minnesota Law Review* (2011): 904–52.

Mullane, Joy Sabino. "Incidence and Accidents: Regulation of Executive Compensation through the Tax Code." *Lewis & Clark Law Review* (Summer 2009): 485–551.

Piketty, Thomas, and Emmanuel Saez. "How Progressive Is the U.S. Federal Tax System? A Historical and International Perspective." *Journal of Economic Perspectives* (Winter 2007): 3–24.

Schoeck, Helmut. *Envy: A Theory of Social Behavior.* Harcourt, Brace & World, 1966.

Slemrod, Joel B. *Tax Progressivity and Income Inequality.* Cambridge University Press, 1994.

Thompson, Earl A. "Taxation and National Defense." *Journal of Political Economy* (July–Aug. 1974): 755–82.

Chapter 8

Taxes and the Business Cycle

E conomists have long sought ways of moderating business cycles so that economies could avoid the boom-and-bust cycle, which has existed throughout modern history. Historically, one problem is that governments were small and had a limited impact on the economy for good or ill. Those inclined to primarily blame government for the business cycle should remember that economic booms and busts also occurred hundreds of years ago, when governments were minuscule by today's standards and before the institution of central banks. Some famous examples are the tulip mania of the seventeenth century and the South Sea bubble of the eighteenth century.

What distinguishes both booms and busts is that they are primarily about large changes in spending—consumer spending and investment spending—which rises rapidly in booms as people buy houses, tech stocks, or whatever characterizes a particular boom, and falls sharply in a downturn as people lose jobs and increase precautionary saving.

Thus economists have long focused on ways of moderating spending during upturns and stimulating it during downturns. Historically, taxation was not seen as having much of a role because before the twentieth century taxes weren't very high and had little impact on the overall economy one way or another.

Recent research suggests that taxes may have played a more significant role in the Great Depression than economists thought. But insofar as spending is concerned, taxes were a nonfactor because on the eve of World War II, only about 3 percent of Americans paid any income taxes at all. Consequently economists continue to focus primarily on the role of the Federal Reserve and other monetary factors such as the gold standard to explain the length and depth of the Depression.

INVESTMENT TAX CREDIT

The first real effort to use tax policy as a countercyclical tool came during the Kennedy administration. One of its early initiatives was the creation of an Investment Tax Credit (ITC), which gave businesses a credit against their tax liability of 7 percent of the purchase price of capital equipment. Thus if a business bought a new machine tool for $100,000, it would be able to deduct $7,000 directly from its tax liability the year in which the machine went into service.

The first ITC went into effect in January 1962 to stimulate growth that was still sluggish following the 1960–61 recession. In 1960 real GDP grew just 2.5 percent, and this figure fell to 2.3 percent in 1961. Investment spending was especially weak. There was zero growth in gross private domestic investment in 1960, and a 0.7 percent contraction in 1961. But institution of the ITC led to a sharp rise of 12.7 percent in investment spending in 1962, which caused real GDP growth to climb 6.1 percent that year—a powerful performance.

Within a few years, however, there was concern that the economy was overheating and inflation was becoming a problem. Congress suspended the ITC in October 1966. But that led to such a sharp decline in investment spending that it was reinstated in March 1967. The ITC was suspended again in April 1969, reinstated in April 1971, and increased to 10 percent in 1975.

In 1979 the economists Alan Auerbach and Larry Summers evaluated the performance of the ITC as an economic stabilization tool and found it seriously flawed. "There is little evidence that a change in the investment tax credit is an effective tool for expansionary fiscal policy," they concluded. Indeed they found that the ITC was destabilizing, leading to overinvestment in equipment at the expense of other types of investment. Partly for this reason Congress abolished the ITC in 1986.

From time to time some economists advocate reinstatement of the ITC. But a 1998 study by the economist Austan Goolsbee has convinced most of them that the main effect of an ITC would be to raise the price of equipment, negating most of its stimulative effect. The ITC would just enrich equipment manufacturers without providing much bang for the buck in terms of increasing overall investment or economic growth.

TAX REBATES

The first use of a tax rebate as a countercyclical tool came in 1975. In 1973 the deepest postwar recession until that time had begun. But inflation was also a problem, and policymakers were reluctant to enact a permanent tax cut lest it raise the deficit too much, thus worsening inflationary expectations. A onetime tax rebate was deemed a reasonable compromise that would put money in people's pockets and stimulate consumer spending. The rebate equaled 10 percent of a taxpayer's 1974 tax liability, with minimum payments of $100 and a maximum of $200. The recession ended in March 1975, just as Congress completed action on the rebate legislation.

Subsequent analysis found that the 1975 rebate had no significant effect on growth because it didn't stimulate spending. By and large people saved the money or used it to pay down debt, the same thing economically. A 1977 study by the economists Franco Modigliani and Charles Steindel found that only about a fourth of the rebate was spent in the three quarters afterward. They concluded that "a rebate is not a particularly effective way of producing a prompt and temporary stimulus to consumption." And the increased saving didn't help growth because the deficit, which is negative saving, increased by exactly the same amount.

In a 1981 study the economist Alan Blinder found that a rebate had less than 40 percent of the impact of a permanent tax cut of similar magnitude, because permanent tax changes induce people to change their behavior in ways that temporary tax changes do not. A key reason is that people tend to have an idea of their "permanent income" and will save windfalls and draw down savings or borrow to cover shortfalls thought to be temporary. Thus policy needs to raise people's perceptions of their permanent income if the goal is to get them to spend more.

Despite the theoretical and empirical evidence throwing cold water on the rebate idea, George W. Bush insisted on trying it again in 2001. Treasury Secretary Paul O'Neill told him it was a bad idea. As he explained in a March 27, 2001, speech, "Some suggest we send a rebate to the taxpayers now. . . . I was here when we tried that in 1975 and it just didn't work. If we want to change consumption patterns, we need to make a permanent change in people's tax burdens." According to the journalist Ron Suskind, Glenn Hubbard, then the chairman of the Council of Economic Advisers, also tried to talk Bush out of another rebate, but to no avail.

As with the 1975 rebate, subsequent analysis found little impact. At the low end of estimates, the University of Michigan economists Matthew Shapiro and Joel Slemrod found that only about a fifth of the rebate was spent, the rest being saved and thus providing no stimulus. At the high end, the economists David Johnson, Jonathan Parker, and Nicholas Souleles found that perhaps two-thirds of the rebate was spent in the quarter it was received and the subsequent quarter combined. This still suggests a rather low impact relative to other policies. The recession ended in November 2001, just as the last of the rebates were being paid out.

Despite the lack of evidence that tax rebates are an effective short-term stimulus measure, Bush went back to the same well in early 2008, proposing yet another tax rebate when it became clear that the second recession of his administration had begun. I wrote op-eds for both the *New York Times* and the *Wall Street Journal* recounting the history of the rebate and explaining that it was a bad idea, but Congress enacted it anyway. The 2008 rebate sent out $106 billion in payments with the same goal of increasing short-term spending that had been refuted by the experiences of 1975 and 2001.

Once again subsequent analysis found little impact from the rebate, certainly little relative to the cost. Studies by the same economists who had studied the 2001 rebate found roughly the same impact. A March 2008 CNN/Opinion Research poll found that only 21 percent of people planned to spend their rebate; 73 percent planned to save it or use it to pay down debt. An April 2008 CBS News/*New York Times* poll found that only 18 percent of people expected to spend the rebate; 78 percent planned to save it or pay down debt. The Bureau of Labor Statistics concluded that 49 percent of the 2008 rebate was used to pay down debt, 18 percent was saved, and only 30 percent was spent.

The failure of the 2008 tax rebate to forestall or even mitigate the impact of the economic crisis led most economists to conclude that government spending needed to compensate for the falloff in household and business spending. This was especially critical since monetary policy was effectively impotent, as it is impossible for the Federal Reserve to cut interest rates below zero. Republicans nevertheless insisted that tax cuts and only tax cuts were capable of reviving growth, even though federal revenues were at their lowest share of GDP in sixty years. They consumed just 14.9 percent of GDP in both 2009 and 2010, down from 18.5 percent in 2007, which is about the postwar average. In the end the Obama administration split the difference, allocating 40 percent of the February 2009 fiscal stimulus package to a general tax credit that lowered taxes for every family with an income below $74,000.

The most interesting thing about the Obama initiative is that it sought to deal with the perceived failure of tax rebates on the basis of behavioral economics. It was thought that people were more inclined to save rebates because these were received in a lump sum. If, on the other hand, a tax cut reduced tax withholding so that people saw more money in their paychecks on a week-to-week basis, they might be more inclined to view this as an increase in their permanent income and spend it. Thus the main focus of the Making Work Pay Credit, which is what the Obama administration called its tax cut, was on increasing take-home pay.

This theory was not bad and shows that the Obama administration was trying to be creative. Unfortunately subsequent research showed that the Making Work Pay Credit had even less impact on spending than the 2008 rebate. Continuing research by the Congressional Budget Office shows that the tax cut was the least stimulative element of the stimulus package.

FINANCIAL TRANSACTIONS TAX

Although most research analyzing cyclical issues has dealt with ways in which tax policy could moderate downturns, some have looked at ways it could dampen booms, thus preventing the buildup of imbalances that often lead to subsequent busts. One suggestion that comes up from time to time is a tax on financial transactions.

The original idea was proposed by the economist John Maynard Keynes, who thought that if the cost of trading stocks was increased by a transactions tax, investors would have more of an incentive to hold assets and not trade so often. He believed this would reduce volatility and thereby moderate the business cycle.

In the 1970s the Yale economist James Tobin extended the idea to currency transactions to moderate wide swings in foreign exchange rates.

In recent years almost all discussion of a tax on securities transactions has been about raising revenue. Since the volume of such transactions is high, a small tax could still raise large revenues. A tax of just 0.5 percent could raise more than $200 billion annually.

The big problem for a single country imposing such a tax is that trading would simply migrate to exchanges in other countries. It would be easy for traders and investors in the United States to move accounts to London, Paris, or Tokyo to evade the tax. Hence it would be necessary for major nations to impose a securities transaction tax together if it were to work. The United Nations floats this proposal from time to time, but it seems unlikely ever to happen.

The other problem is that a securities tax would reduce liquidity in capital markets and raise the cost of capital. And insofar as it reduced trading volume, the revenue yield would also fall. A 2011 study by the International Monetary Fund concluded that a securities transaction tax is "an inefficient instrument for regulating financial markets and preventing bubbles."

REVENUE VOLATILITY

Insofar as the business cycle relates to taxation, the biggest problem may be that it leads to extreme volatility in revenues. During booms, revenues from income taxes pour into the Treasury. Congress inevitably tends to view this bounty as free money to be spent on new spending programs or tax cuts, which may add fuel to the boom and make the subsequent bust even more painful. The sharp downturn in revenue during recessions adds to the deficit and leaves the nation with a higher burden of debt and interest payments when they finally end.

Economists know that certain tax bases are more volatile than others. Capital gains taxes, in particular, are volatile, booming when times are good and crashing when times are bad. Income taxes in general are more volatile than property or consumption taxes. Another virtue of moving toward a more consumption-based tax system would be to stabilize government revenues and make budgeting more predictable. It would also avoid the common problem of politicians treating revenue inflows during boom periods as free money to spend on new programs and tax cuts that often make the retrenchment during bust periods more painful than necessary.

FURTHER READINGS

Auerbach, Alan J., and Lawrence H. Summers. "The Investment Tax Credit: An Evaluation." National Bureau of Economic Research Working Paper No. 404 (Nov. 1979).

Bartlett, Bruce. "Feel-Good Economics." *Wall Street Journal* (Jan. 19, 2008).

Bartlett, Bruce. "Maybe Too Little, Always Too Late." *New York Times* (Jan. 23, 2008).

Blinder, Alan S. "Temporary Income Taxes and Consumer Spending." *Journal of Political Economy* (Feb. 1981): 26–53.

Bureau of Labor Statistics. "Consumer Expenditure Survey Results on the 2008 Economic Stimulus Payments (Tax Rebates)." Consumer Expenditure Survey (Oct. 15, 2009).

Congressional Budget Office. *Did the 2008 Tax Rebates Stimulate Short-Term Growth?* June 10, 2009.

Garber, Peter M. *Famous First Bubbles.* MIT Press, 2000.

Goolsbee, Austan. "Investment Tax Incentives, Prices, and the Supply of Capital Goods." *Quarterly Journal of Economics* (Feb. 1998): 121–48.

Johnson, David S., Jonathan A. Parker, and Nicholas S. Souleles. "Household Expenditure and Income Tax Rebates of 2001." *American Economic Review* (Dec. 2006): 1589–610.

Matheson, Thornton. "Taxing Financial Transactions: Issues and Evidence." International Monetary Fund Working Paper No. WP/11/54 (Mar. 2011).

McGrattan, Ellen R. "Capital Taxation during the Great Depression." National Bureau of Economic Research Working Paper No. 16588 (Dec. 2010).

Modigliani, Franco, and Charles Steindel. "Is a Tax Rebate an Effective Tool for Stabilization Policy?" *Brookings Papers on Economic Activity* (1977): 195–203.

Parker, Jonathan, et al. "Consumer Spending and the Economic Stimulus Payments of 2008." National Bureau of Economic Research Working Paper No. 16684 (Jan. 2011).

Sahm, Claudia R., Matthew D. Shapiro, and Joel B. Slemrod. "Check in the Mail or More in the Paycheck: Does the Effectiveness of Fiscal Stimulus

Depend on How It Is Delivered?" National Bureau of Economic Research Working Paper No. 16246 (July 2010).

Sahm, Claudia R., Matthew D. Shapiro, and Joel B. Slemrod. "Household Response to the 2008 Tax Rebate: Survey Evidence and Aggregate Implications." *Tax Policy and the Economy* 24 (2010): 69–110.

Shapiro, Matthew D., and Joel Slemrod. "Consumer Response to Tax Rebates." *American Economic Review* (Mar. 2003): 381–96.

Chapter 9

How Other Countries Tax Themselves

Obviously there is great variety in the way other countries tax themselves. Nevertheless some broad conclusions can be drawn by looking at countries with advanced economies and populations that are demographically similar to that of the United States.

1. Other major countries tax themselves more heavily than the United States does, but their governments also deliver services that Americans pay for out of pocket.

The Organization for Economic Cooperation and Development (OECD) collects internationally comparable data on all the major market-oriented economies. In 2008 the average tax burden in the OECD area was 34.8 percent of GDP, compared with 26.1 percent of GDP in the United States. These data include all levels of government: federal, state, and local. Most countries have unitary government structures with no meaningful separation between the federal, state, and local sectors in terms of fiscal affairs. But in other countries, particularly the United States, looking only at the central government would give a distorted picture of tax policy.

By and large, the wealthier a country, the heavier its tax burden. The most heavily taxed countries are in Scandinavia and Western Europe. Denmark had a tax/GDP ratio of 48.2 percent in 2008, followed by Sweden (46.3), Belgium (44.2), Italy (43.3), and France (43.2). Some economists believe these high tax ratios result from "Wagner's Law," named for the German economist Adolph Wagner, who hypothesized that once people had secured the necessities of life, they were more inclined to want additional government services.

Economists have speculated on why Europeans have been more receptive to higher taxes than Americans have. One theory is that the devastation of World War II made them more security-conscious and more willing to tolerate higher taxes in return for a broader welfare state that protected them from economic adversity. Another theory, advanced by the Harvard economists Alberto Alesina and Edward Glaeser, is that European countries have tended to be more homogeneous racially, ethnically, religiously, and historically than the United States, which has always been much more diverse. Thus Europeans have seen welfare state policies as benefiting people like themselves, whereas Americans tend to view such policies as benefiting outsiders and the "undeserving." An August 2011 Rasmussen poll, for example, found that 71 percent of Americans believe that those on welfare don't deserve it. Constitutional differences between the United States and Europe are also important in explaining their divergent approaches toward taxation and the welfare state.

Another important factor is that European welfare states deliver benefits to all their citizens in ways that the United States does not. All Europeans get health insurance from their government. Thus an apples-to-apples comparison of U.S. and European tax levels would add to those in the United States the heavy burden of private health insurance that Europeans don't pay. That amounts to 9 percent of GDP in the United States and close to zero in countries with national health insurance.

Also, most European countries provide extensive cash benefits for all families with children. If one thinks of such payments as negative taxes, they reduce the effective tax burden significantly. For example, in Luxembourg, which has a tax/GDP ratio 10 percentage points higher than the United States, a typical middle-class married couple with two children paid an average tax rate of 16.5 percent in 2010, according to the OECD. But deducting family allowances from their taxes reduced their effective tax burden to just 1 percent.

Europeans are also less inclined to channel spending through the tax system, as Americans do. This gives the appearance of higher spending in Europe and lower taxes in the United States, but in many cases this is just an optical illusion. If Europeans used refundable tax credits, as we do, instead of direct spending, their tax burdens would appear lower, but nothing meaningful would change in terms of the size of government as a share of the economy.

2. Other countries tend to have higher tax rates but less progressivity than the United States.

Calculating the top tax rate across countries is not a simple matter. Indeed it's not a simple matter even within the United States because the final tax rate depends on the state one lives in and the form of one's income. Wage income is taxed as much as 35 percent by the federal income tax, and part of the payroll tax applies as well, whereas capital gains and dividends face a top federal rate of just 15 percent and are not covered by the payroll tax. Moreover the deductibility of state taxes at the federal level affects the effective top rate. The same problem exists in other countries as well.

That said, the OECD tries to estimate the top rate across countries, taking into account all the different levels of taxation and their interaction. Table 9.1 shows the top statutory personal income tax rate in selected countries in 2010 and the all-in rate that includes payroll taxes as well. The threshold income at which the top rate takes effect is measured as a multiple of the income earned by the average worker.

Table 9.1 Top Marginal Personal Income Tax Rate for Employees, 2010

Country	Top Statutory Rate	All-in Rate	Threshold Multiple
Australia	46.5	46.5	2.8
Canada	46.4	46.4	2.9
Denmark	51.6	62.8	1.0
France	45.8	49.8	2.8
Germany	47.5	47.5	6.2
Italy	44.9	50.7	3.2
Japan	50.0	47.7	4.6
Sweden	56.5	56.5	1.5
U.K.	40.0	51.0	1.3
U.S.	41.9	43.2	9.6

Source: OECD.

As you can see, the United States has the lowest top rate. But more important, the income threshold at which the top rate takes

effect is much higher in the United States. In most European countries, the top rate takes effect at a much lower income level. Indeed
the average worker making an annual income in the $40,000-to-
$50,000 range is in the top marginal tax bracket. Such countries
effectively have flat-rate tax systems, and this is one reason they
can have both higher rates and less progressivity.

Another important distinction between U.S. and foreign tax
systems is that other countries rely much more heavily on consumption taxes than the United States does (see Table 9.2). Since consumption taxes are far more efficient than income taxes—imposing
less of an economic cost per $1 raised—the overall burden of taxes
in other countries is lower than it appears if we look only at the
tax/GDP ratio. Consumption taxes are also regressive, taking more
in percentage terms from those with low incomes, whereas income
taxes are progressive. This is another reason the U.S. tax system
is more progressive and European tax systems are less progressive
than commonly believed.

Table 9.2 Tax Structure in OECD Countries, 2008 (percentage)

Tax	OECD Average	U.S.
Personal income tax	25.0	38.1
Corporate income tax	10.1	7.1
Payroll tax	26.4	25.1
Property tax	5.4	12.1
General consumption taxes (e.g., VAT, retail sales tax)	19.5	8.1
Specific consumption taxes (e.g., gasoline, tobacco)	10.4	6.3
Other taxes	3.2	3.2
Total	100.0	100.0

Source: OECD.

3. Countries with low tax/GDP ratios don't necessarily grow faster than those with high tax/GDP ratios.

It is an article of faith among conservatives that the overall level
of taxation has a powerful effect on economic growth. They also
believe strongly that the United States has long grown faster than
high-tax European countries for this reason. This is not true, as
much research and Table 9.3 indicate.

Table 9.3 Average Annual Growth in Real GDP per Capita, 1979–2010, and Taxes as a Share of GDP, 1979

Country	Growth	Tax/GDP	Country	Growth	Tax/GDP
Ireland	3.2	28.4	Netherlands	1.7	42.6
Finland	2.0	35.6	Sweden	1.7	46.7
Norway	2.0	40.8	Belgium	1.6	43.0
Japan	1.9	24.3	U.S.	1.6	26.0
Spain	1.9	22.0	Canada	1.4	30.1
Australia	1.8	25.0	Denmark	1.4	42.1
U.K.	1.8	31.9	France	1.3	38.7
Austria	1.7	38.4	Italy	1.2	26.1

Sources: OECD and Bureau of Labor Statistics.

European tax structures are less harmful to growth than many Americans believe. Europeans tax capital relatively lightly and derive much more of their revenue from consumption taxes. But another key factor is that the structure of government spending is more growth-oriented in Europe.

More of European spending goes to provide goods and services, such as health care, while the bulk of U.S. federal spending goes to income transfers to the elderly and for national defense. The United States spends roughly twice as much as a share of GDP on defense compared with European countries. Many economists believe that such spending is essentially economic waste, indisputably so in the case of resources consumed by war. European countries also spend more on public works, which enhance growth insofar as they are genuine public goods, while such spending has been declining in the United States. The cutback in government spending on goods and services and public infrastructure has been blamed for the slowdown in growth in the United States since the 1970s.

Additionally, while European tax levels may discourage labor supply to some extent, other policies enhance it. Public provision of day care in Europe makes it easier for women to work. Better public transportation systems reduce time wasted commuting. Broader measures of well-being that go beyond per capita GDP—such as higher life expectancy, more leisure time, greater income equality, and less poverty—show that Europeans are better off than Americans in many important ways despite paying more taxes.

TAX IDEAS FROM OTHER COUNTRIES

Americans tend to be provincial when it comes to taxation; they seldom look to other countries for guidance. However, just as American states learn from and copy each other all the time, the federal government could learn from the experiences of other countries. Here are a few ideas that may be worth thinking about.

DUAL INCOME TAX. The Nordic countries have what is called a dual income tax under which labor income and income from capital are taxed separately, rather than being aggregated as in most countries. Each form of income has its own rate schedule. In general, capital income is taxed at a low flat rate, while labor income is taxed at much higher progressive rates. Capital income is defined broadly and does not make distinctions among capital gains, interest, and dividends, as the U.S. tax system does. The low taxation of capital in a dual income tax system is a key reason Nordic countries do not suffer economically from high tax rates. Those rates apply primarily to labor income.

WEALTH TAXES. Many European countries have national taxes on net wealth. Such taxes are assessed annually at a low rate of around 1 percent above some threshold. From time to time such a tax has been proposed for the United States for both equity and revenue reasons. The version of this tax in the Netherlands is particularly interesting. It's similar to the Nordic system except that it has three "boxes" in which income is allocated. The first box is for wages, rent, and business income; the second involves cases where someone has a substantial ownership share in a business; and the third contains saving and investment income. The wealth tax element comes into play in the third box because taxpayers report their net assets rather than the income from those assets, as is the case in the United States. They are assumed to get a 4 percent annual rate of return on them, which is taxed whether they actually get 4 percent or not. The Netherlands wealth tax is a substitute for the taxation of capital income that is neutral as to the form of capital. One advantage is that Dutch taxpayers have no incentive to avoid realizing capital gains for tax reasons. Realization is irrelevant to the taxation of capital assets.

ENVIRONMENTAL TAXES. All major countries except the United States and Mexico raise substantial revenues from environmental taxes, which include taxes on motor vehicles, fuel, organic compounds, waste, and environmentally harmful activities. On average OECD countries raised 2.2 percent of GDP in revenue from such taxes in 2008, compared with 0.8 percent in the United States. Denmark and the Netherlands raised more than 4 percent of GDP in revenue from environmental taxes—three times what the United States raises from the corporate income tax. Many economists believe that taxing energy has the double advantage of improving the environment while raising revenue in a way that does little damage to incentives. Thus some sort of tax on energy, such as a carbon tax, might be the ideal way to raise revenue to pay for tax rate reductions in a revenue-neutral tax reform.

TAXING CITIZENS ABROAD. Every other country exempts from domestic taxation the earned income of its citizens living in other countries. The United States, by contrast, taxes its citizens wherever in the world they may live, even if all their income is earned outside the United States. To avoid U.S. taxes legally, American citizens must renounce their citizenship. Many analysts believe that this provision of the U.S. tax system is unfair, anachronistic, and counterproductive because it discourages U.S.-based multinationals from staffing their foreign operations with Americans. There is good reason to believe that this leads to reduced exports from the United States, since foreign nationals are more inclined to purchase goods and services for their employers from their home country.

Of course, there are an almost infinite number of ways we could alter our tax system that would benefit from the experiences of other countries, many of which are suggested in other chapters. For example, many countries don't allow mortgage interest to be deducted, yet have home ownership rates similar to those in the United States. The point simply is to learn from the experiences of others as we do already among the states.

Perhaps the big lesson from other countries is that large welfare states require very conservative tax systems that tax capital lightly and consumption heavily. That allows large revenues to be raised without reducing economic growth. European countries accepted this trade-off long ago, but the United States has not. Conservatives still believe that the welfare state can be controlled by slashing spending, while liberals resist regressive tax systems as unfair. In coming years both groups may find useful lessons in the European experience.

FURTHER READINGS

Alesina, Alberto, and Edward L. Glaeser. *Fighting Poverty in the U.S. and Europe*. Oxford University Press, 2004.

Arslanalp, Serkan, et al. "Public Capital and Growth." International Monetary Fund Working Paper No. WP/10/197 (July 2010).

Avi-Yonah, Reuven S. "The Case against Taxing Citizens." *Tax Notes* (May 10, 2010): 680–84.

Baldwin, Peter. *The Narcissism of Minor Differences: How America and Europe Are Alike*. Oxford University Press, 2009.

Brooks, Neil, and Thaddeus Hwong. *The Social and Economic Costs of Taxation: A Comparison of High- and Low-Tax Countries*. Canadian Centre for Policy Alternatives (Dec. 2006).

Castles, Francis G., et al. *The Oxford Handbook of the Welfare State*. Oxford University Press, 2010.

Cnossen, Sijbren, and Lans Bovenberg. "Fundamental Tax Reform in the Netherlands." *International Tax and Public Finance* (Aug. 2001): 471–84.

European Commission. "The Quality of Public Finances and Growth: A Conceptual Framework." *Public Finances in EMU* (2008): 127–65.

European Commission. *Taxation Trends in the European Union*. 2011.

Ganghof, Steffen. "The Political Economy of High Income Taxation." *Comparative Political Studies* (Sept. 2007): 1059–84.

Ganghof, Steffen. "Tax Mixes and the Size of the Welfare State: Causal Mechanisms and Policy Implications." *Journal of European Social Policy* (Nov. 2006): 360–73.

Jones, Charles I., and Peter J. Klenow. "Beyond GDP? Welfare across Countries and Time." National Bureau of Economic Research Working Paper No. 16352 (Sept. 2010).

Kato, Junko. *Regressive Taxation and the Welfare State*. Cambridge University Press, 2003.

Kenworthy, Lane. "Tax Myths." *Contexts* (Summer 2009): 28–32.

Kleinbard, Edward J. "An American Dual Income Tax: Nordic Precedents." *Northwestern Journal of Law and Social Policy* (Spring 2010): 41–86.

Kneller, Richard, Michael Bleaney, and Norman Gemmell. "Fiscal Policy and Growth: Evidence from OECD Countries." *Journal of Public Economics* (Nov. 1999): 171–90.

Lehner, Moris. "The European Experience with a Wealth Tax: A Comparative Discussion." *Tax Law Review* (Spring 2000): 615–91.

Lindert, Peter H. *Growing Public: Social Spending and Economic Growth since the Eighteenth Century*, 2 vols. Cambridge University Press, 2004.

Mares, Isabela. "The Economic Consequences of the Welfare State." *International Social Security Review* (Apr.–Sept. 2007): 65–81.

Messere, Ken. *The Tax System in Industrialized Countries*. Oxford University Press, 1998.

Mutti, John H. "The American Presence Abroad and U.S. Exports." *Southern Economic Journal* (July 1980): 40–50.

Myles, Gareth D. "Economic Growth and the Role of Taxation: Aggregate Data." Organization for Economic Cooperation and Development Economics Department Working Paper No. 714 (July 15, 2009).

Norregaard, John, and Tehmina S. Khan. "Tax Policy: Recent Trends and Coming Challenges." International Monetary Fund Working Paper No. WP/07/274 (Dec. 2007).

Organization for Economic Cooperation and Development. *Choosing a Tax Base–Low Rate Approach to Taxation*. Tax Policy Study No. 19 (2010).

Organization for Economic Cooperation and Development. *Fundamental Reform of Corporate Income Tax*. Tax Policy Study No. 16 (2007).

Organization for Economic Cooperation and Development. *Fundamental Reform of Personal Income Tax*. Tax Policy Study No. 13 (2006).

Organization for Economic Cooperation and Development. *Recent Tax Policy Trends and Reforms in OECD Countries*. Tax Policy Study No. 9 (2004).

Organization for Economic Cooperation and Development. *Revenue Statistics, 1965–2009*. 2010.

Organization for Economic Cooperation and Development. *Tax Expenditures in OECD Countries*. 2010.

Organization for Economic Cooperation and Development. *Tax Policy Reform and Economic Growth*. Tax Policy Study No. 20 (2010).

Organization for Economic Cooperation and Development. *Taxation, Innovation and the Environment*. 2010.

Organization for Economic Cooperation and Development. *Taxing Wages, 2008–2009*. 2009.

Owens, Jeffrey. "Fundamental Tax Reform: The Experience of OECD Countries." Tax Foundation Background Paper No. 47 (Feb. 2005).

Peter, Klara S., Steve Buttrick, and Denvil Duncan. "Global Reform of Personal Income Taxation, 1981–2005: Evidence from 189 Countries." *National Tax Journal* (Sept. 2010): 447–78.

Prasad, Monica, and Yingying Deng. "Taxation and the Worlds of Welfare." *Socio-Economic Review* (July 2009): 431–57.

Prescott, Edward C. "Why Do Americans Work So Much More Than Europeans?" *Federal Reserve Bank of Minneapolis Quarterly Review* (July 2004): 2–13.

Rogerson, Richard. "Taxation and Market Work: Is Scandinavia an Outlier?" *Economic Theory* (July 2007): 59–85.

Sørensen, Peter B. "From Global Income Tax to the Dual Income Tax: Recent Tax Reforms in the Nordic Countries." *International Tax and Public Finance* (Feb. 1994): 57–79.

Weber, Christian E. "Government Purchases, Government Transfers, and the Post-1970 Slowdown in U.S. Economic Growth." *Contemporary Economic Policy* (Jan. 2000): 107–23.

Wilensky, Harold L. "Trade-offs in Public Finance: Comparing the Well-being of Big Spenders and Lean Spenders." *International Political Science Review* (Oct. 2006): 333–58.

Part II

SOME PROBLEMS

Chapter 10

Spending Through the Tax Code

I t's common for almost everyone to write and think about government budgets as if there is a clear delineation between taxes and spending. Taxes take money out of people's pockets and spending puts money in people's pockets, they believe. It's the difference between giving, on the one hand, and receiving, on the other. Since the giving is done under the threat of force, many say it is inherently immoral, and it follows that anything that allows taxpayers to keep their own money is therefore legitimate.

Unfortunately, in the real world the simple distinction between taxes and spending falls apart. There are, for example, large revenues collected by the federal government that are not counted as revenues at all, but as negative spending. That is, the budget shows that they reduce spending rather than raise revenue. Called "offsetting receipts" or "offsetting collections," the best known is Medicare Part B premiums, which came to $61 billion in 2010. Other receipts that are netted against outlays rather than counted as revenues include those from the government's business-like activities, such as the sale of electric power through the Tennessee Valley Authority.

The budgetary convention of treating some government revenues as negative spending has no effect on the deficit, but makes the government's impact on the economy appear smaller than it is. In 2010 both revenues and expenditures were lower by $600 billion than they would be if offsetting receipts were counted as revenues rather than negative spending. In short, the federal government is 4 percent of the gross domestic product larger, in terms of both revenues and expenditures, than the standard data indicate.

Just as some revenues are counted as negative spending, some tax preferences are, in effect, spending programs. These provisions, which economists call "tax expenditures," are a major source of complexity, unfairness, and economic distortion. Sometimes they reduce the tax liability of a business or family by exempting or excluding income from taxation; at other times they involve tax credits that reduce tax payments directly. And in some cases these credits are refundable for those with no income tax liability to offset, making them identical to a direct spending program in all but name.

HORIZONTAL EQUITY

Both common sense and basic principles of taxation tell us that people with roughly the same income ought to pay roughly the same amount of income taxes. Economists call this idea "horizontal equity." Not only is it unfair to tax two people in roughly the same circumstances much differently, but it encourages a lot of wasteful efforts by people to shift their income and investments to lower their tax liability.

Probably the best-known way that the tax system violates horizontal equity involves housing. One homeowner may deduct both mortgage interest and property taxes from her income, and in addition she will generally not have to pay taxes on any capital gains when she sells her home. (But neither can she deduct any capital losses.) By contrast, her next-door neighbor, who rents an identical house, will receive no tax advantage even though his rent to some extent embodies the interest and taxes paid by his landlord.

Although most homeowners make monthly payments to their mortgage company that are probably in excess of what renters pay for similar accommodations, that so much of the payment is tax deductible often makes ownership cheaper than renting. Moreover the owner captures the gain when home prices rise. If she has a fixed mortgage she knows her payments will not rise even if interest rates or home prices rise. By contrast, the renter can expect his rent to rise annually along with the cost of living. For these reasons, most people prefer to own rather than rent, if possible.

For many years lawmakers have believed that encouraging homeownership is per se a good thing. It helped create a stable middle class, whose members took more of an interest in their communities, supported local schools, and so on. And for many middle-class families, the equity in their home represents a substantial portion of their total saving.

Unfortunately, in recent years many homeowners treated their home equity like a piggy bank to raid with home equity loans, a key attraction of which is the deductibility of interest, to finance vacations and other frivolous expenditures. This habit put them in dire straits when home prices fell. Furthermore economists believe that the nation as a whole has suffered because too much of national investment went into housing rather than industry.

TAX LOOPHOLES

Once upon a time, special tax deals such as the mortgage interest deduction were known as "tax loopholes." I seldom hear this term anymore. The attitude that everyone is entitled to save as much in taxes as he or she can get away with has become so ingrained that no one seems to care any more that some people pay far less in taxes than others in similar circumstances. It's as if the concept of taxation as theft—rather than as a shared burden that all should contribute toward as the cost of maintaining a civil society—is now so widely shared that many people applaud those who have figured out how to game the system and pay less than their fair share rather than condemn them as social parasites who claim society's benefits without paying for them.

In 2010 the Tax Policy Center produced an interesting table that illustrates the extreme variation in effective federal income tax rates (taxes divided by income) among those with roughly similar incomes (Table 10.1). Looking just at the figures for the top 1 percent of taxpayers, who had an average income of about $2 million, it shows that the bottom 10 percent of those in this income class paid only 2.6 percent in federal income taxes, while those in the top 10 percent of the top 1 percent paid 26.9 percent, or ten times more. Thus many taxpayers in the top 1 percent paid less of their income in federal income taxes than the top quarter of those in the second income quintile (20 percent of households). In 2007 it took an income of more than $350,000 to be in the top 1 percent; the income threshold for the second income quintile was just $20,500.

Table 10.1 Variation in Effective Federal Income Tax Rates, 2010

Cash Income	Percentiles				
	10th	25th	Median	75th	90th
Lowest quintile	-39.4	-12.2	-4.2	0.0	0.0
Second quintile	-20.8	-6.0	0.0	3.2	5.9
Middle quintile	-4.5	-0.1	3.2	7.5	9.0
Fourth quintile	0.5	3.3	6.4	9.3	13.0
Top quintile	3.8	7.1	10.8	14.1	18.6
Top 1 percent	2.6	10.7	18.8	24.4	26.9
All	**-12.8**	**-2.3**	**1.5**	**7.1**	**11.4**

Source: Tax Policy Center.

People used to be incensed when the rich paid tax rates lower than those barely in the middle class. Today they don't seem to care. Why, I don't know. I think it may have to do with the decline of the balanced budget as the expected norm in budget policy. When that was the case, people understood that if one group of taxpayers didn't pay their fair share, others had to pay more. But since 2001 Republicans have insisted that "deficits don't matter," as former vice president Dick Cheney once said, and that big tax cuts are always justified even when the budget is grossly out of balance. An effect of this widely shared attitude appears to be that taxpayers no longer feel that one taxpayer's exploitation of tax loopholes comes at their expense.

REFUNDABLE TAX CREDITS

Another fact illustrated by Table 10.1 is that many tax filers not only pay no federal income taxes but actually get a check from the government. That is what it means when we say people have a negative tax liability. This results principally from a program called the Earned Income Tax Credit (EITC). Originally designed to offset the payroll tax for those with incomes too low to owe federal income taxes, the EITC has expanded over the years to be an all-purpose welfare program for workers with children.

Almost all economists praise the EITC as an effective program for aiding the working poor. In 2008 it put $51 billion into their pockets. The vast bulk of this—more than $44 billion—was the refunded portion, with the rest offsetting federal income taxes that would otherwise have been owed. This $44 billion, while treated as a "tax cut" in the tax distribution tables, is obviously a government spending program.

The EITC was first introduced during the Gerald Ford administration. Republicans reasoned that it was a good idea to help the working poor and strengthen work incentives, in contrast to those who didn't work at all and collected welfare checks. Ronald Reagan and George H. W. Bush also favored raising the EITC as a better way of helping the poor than increasing the minimum wage.

Tax credits were once anathema to Republican thinking. They preferred tax deductions and exemptions because these means benefited those in high tax brackets more and didn't benefit those with no tax liability. But in the 1990s Republicans began to embrace tax credits for a variety of purposes, in part because tough budget caps enacted by George H. W. Bush and Bill Clinton left a loophole for spending disguised as a tax cut.

In 1997 Republicans created a child credit of $400 that was partially refundable. But under the George W. Bush administration, it was raised to $1,000 per child and the refundability was expanded. In 2009 Democrats also got on the refundable tax credit bandwagon, creating one for first-time home buyers and an all-purpose credit called the Making Work Pay Credit. There are also refundable credits for adoption, health insurance, and other purposes.

The proliferation of tax credits has created many problems. The biggest is that they have produced a huge class of people who file income tax returns but pay nothing. In 2011, 47 percent of all tax filers paid no federal income taxes, and refundable credits offset all of the payroll tax liability as well for 22.9 percent of filers. Many of those paying no federal income taxes are fairly well-to-do. The *Wall Street Journal* calls them "lucky duckies."

Other problems include strong incentives for tax fraud. In early 2011 the Treasury Department's inspector general for tax administration reported that in 2009, $11 billion to $13 billion of EITC payments had been claimed improperly. Some political scientists worry that having such a large class of people who contribute nothing to the federal government's general operations undermines democracy and makes them less engaged in what their government does. Finally, having a large class of people with a zero or negative tax liability is a severe barrier to tax reform. For example, the flat tax, which many conservatives support, would constitute a significant tax increase for everyone with a negative tax liability, as the least amount of taxes one could pay under the flat tax would be zero.

THE HIDDEN AMERICAN WELFARE STATE

When one properly accounts for tax expenditures, the American welfare state is far larger than most people imagine. They tend to look at taxes and spending as a share of GDP, see that those percentages are much lower in the United States than in countries in Europe that have long embraced "big government," and conclude that we are fundamentally different. But it's more a difference of semantics than substance, economists increasingly conclude.

Take health care. As we saw in 2009, there is strong opposition to national health insurance in the United States. The idea of a "public option" was rejected even by Democrats during debate on the Affordable Care Act. But the tax expenditure for employer-provided health insurance is $184 billion. In effect, the federal government directs that $184 billion of the nation's resources be channeled into health care. But because it is done through the tax code rather than by providing health care to people through national health insurance, as in other nations, we pretend that we have a smaller public sector than nations with government-run health systems.

In other countries people basically pay taxes for health insurance, whereas Americans have that cost deducted from their compensation or pay it out of their pockets. If we had national health insurance, people would be able to stop paying out of pocket, and their wages would rise by the cost their employers now pay for health insurance. If their taxes rose by the same amount, they would be no worse off than they are now, but taxes and government spending would both be higher. This explains almost all of the difference in tax burdens between the United States and Europe.

Similarly, in terms of housing, the federal government "spends" close to $100 billion through the mortgage interest deduction, encouraging people to buy a house rather than rent, plus another $35 billion by effectively exempting taxation on home sales, and still another $25 billion by allowing homeowners to deduct their property taxes. It also spends $67 billion encouraging people to save for retirement through 401(k) plans, $45 billion for defined benefit pensions provided by employers, $17 billion for Keogh plans for the self-employed, and $16 billion for Individual Retirement Accounts. In other countries people pay higher taxes and in return receive much more generous government pensions at retirement.

There may be reasons to think that privately provided social welfare benefits are superior to those provided by government. But the idea that they are cheaper is not one of them. According to the OECD, Americans spend more of their income on health care than the citizens of any other country—about 17 percent of GDP. That's 5 percent of GDP more than the country with the next largest amount of health care spending as a share of its economy. And, contrary to popular belief, many studies show that on balance Americans don't have better health or health care than people in countries with significantly lower levels of health care spending or with national health insurance.

A recent OECD study calculated social spending as a share of GDP in major countries, taking account of things such as tax expenditures that consume economic resources without showing up in the budget or standard measures of government as a share of GDP. According to this study, net public social welfare outlays consumed 27.2 percent of GDP in the United States in 2005—well above the percentages for countries generally thought to have big governments, such as Denmark (see Table 10.2).

Table 10.2 Net Social Spending as a Share of GDP, 2005

France	33.6	Denmark	25.7	Spain	21.4
Belgium	30.3	Portugal	25.7	Norway	21.2
Germany	30.2	Finland	24.4	Czech Republic	20.1
U.K.	29.5	Canada	23.3	Poland	19.7
Sweden	29.3	OECD average	23.3	New Zealand	18.8
U.S.	27.2	Luxembourg	23.0	Ireland	18.3
Italy	26.6	Japan	22.8	Slovak Republic	17.6
Austria	26.5	Iceland	22.1	Korea	10.7
Netherlands	25.8	Australia	21.7	Mexico	9.4

Source: OECD.

BUDGET SEMANTICS

Some years ago the economist David Bradford explained how conventional concepts of taxing and spending distort our understanding of how government affects the economy. As he hypothesized, suppose the Defense Department decided to pay for a new bomber by giving the contractor a tradable, refundable tax credit instead of just writing a check. The contractor would save an amount of taxes exactly equal to what it would otherwise charge DOD, and if its tax liability wasn't large enough, it could simply sell the tax credit to another company.

In this example, government spending will be lower by the cost of the bomber, and taxes will also be lower by the amount of the tax credit. Superficially it would appear that we have achieved a magical way of cutting the size of government costlessly. But it is just sleight of hand. Exactly the same resources—the labor, technology, energy, and materials necessary to build a bomber—have been taken out of the private economy and preempted for government use, just as they would if DOD paid for the bomber directly.

Nevertheless many conservatives solemnly proclaim that there is a fundamental difference between government spending and tax expenditures. As Sen. Orrin Hatch (R-UT), the ranking Republican on the Senate Finance Committee, explained in a statement on July 12, 2011:

> The federal government cannot spend money that it never touched and never possessed. Tax Expenditures let taxpayers keep more of their own money. And only by the public consent is the government permitted to take some of it in taxation to pay for certain public goods. When tax hike proponents say we are giving businesses and individuals all this money in tax expenditures, they are incorrectly assuming that the government has that money to give in the first place, when in fact it does not. To the contrary, the government never touches the money that a taxpayer keeps due to benefitting from a tax expenditure, whereas with spending, the government actually collects money from taxpayers and then spends it.

Another difference between tax expenditures and spending is that reducing or eliminating a tax expenditure without an offsetting tax cut to reach a revenue neutral level will cause the size of the federal government to grow, while reducing or eliminating spending causes the size of the federal government to shrink.

This statement is complete nonsense. If a tax expenditure encourages taxpayers to spend or invest funds in a way other than the way they would have done in the absence of the tax expenditure, there is no difference, economically, than if the government taxed the money and spent it the same way the taxpayers did only because of the tax expenditure. By Sen. Hatch's logic, we could reduce the size of government by passing laws forcing people to spend their own labor and money to build roads—which is exactly how roads got built until the modern era.

In the end what matters is the extent to which national resources are being redirected out of those governed by economic fundamentals and into those directed by government. Tax expenditures can do this just as taxes and spending can. It's sophistry to think that all tax cuts reduce the role of government in the economy. And it's wrong to assume that taxes and spending as a share of GDP are meaningful measures of government's impact on the economy and society.

The goal of tax reform should be to create neutrality to the greatest extent possible. Let businesses and families make economic decisions without being biased or even pressured to do one thing rather than another, such as buy rather than rent a home, just because the tax code makes it worthwhile. Tax reform should also strive to restore horizontal equity and eliminate the wide disparity in effective tax rates among those in similar circumstances.

FURTHER READINGS

Bartlett, Bruce. "Tax Aspects of the 1997 Budget Deal." *National Tax Journal* (Mar. 1998): 127–41.

Batchelder, Lily L., Fred T. Goldberg Jr., and Peter T. Orszag. "Efficiency and Tax Incentives: The Case for Refundable Tax Credits." *Stanford Law Review* (Oct. 2006): 23–76.

Commonwealth Fund. *Mirror, Mirror on the Wall: How the Performance of the U.S. Health Care System Compares Internationally.* June 2010.

Congressional Research Service. "An Analysis of the 'Buffet Rule.'" Report No. R42043 (Oct. 7, 2011).

Congressional Research Service. "Tax Expenditures and the Federal Budget." Report No. RL34622 (June 1, 2011).

Congressional Research Service. *Tax Expenditures: Compendium of Background Material on Individual Provisions.* Committee Print, Senate Budget Committee (Dec. 2010).

Congressional Research Service. "U.S. Health Care Spending: Comparison to Other OECD Countries." Report No. RL34175 (Sept. 17, 2007).

Cuny, Thomas J. "Offsetting Collections in the Federal Budget." *Public Budgeting & Finance* (Autumn 1988): 96–110.

Howard, Christopher. *The Welfare State Nobody Knows.* Princeton University Press, 2007.

Iyer, Govind S., Anath Seetharaman, and Ted D. Englebrecht. "An Analysis of the Distributional Effects of Replacing the Progressive Income Tax with a Flat Tax." *Journal of Accounting and Public Policy* (Summer 1996): 83–110.

Joint Committee on Taxation. "Present Law and Background Relating to Tax Treatment of Household Debt." Report No. JCX-40-11 (July 11, 2011).

Lim, Katherine, and Jeffrey Rohaly. "Variation in Effective Tax Rates." *Tax Notes* (Feb. 8, 2010): 785.

Marron, Donald B. "Spending in Disguise." *National Affairs* (Summer 2011): 20–34.

Musgrave, Richard A. "Horizontal Equity, Once More." *National Tax Journal* (June 1990): 113–22.

"The Non-Taxpaying Class: Those Lucky Duckies!" *Wall Street Journal* (Jan. 20, 2003).

Organization for Economic Cooperation and Development. "How Expensive Is the Welfare State? Gross and Net Indicators in the OECD Social Expenditure Database." Social, Employment and Migration Working Paper No. 92 (Nov. 19, 2009).

U.S. Government Accountability Office. "Opportunities to Reduce Potential Duplication in Government Programs, Save Tax Dollars, and Enhance Revenue." Report No. GAO-11-318SP (Mar. 2011).

Williams, Roberton. "Why Nearly Half of Americans Pay No Federal Income Tax." *Tax Notes* (June 7, 2010): 1149.

Chapter 11

Taxes and the Health System

Taxation has an enormous influence on health policy. Key features of the American health care system, such as the widespread provision of employer-provided health insurance, exist primarily because tax policy made them advantageous. It would have been better to have dealt with the tax aspects of health care policy during debate on the Affordable Care Act in 2009, but that, unfortunately, didn't happen. Tax reform may present another opportunity to address these issues and perhaps improve both the tax system and the health care system at the same time.

The most important way tax policy affects health care policy is that employer-provided health insurance is deductible as a business expense but not taxable to workers. Indeed it is excluded from the tax base and need not even be reported on individual tax returns. Moreover, neither employers nor employees pay payroll taxes on health insurance benefits even though these are clearly part of the employees' wages. (The self-employed get an income tax deduction for health insurance but, unfairly, get no relief from the payroll tax.)

Additionally, individuals are not required to pay taxes on the large benefits they receive from Medicare over and above their contributions. Furthermore unreimbursed medical costs that exceed 7.5 percent of adjusted gross income (10 percent beginning in 2013) are tax deductible. And some individuals may establish health care savings accounts, which allow them to make tax-deductible contributions in order to pay nonreimbursed medical expenses.

EXCLUSION FOR HEALTH INSURANCE

The exclusion for employer-provided health insurance is far and away the largest of all tax expenditures. In 2012 it reduced federal income tax revenues by more than $184 billion and payroll taxes by another $250 billion. The next largest tax expenditure, for mortgage interest, reduced federal revenues less than $100 billion.

Before World War II health insurance was not widely available. Medical costs were low, largely because medical technology was primitive. Hospitalization was rare, and most people received medical care at home. Convalescence was the main cure for most medical problems, and the main cost of sickness was lost wages rather than out-of-pocket expenses for doctors and medicine.

But as medical technology improved, its cost increased. Hospitals acquired X-ray machines and other modern equipment, and established laboratories for analyzing diseases and other medical conditions. Training for medical doctors improved, as did surgical techniques, and ever-advancing pharmaceuticals became more expensive. These led to improvements in medical outcomes that increased the demand for medical services.

Hospitals developed the first medical insurance, the Blue Cross system. In 1929 Baylor University Hospital contracted with local Dallas teachers to provide up to twenty-one days of hospitalization for $6 annually (about $75 today). Doctors, however, were skeptical of health insurance. They feared that insurance companies would interfere with their practice. But in the 1930s they banded together to create the Blue Shield system, in part out of fear that a government-run program would be established unless private health insurance was widely available.

In 1940 only about 12 million people in a population of 132 million had health insurance. During the war the federal government imposed wage and price controls to keep inflation in check. But because so many men had been called up for military service, there was a severe labor shortage. Businesses looked for ways to increase de facto wages to attract workers. One way was to offer free health insurance, permitted by the Stabilization Act of 1942.

In 1943 the Internal Revenue Service issued a ruling that premiums on health insurance for workers paid directly to insurance companies were not taxable to the worker. In 1954 Congress codified this ruling and expanded the scope of the exclusion for health insurance. Given that the high tax rates during World War II and the Korean War remained in effect until 1964, workers were receptive to receiving tax-free income in the form of health benefits. As a consequence, health insurance coverage soared. By 1960, in a population of 179 million, 122 million Americans had health insurance.

EXCESSIVE CONSUMPTION

In the 1970s economists grew concerned that the exclusion for health insurance was incentivizing people to buy excess health insurance. Instead of providing protection for unforeseen events, analogous to fires in the case of homeowners insurance or accidents in the case of auto insurance, health insurance evolved into something broader. In effect, people were paying for ordinary consumption with before-tax dollars by having their health insurance cover regular doctors' visits, prescription drugs, and other medical services that were not unforeseen or not catastrophic. It was as if one's auto insurance covered not only accidents but routine maintenance and gasoline as well.

Overbuying health insurance and the declining amount of medical care paid out of pocket led to a vast increase in demand for such services and raised their cost. Medical cost inflation drove up health insurance premiums, which consumed a rising share of employee compensation. This is a key reason cash wages have stagnated since the 1970s. Productivity gains have largely been channeled into increasingly expensive benefits rather than paychecks. In 1970 pension and health benefits constituted just 4.5 percent of total employee compensation; by 2010 that figure had almost doubled to 8.5 percent—more than $1 trillion.

For many years a number of proposals have been put forward to cap or abolish the exclusion for health insurance. During the 2008 campaign, for example, Sen. John McCain (R-AZ), the Republican presidential nominee, said he would eliminate the exclusion and use the revenue to give individuals a $5,000 refundable tax credit with which to buy individual health insurance policies.

An important benefit of the McCain plan would have been to "delink" health insurance from employment. The current system often forces workers to remain in a job just to hold on to their health insurance. Delinking would promote worker mobility and make it easier for small businesses, which are less likely to offer much in the way of benefits, to compete with big companies more likely to offer a full range of benefits.

Converting the health insurance exclusion to a refundable tax credit would also improve fairness. As with tax deductions, an exclusion benefits those in high tax brackets more than those in lower brackets, as the tax saving is a function of one's tax rate, whereas a refundable tax credit benefits everyone equally, regardless of income. The MIT economist Jonathan Gruber estimates that five-sixths of the tax savings from the exclusion for health insurance benefits those in the top half of the income distribution.

Lack of fairness is also a key problem with the deduction for medical expenses. It's of no value to those who don't itemize their tax returns or who have no federal income tax liability. Therefore the benefits accrue almost exclusively to those with high incomes rather than those with the heaviest burden of unreimbursed medical expenses. According to the Joint Committee on Taxation, 88 percent of the benefits of the medical deduction went to households with incomes over $50,000 in 2009.

PERVERSE EFFECTS

Another concern about the medical deduction is that it may discourage those who can easily afford health insurance from buying it because the federal government will partially share the costs when large medical outlays are necessary. The Harvard law professor Louis Kaplow calls the deduction "an odd sort of free, partial, quasi-compulsory insurance: for no explicit premium (except higher taxes generally), some individuals (those who itemize) receive partial coverage (for losses above a floor) at a level equaling their tax rate (and thus higher for the more wealthy) for qualifying losses (with privately insured losses not qualifying)."

For many years conservative economists argued that having most health care costs paid by insurance companies discouraged individuals from comparing prices for health care expenses and shopping around for the best price, and that this arguably contributed to medical cost inflation. They suggested that if people could set up health care savings accounts to pay routine medical costs they would become more price-sensitive, thereby holding down costs.

Congress established health savings accounts (HSAs) in 2003 in the legislation that established Medicare Part D. Individuals with high deductible health insurance policies are permitted to establish

HSAs and deduct the contributions from their taxable income. Qualified health care expenses may be paid from the accounts and are not taxable. Certain types of insurance may also be purchased with funds from HSAs. Withdrawals from them not used for qualified health care expenses are taxable, and also subject to a 20 percent penalty. But after age sixty-five the penalty is waived.

Conservative economists were confident that HSAs would be popular with both individuals and employers, which are permitted to set them up and make contributions for their employees. The Harvard economist Martin Feldstein said they had the potential "to transform health care finances, bringing costs under control and making health care reflect what patients and their doctors really want." However, in the years since HSAs were established, relatively few businesses and individuals have taken advantage of them. Critics charge that they primarily benefit the healthy and wealthy.

TAX-FREE MEDICARE BENEFITS

An important but seldom noted tax benefit is the tax-free status of Medicare. Insofar as lifetime Medicare benefits exceed lifetime contributions (not including the employer's share because it is tax-deductible), that constitutes income to individuals and in principle ought to be included in the tax base.

If Medicare contributions were actuarially fair and people paid fully for aggregate Medicare benefits through taxes and premiums, it wouldn't matter that some people got more benefits than they paid for, as others would get less. That is the nature of a true insurance system. Gains and losses would offset each other, and there would be no net income to Medicare beneficiaries.

However, Medicare taxes and premiums cover only a fraction of benefits, and almost all beneficiaries receive a large net transfer that improves their well-being and is income in every meaningful sense of the term. According to an Urban Institute study, the average person retiring at age sixty-five in 2011 will receive lifetime Medicare benefits that are three times greater than his or her contribution. Men will get back $170,000 in benefits for a lifetime contribution of $60,000. Because of their greater longevity, women will get back $188,000 in benefits.

The tax-free status of Medicare benefits is not part of the law, but based on a 1970 revenue ruling by the IRS. Since Social Security benefits were tax-free, the IRS figured Medicare should be treated symmetrically.

But in 1993 Congress began subjecting some Social Security benefits to taxation. Many legal scholars believe that all benefits should be taxable in the same way that private pensions are taxed. Not only would this raise revenue that could be channeled into the Social Security trust fund to stabilize its finances, but it would improve the fairness of the system by imposing de facto means testing: reducing net benefits for the well-to-do while exempting the poor. It has also been argued that equalizing the tax treatment of Social Security and private pensions would strengthen Social Security politically by solidifying its status as an earned benefit rather than as a government giveaway.

According to the Congressional Research Service, the tax expenditure for Medicare is substantial. In 2012 the revenue loss associated with Part A, which pays for hospitalization, was $36 billion. The tax expenditure for Part B, which covers doctors' visits, was $25 billion. (Note that Part B premiums are fixed by law to cover only 25 percent of the program's costs, with the balance coming from general revenues.) And the tax expenditure for Part D, which pays for prescription drugs, is $7 billion. Thus the total revenue loss associated with the nontaxation of Medicare benefits is close to $70 billion.

As noted earlier, it would have been better to reexamine the tax treatment of health care benefits in the context of health care reform. Unfortunately, except for a new 40 percent tax on certain high-cost health plans taking effect in 2018, tax issues were not considered when Congress debated the Affordable Care Act. This was a gross oversight.

REFORM OPTIONS

A variety of proposals have been put forward over the years for limiting and better targeting tax subsidies for health insurance and care. A 2008 Congressional Budget Office report listed these options:

- Reduce the tax exclusion for employment-based health insurance and the health insurance deduction for self-employed individuals.

- Replace the income tax exclusion for employment-based health insurance with a deduction.

- Replace the income and payroll tax exclusion with a refundable credit.

- Allow self-employed workers to deduct health insurance premiums from income that is subject to payroll taxes.

- Expand eligibility for an "above the line" deduction for health insurance premiums.

- Disallow new contributions to health savings accounts.

- Allow health insurance plans with coinsurance of at least 50 percent to qualify for the health savings account tax preference.

- Levy an excise tax on medigap plans.

Obviously this list doesn't exhaust the available alternatives. Given that tax policy has been blamed for many of the problems in our health care system, Congress should consider revisiting tax provisions related to health care when it considers tax reform.

FURTHER READINGS

Ball, Robert M. "Raise Social Security Taxes." *New York Times* (July 2, 1993).

Blumenthal, David. "Employer-Sponsored Health Insurance in the United States—Origins and Implications." *New England Journal of Medicine* (July 6, 2006): 82–88.

Buchmueller, Thomas, et al. "Cost and Coverage Implications of the McCain Plan to Restructure Health Insurance." *Health Affairs* (Sept. 16, 2008): w472–w481.

Burman, Leonard E. "A Blueprint for Tax Reform and Health Reform." *Virginia Tax Review* (Fall 2008): 287–323.

Christensen, Sandra. "The Subsidy Provided under Medicare to Current Enrollees." *Journal of Health Politics, Policy and Law* (Summer 1992): 255–64.

Cogan, John F., R. Glenn Hubbard, and Daniel P. Kessler. "The Effect of Tax Preferences on Health Spending." *National Tax Journal* (Sept. 2011): 795–816.

Congressional Budget Office. *Budget Options,* Vol. 1: *Health Care.* Dec. 2008.

Congressional Budget Office. *The Tax Treatment of Employment-Based Health Insurance.* Mar. 1994.

Congressional Research Service. "The Tax Exclusion for Employer-Provided Health Insurance: Policy Issues Regarding the Repeal Debate." Report No. RL34767 (Nov. 21, 2008).

Congressional Research Service. *Tax Expenditures: Compendium of Background Material on Individual Provisions.* Committee Print, Senate Budget Committee (Dec. 2010).

Cunningham, Laura E. "National Health Insurance and the Medical Deduction." *Tax Law Review* (Winter 1995): 237–64.

Feldstein, Martin. "Health and Taxes." *Wall Street Journal* (Jan. 19, 2004).

Feldstein, Martin. "The Welfare Cost of Excess Health Insurance." *Journal of Political Economy* (Mar.–Apr. 1973): 251–80.

Feldstein, Martin, and Bernard Friedman. "Tax Subsidies, the Rational Demand for Insurance and the Health Care Crisis." *Journal of Public Economics* (Apr. 1977): 155–78.

Forman, Jonathan B. "Reconsidering the Income Tax Treatment of the Elderly: It's Time for the Elderly to Pay Their Fair Share." *University of Pittsburgh Law Review* (1995): 589–626.

Furman, Jason. "Health Reform through Tax Reform: A Primer." *Health Affairs* (May–June 2008): 622–32.

Gillette, Robert, et al. "The Impact of Repealing the Exclusion for Employer-Sponsored Insurance." *National Tax Journal* (Dec. 2010): 695–708.

"Group Health Plans: Some Legal and Economic Aspects." *Yale Law Review* (Dec. 1943): 162–82.

Gruber, Jonathan. "Taxes and Health Insurance." *Tax Policy and the Economy* 16 (2002): 37–66.

Gruber, Jonathan. "The Tax Exclusion for Employer-Sponsored Health Insurance." *National Tax Journal* (June 2011): 511–30.

Gruber, Jonathan. "Tax Policy and Health Insurance." *Tax Policy and the Economy* 19 (2005): 39–63.

Joint Committee on Taxation. "Present Law and Analysis Relating to the Tax Treatment of Health Care Expenses." Report No. JCX-12–06 (Mar. 6, 2006).

Joint Committee on Taxation. "Present Law Tax Treatment of the Cost of Health Care." Report No. JCX-81–08 (Oct. 24, 2008).

Kaplow, Louis. "The Income Tax as Insurance: The Casualty Loss and Medical Expense Deductions and the Exclusion of Medical Insurance Premiums." *California Law Review* (Dec. 1991): 1485–510.

Pauly, Mark V. "Taxation, Health Insurance, and Market Failure in the Medical Economy." *Journal of Economic Literature* (June 1986): 629–75.

Saito, Blaine G. "The Value of Health and Wealth: Economic Theory, Administration, and Valuation Methods for Capping the Employer Sponsored Insurance Tax Exemption." *Harvard Journal on Legislation* (2011): 235–70.

Sessions, Samuel Y., and Philip R. Lee. "Using Tax Reform to Drive Health Care Reform." *Journal of the American Medical Association* (Oct. 22–29, 2008): 1929–31.

Steuerle, Eugene. "Taxing the Elderly on Their Medicare Benefits." *Tax Notes* (July 21, 1997): 427–28.

Steuerle, C. Eugene, and Stephanie Rennane. "Social Security and Medicare Taxes and Benefits over a Lifetime." Urban Institute (June 2011).

"Taxation of Employee Accident and Health Plans before and under the 1954 Code." *Yale Law Journal* (Dec. 1954): 222–47.

Thomasson, Melissa A. "From Sickness to Health: The Twentieth-Century Development of U.S. Health Insurance." *Explorations in Economic History* (July 2002): 233–53.

Thomasson, Melissa A. "The Importance of Group Coverage: How Tax Policy Shaped U.S. Health Insurance." *American Economic Review* (Sept. 2003): 1373–84.

Chapter 12

Tax Preferences for Housing

Almost every time tax reform comes up, the question of whether the mortgage interest deduction will be abolished or restricted also comes up. And, just as predictably, home-owners resist and powerful trade associations such as the National Association of Realtors and the National Association of Home Builders lobby Congress to drop the idea, which it does.

It would be easier to just forget about tampering with the mort-gage interest deduction, but the problem is that there are good reasons why it is a bad idea. It's a key area where tax policy could encourage people to change their behavior in ways that would be beneficial both to themselves and to the economy as a whole.

The mortgage interest deduction is one of the largest tax expen-ditures. If we want to reduce tax rates by broadening the tax base, it becomes much harder to do if the mortgage interest deduction is taken off the table right from the beginning. Moreover giving it a pass means that the next most popular deduction will be much harder to eliminate than it would be if all options were on the table.

Although mortgage interest is the most important tax preference for real estate, there are others as well. The biggest is the deduction for property taxes, but the special tax treatment of capital gains on home sales is also important.

MORTGAGE INTEREST DEDUCTION

The deduction for mortgage interest is undoubtedly the most well-liked preference in the tax code. It saves homeowners a tremendous amount of taxes, and that tax saving is capitalized in home values. Thus even if homeowners might pay less tax in a reform that scaled back the mortgage interest deduction, they would probably still oppose it if they thought it would reduce the value of their principal asset. And because the mortgage interest deduction is such a large one for most homeowners, it generally pushes deductions above the threshold of the standard deduction and thus allows homeowners to itemize other deductions that they might not otherwise be able to take advantage of.

Contrary to popular belief, the mortgage interest deduction was not created to encourage homeownership. When the income tax was created in 1913, it allowed a deduction for all interest paid for whatever reason. In those days people tended to pay cash when they bought a house, and consumer borrowing was far less prevalent than it is today. Congress reasoned that most interest paid was for business purposes and thus a legitimate business expense.

From the beginning there have been two major criticisms of the mortgage interest deduction. The first is that it primarily benefits the well-to-do. They are more likely to own a home rather than rent and are also more likely to be in a high tax bracket. Thus someone in the 35 percent bracket saves 35 cents in taxes for every $1 of mortgage interest paid, but someone in the 15 percent bracket saves only 15 cents for every $1 of mortgage interest paid. Therefore it is not surprising that the bulk of mortgage interest is paid by those with incomes above $50,000 per year (see Table 12.1).

Table 12.1 Distribution of the Mortgage Interest Deduction, 2009

Income Class	Number of Returns	Amount Deducted
Below $10,000	>500	>$500,000
$10,000–$20,000	311,000	$88,000,000
$20,000–$30,000	1,000,000	$521,000,000
$30,000–$40,000	2,023,000	$1,292,000,000
$40,000–$50,000	2,923,000	$2,329,000,000
$50,000–$75,000	7,603,000	$9,332,000,000
$75,000–$100,000	6,754,000	$10,066,000,000
$100,000–$200,000	10,594,000	$30,261,000,000
$200,000 and over	3,424,000	$22,768,000,000
Total	**34,632,000**	**$76,656,000,000**

Source: Joint Committee on Taxation.

A second criticism is that the mortgage interest deduction is unfair to those who rent, since rental payments are nondeductible. The mortgage interest deduction was undoubtedly a major factor in the decline of rental housing after World War II and the vast migration of the middle class out of the cities into suburbs, where homeownership predominates. The rise in taxes during World War II, which increased the percentage of people paying income taxes ten times, was also an important factor because many more people needed tax preferences available to the middle class.

EXCESSIVE HOMEOWNERSHIP

Another concern economists have expressed is that by encouraging excessive homeownership, the mortgage interest deduction may have discouraged people from investing in bonds and common stock, which would provide capital to industry that would increase economic growth, productivity, and wages. Instead people have tended to put far too much of their saving into illiquid housing, where it earned a low return and made them vulnerable to downturns in the housing market. According to the Federal Reserve, between 2006 and 2010 the downturn in housing prices wiped out more than $6 trillion in homeowner wealth and saving.

Many economists believe that the decline in real estate wealth was at the core of the Great Recession. The easy availability of second mortgages and home equity loans in recent years encouraged homeowners to tap their real estate wealth for consumption. Estimates suggest that homeowners spend about $5 for every $100 increase in their financial wealth, but as much as $9 for every $100 increase in housing wealth because they view it as more stable. Thus the loss of $6 trillion in such wealth probably pulled $500 billion per year in spending out of the economy and accounted for much of the severity of the downturn.

Economists also note that unemployment was exacerbated by the fact that many of the unemployed could not move to where jobs were available because they could not sell their home for a price that would cover their mortgage. Even in times when unemployment was less of a problem and the housing market was more robust, the difficulty of selling homes created immobility in the labor market, which made it harder for employers to find workers and workers to find jobs.

Despite these problems, however, Americans are devoted to homeownership and disinclined to support measures that would make it more expensive or reduce the value of their largest asset. An April 2011 Gallup poll is typical. It found that 61 percent of people oppose eliminating the mortgage interest deduction even if tax rates are reduced simultaneously. Only 31 percent of people were in favor. Not surprisingly, the former percentage approximately equals the homeownership rate.

As noted earlier, a key and not unreasonable concern homeowners have is that withdrawal of the mortgage interest deduction would cause home prices to fall. In 1995, when there was a brief boomlet for the flat tax, which would eliminate all personal deductions in the tax code, the Realtors Association contracted with the prominent economic consulting firm DRI/McGraw-Hill to calculate the impact on home prices. It concluded that the flat tax would cause a 15 percent drop. Although some economists raised serious questions about the methodology of the study and thought the impact on home prices was overstated, whatever support there was for the flat tax evaporated.

One point worth keeping in mind should this issue come up again is that whatever negative effect there may be on home prices would be a one-time-only effect. Once mortgage deductibility was gone and home prices were adjusted, the prices would rise at the same rate they would have risen otherwise.

We know this because many other countries, such as Australia, Canada, Germany, Israel, and Japan, do not allow mortgage interest to be deducted, have homeownership rates comparable to or even greater than those in the United States, and in many cases have seen historical home appreciation even greater than that in the United States. Great Britain abolished the deduction for mortgage interest in April 2000, yet housing prices rose more over the next decade than they did in the United States despite predictions to the contrary.

Of course, there are options for scaling back the mortgage interest deduction short of complete abolition. The United States capped the amount of a mortgage on which interest could be deducted at $1 million in 1987 (principal and secondary residences combined). That amount could be further reduced. In 1993 Finland changed its law so that all taxpayers deducted mortgage interest at the same rate, thus reducing the advantage that high-income homeowners had relative to those with lower incomes. A number of economists have suggested limiting the deduction for mortgage interest to a certain percentage of income or converting the deduction into a tax credit as a way of limiting it and improving fairness.

PROPERTY TAXES AND CAPITAL GAINS

Although the mortgage interest deduction is the best-known tax preference to benefit housing, it is not the only one. Another is the deductibility of property taxes, which renters pay implicitly through their rent but cannot deduct. As with the mortgage interest deduction, the benefits of property tax deductibility go primarily to the wealthy. In 2007, 70 percent of the value of the property tax deduction went to those with incomes above $100,000. Keep in mind that even if interest can't be deducted above a $1 million mortgage, property taxes are deductible no matter how expensive a home is.

As with mortgage interest, the deductibility of property taxes dates back to the original income tax in 1913 and was based on the theory that all taxes should be deductible. But in the years since, Congress has gradually taken away the deduction for many taxes. Most recently the Tax Reform Act of 1986 eliminated the deduction for state and local sales taxes. (Limited deductibility was restored in 2004 for people living in states with no income taxes.) The deductibility of property taxes is also subject to a phaseout for those with high incomes.

Additionally, capital gains on sales of owner-occupied residences receive special tax treatment. Beginning in 1951 it was possible to defer taxes on capital gains as long as the seller bought a new home of equal or greater value within a certain time period. This often imposed a severe burden on those forced to sell a home because of a divorce or job transfer, and on those moving from parts of the country where home prices are high to those where they are lower. I know someone who had gold fixtures installed in his bathroom in order to raise the price of a house he bought to be able to roll over the capital gain. (Improvements to a newly purchased home went into the purchase price for tax purposes.)

Beginning in the 1960s Congress created special rules for the elderly. Eventually those over age fifty-five were permitted a one-time exclusion of up to $125,000 in gains on home sales. In 1997

Congress decided that all taxpayers should benefit, and the law was changed to allow homeowners to realize up to $250,000 in capital gains on owner-occupied residences every two years tax-free ($500,000 for couples filing jointly). Research shows that home price appreciation from that date was much greater for homes below the $500,000 threshold. Some economists blame this provision for fueling the housing bubble in the 2000s.

A first-time home buyer tax credit was enacted in 2008 as a temporary measure to stimulate home purchases. Despite a lack of evidence that it accomplished much and a lot of evidence that people claimed the credit improperly, Congress renewed it twice. Although there was pressure to continue the credit, it was allowed to expire in early 2010.

Having spent a number of years in the 1990s advocating abolition of the mortgage interest deduction as part of a flat-tax reform that would eliminate all deductions, I know how devoted people are to that particular deduction and how difficult it will be to restrict it. Nevertheless there is a case for doing so because mortgage interest is the second largest tax expenditure, reducing federal revenues by almost $100 billion in 2012 alone.

FURTHER READINGS

Bartlett, Bruce. "Will the Flat Tax KO Housing?" *Wall Street Journal* (Aug. 2, 1995).

Congressional Research Service. "An Economic Analysis of the Homebuyer Tax Credit." Report No. R40955 (Dec. 1, 2009).

Congressional Research Service. "The Flat Tax and Other Proposals: Effects on Housing." Report No. 96–379E (Apr. 29, 1996).

Congressional Research Service. "Fundamental Tax Reform: Options for the Mortgage Interest Deduction." Report No. RL33025 (Aug. 8, 2005).

Ferreira, Fernando, Joseph Gyourko, and Joseph Tracy. "Housing Busts and Household Mobility." *Journal of Urban Economics* (July 2010): 34–45.

Hendershott, Patric, and Gwilym Pryce. "The Sensitivity of Homeowner Leverage to the Deductibility of Home Mortgage Interest." *Journal of Urban Economics* (July 2006): 50–68.

Hendershott, Patric, Gwilym Pryce, and Michael White. "Household Leverage and the Deductibility of Home Mortgage Interest: Evidence from U.K. House Purchasers." *Journal of Housing Research* (2003): 49–82.

Hilbers, Paul, et al. "House Price Developments in Europe: A Comparison." International Monetary Fund Working Paper No. WP/08/211 (Oct. 2008).

Joint Committee on Taxation. "Present Law, Data, and Analysis Relating to Tax Incentives for Homeownership." Report No. JCX-50–11 (Sept. 30, 2011).

Lehman, H. Jane. "Flat Tax Could Cost Owners: Study Predicts 15% Dip in Home Values." *Washington Post* (July 1, 1995).

Mathias, William T. "Curtailing the Economic Distortions of the Mortgage Interest Deduction." *University of Michigan Journal of Law Reform* (Fall 1996): 43–78.

Mills, Edwin S. "Dividing Up the Investment Pie: Have We Overinvested in Housing?" *Federal Reserve Bank of Philadelphia Business Review* (Mar.–Apr. 1987): 13–23.

Saarimaa, Tuukka. "Tax Incentive and Demand for Mortgage Debt: Evidence from the Finnish 1993 Tax Reform." *International Journal of Housing Policy* (Mar. 2010): 19–40.

Shan, Hui. "The Effect of Capital Gains Taxation on Home Sales: Evidence from the Taxpayer Relief Act of 1997." *Journal of Public Economics* (Feb. 2011): 177–88.

Taylor, Lori L. "Does the United States Still Overinvest in Housing?" *Federal Reserve Bank of Dallas Economic Review* (2nd Quarter 1998): 10–18.

Tsounta, Evridiki. "Home Sweet Home: Government's Role in Reaching the American Dream." International Monetary Fund Working Paper No. WP/11/191 (Aug. 2011).

Ventry, Dennis J. "The Accidental Deduction: A History and Critique of the Tax Subsidy for Mortgage Interest." *Law and Contemporary Problems* (Winter 2010): 233–84.

Woodward, Susan E., and John C. Weicher. "Goring the Wrong Ox: A Defense of the Mortgage Interest Deduction." *National Tax Journal* (Sept. 1989): 301–13.

Chapter 13

How Federal Taxes Affect the States

Discussions of tax reform tend to ignore the impact on state and local governments because they have their own tax systems. But state and federal taxes are intertwined, and tax changes at the federal level ripple throughout the states. A key reason is that the states follow the federal tax base, federal definitions of income, and so on to a large extent. Most states use the same tax base as the IRS does, with state tax rates applying to the income reported on federal 1040 forms. The states also depend on IRS enforcement, as the IRS notifies states when it uncovers a tax problem with one of their residents. Moreover there are certain federal tax provisions that affect state and local governments directly, in particular the deduction for state and local income and property taxes and the exclusion of interest on state and local government bonds. Since these are major targets for tax reformers, states and localities have a large stake in federal tax reform.

State and local income and property taxes paid have been fully deductible since the beginning of the modern income tax in 1913. Deductibility of state sales taxes was abolished in 1986, but in 2004 it was restored for those who live in states without an income tax, such as Texas and Florida. Likewise the exclusion of interest on state and local government bonds has existed for as long as there has been a federal income tax. In 2012 the Treasury Department estimated that the deduction for state and local taxes reduced federal revenues by $49 billion, and the exclusion for interest on state and local government bonds reduced federal revenues by $37 billion.

EFFECTS OF THE TAXES PAID DEDUCTION

Critics of the deduction for state and local taxes often focus on the idea that it causes such taxes to be higher than they would be in the absence of deductibility. Assuming that there is a political and economic limit to taxation by state and local governments, deductibility allows them to tax more than they would otherwise be able to do.

Consider those in the 25 percent tax bracket who itemize their returns. If they pay $1,000 in state income taxes, their true burden is only $750 because they will save $250 in federal income taxes as a result of deductibility. Similarly federal deductibility reduces the progressivity of state income tax rates. At present the highest state income tax rate is 11 percent, in both Hawaii and Oregon. Since the top federal income tax rate is 35 percent, the effective top state tax rate is 35 percent less. That makes the effective top rate a little over 7 percent in both states.

It's hard to prove how much higher state taxes are because of federal deductibility, but there's no question that they are higher. Indeed economists have long recommended that states impose higher and more graduated tax rates precisely because a good part of the burden is in effect shifted to the federal government. This was especially so in the 1970s, when the top federal income tax rate was 70 percent. State taxpayers received a de facto 70 percent subsidy on their deductible state and local taxes. In an article published in 1972 the Federal Reserve Bank of Boston economist Edward Moscovitch explained why states with flat-rate income taxes would benefit from switching to graduated rates:

> A graduated tax allows the state to shift a large part of the tax burden onto the federal government. Since all major state and local taxes are deductible for federal income-tax purposes, the federal government in effect bears part of the burden of state taxes. By shifting state taxes onto those taxpayers in the highest federal tax brackets, the adoption of graduated rates increases the total amount of federal tax savings, and thereby reduces the total burden of a state income-tax. In effect, adoption of graduated rates offers an opportunity for the state to participate in a form of state-initiated revenue-sharing.

As with all deductions, the value increases the higher one's income tax bracket is. Consequently the bulk of the tax savings from the deduction for state and local taxes accrues to the wealthy. According to the Joint Committee on Taxation, just 2.5 percent of the aggregate tax savings from this deduction in 2009 went to those with incomes below $50,000, and 16 percent went to those with incomes between $50,000 and $100,000. The rest, 81 percent of the aggregate tax savings, went to those with incomes above $100,000, with 60 percent of these benefits going to those with incomes above $200,000.

EFFECTS ON STATE SPENDING

Another concern raised by economists is that the deduction for state and local taxes encourages state and local governments to take on responsibilities that could be better handled by the private sector. Trash collection is a good example. If a private company picks up your trash, you can't deduct the fee, but if your town picks it up and includes the cost in your property taxes, it is deductible. Not only does this system discourage governments from privatizing services, but it also discourages them from charging fees for such services because only taxes are deductible, not fees, even if paid to a state or local government.

Low-tax states also assert that the deduction for state and local taxes constitutes a de facto subsidy from them to high-tax states. According to this argument, since taxpayers in low-tax states get less benefit from deductibility and because it reduces overall federal revenues that must be collected in other ways, they pay higher federal taxes than would be the case if high-tax states didn't receive a tax subsidy from the federal government.

For these reasons, tax reformers have long targeted the deduction for state and local taxes for elimination. The first major effort to do so was in 1984, when the Treasury Department recommended it in a report to President Reagan. Treasury said that the deduction was unnecessary as a matter of principle. Its major justification, it said, was to prevent the combined state and federal tax rate from exceeding 100 percent during the era when the top federal tax rate was 90 percent or more. In 1984, however, the top rate was 50 percent; today the top federal income rate is just 35 percent.

Therefore the rationale that a deduction for state and local taxes is necessary to prevent confiscatory taxation is no longer valid.

Treasury was also concerned that people could shift private consumption spending onto government by, for example, having local governments establish municipal swimming pools, tennis courts, golf courses, and other means of entertainment unconnected to the essential nature of government. And despite laws in most states that try to equalize per pupil education spending, it's obvious that those in wealthy communities have better schools than those in central cities and poor areas. Wealthy people, who could afford private tuition for their children, save that expense because they are able to send their children to public schools paid for with deductible taxes. As the Treasury report explained:

> Expenditures by state and local governments provide benefits primarily for residents of the taxing jurisdiction. To the extent that state and local taxes merely reflect the benefits of services provided to taxpayers, there is no more reason for a federal subsidy for spending by state and local governments than for private spending. . . . It would be better—fairer, simpler, and more neutral—to have lower federal tax rates and have state and local government services—like private purchases— funded from after-tax dollars.

The proposal never went anywhere due to intense opposition from high-tax states. Governor Mario Cuomo of New York, in particular, aggressively fought the idea of abolishing or even limiting the deduction for state and local taxes. Whenever the idea has come up, politicians from New York have always been in the forefront of opposition. In 1996, for example, Mayor Rudolph Giuliani of New York City was critical of Republican presidential aspirant Steve Forbes's support for the flat tax because it would eliminate the deduction for state and local taxes along with all other deductions. When President George W. Bush appointed a tax reform commission in 2005, it recommended abolition of the deduction for state and local taxes. Not surprisingly, Sen. Charles Schumer of New York was the strongest critic. The proposal went nowhere.

ALTERNATIVE MINIMUM TAX UNDERMINES DEDUCTION

Despite the strong political support for the deduction for state and local taxes, it has nevertheless been substantially eroded by two provisions of the tax code. First is the Alternative Minimum Tax (AMT). Second is a provision popularly known as "Pease," after the congressman who was its author, which phased out personal exemptions for those with high incomes. Although repealed temporarily, Pease will come back in 2013 without congressional action.

The AMT was established in 1969 to prevent wealthy people from eliminating their income tax liability through aggressive use of legal tax preferences. It's been revised several times since. The way it works now, people have to calculate their federal income taxes twice: first under the regular income tax and again under an alternative tax system. In this alternative tax system, they lose some important income adjustments, such as the personal exemption and the deduction for state and local taxes. There are two tax rates for the AMT: 26 percent on the first $175,000 and 28 percent on the rest, plus a large exemption. People pay whichever system yields a higher tax payment. In 2009, 4 million taxpayers paid $32 billion more in taxes because of the AMT.

Thus we see that taxpayers covered by the AMT already lose the value of the deduction for state and local taxes. And those losing the deduction tend to live in high-tax states like New York. That's why the AMT is often called a tax on the so-called blue states that tend to be controlled by Democrats and have high taxes.

Under Pease, the value of all itemized deductions was phased out for those with high incomes. In 1991 the threshold was established at $100,000 of adjusted gross income for joint filers and $50,000 for singles, indexed for inflation. Above those income levels, taxpayers lost 3 percent of their itemized deductions, including the deduction for state and local taxes. However, the provision was capped so that no taxpayers lost more than 80 percent of their itemized deductions.

TAX-EXEMPT BONDS

The tax exclusion for interest on state and local government bonds is another way that federal tax law affects state and local governments. Economists generally view this exclusion as a subsidy from the federal government to state and local governments, which are able to sell bonds at interest rates well below equivalent taxable bonds. Economists assume that the difference between the taxable bond rate and the rate on tax-exempt bonds approximately equals the average marginal tax rate. Movements in the spread, therefore, tell us what is the market's perception of changes in implicit marginal tax rates.

For many years economists and tax theorists have argued that the exemption for interest on state and local government bonds should be abolished. By subsidizing only one aspect of state and local government budgets, the exemption is inefficient and leads to overbuilding and misuse of the tax exclusion for projects such as sports stadiums that seldom justify their cost. Historically a key reason such arguments were rejected is that it was thought that the constitutional principle of federalism required a tax exemption for state and local government bonds. However, in the case of *South Carolina v. Baker* (1988), the Supreme Court rejected this argument. Consequently there would be no constitutional barrier to eliminating or scaling back the tax exemption for state and local government bonds.

State and local governments will resist any federal tax change that affects them negatively. However, it may be possible to mitigate the affects through some sort of on-budget program such as revenue sharing that would hold them harmless while cleaning up the tax code and eliminating distortions that may impose economic costs on society. Since many taxpayers already lose many of the tax benefits related to state and local government taxation through the AMT and other federal tax provisions, they may be less resistant to losing the deduction for state and local government taxes than politicians think, if they get something worthwhile in return.

It has been argued that the strong incentive for states to conform to the federal tax base, the nondeductibility of fees for government services, and various laws and court decisions restricting state taxing authority have imposed on states tax systems that tend to make their revenues highly volatile. Revenues rise in cyclical upswings—a situation that encourages tax cuts and new spending programs—and crash in economic downturns. Hard balanced budget requirements forced states to cut spending and raise taxes during the economic downturn that began in 2007. Many economists believe that this fiscal contraction was so pronounced in the aggregate that it lengthened and deepened the downturn despite an increase in state aid in the 2009 Recovery Act. To the extent that tax reform encouraged states to adopt more stable revenue sources it would be beneficial.

FURTHER READINGS

Congressional Budget Office. *The Deductibility of State and Local Taxes.* Feb. 2008.

Congressional Budget Office. *The Individual Alternative Minimum Tax.* Jan. 2010.

Congressional Research Service. "Federal Deductibility of State and Local Taxes." Report No. RL32781 (Nov. 28, 2007).

Congressional Research Service. "Imposing a Ceiling on the Deduction for State Income Taxes: Horizontal Equity and Other Issues." Report No. 90–443E (Sept. 13, 1990).

Feldstein, Martin S., and Gilbert E. Metcalf. "The Effect of Federal Tax Deductibility on State and Local Taxes and Spending." *Journal of Political Economy* (Aug. 1997): 710–36.

Galle, Brian. "Federal Fairness to State Taxpayers: Irrationality, Unfunded Mandates, and the 'SALT' Deduction." *Michigan Law Review* (Mar. 2008): 805–52.

Johnson, Calvin H. "Repeal Tax Exemption for Municipal Bonds." *Tax Notes* (Dec. 24, 2007): 1259–63.

Johnson, Calvin H. "A Thermometer for the Tax System: The Overall Health of the Tax System as Measured by Implicit Tax." *SMU Law Review* (2003): 13–52.

Joint Committee on Taxation. "Present Law and Background Relating to State and Local Government Bonds." Report No. JCX-14–06 (Mar. 14, 2006).

Kaplow, Louis. "Fiscal Federalism and the Deductibility of State and Local Taxes under the Federal Income Tax." *Virginia Law Review* (Apr. 1996): 413–92.

Keller, Robert I. "The Case for Highly Graduated Rates in State Income Taxes." *Maryland Law Review* (1976): 617–50.

Leonhardt, David. "Case of Vanishing Deductions: Alternative Tax Called Culprit." *New York Times* (Feb. 21, 2005).

Mason, Ruth. "Federalism and the Taxing Power." *California Law Review* (Aug. 2011): 975–1036.

Metcalf, Gilbert E. "Assessing the Federal Deduction for State and Local Tax Payments." *National Tax Journal* (June 2011, pt. 2): 565–90.

Moscovitch, Edward. "State Graduated Income Taxes—A State-Initiated Form of Revenue Sharing." *National Tax Journal* (Mar. 1972): 53–64.

President's Advisory Panel on Federal Tax Reform. *Simple, Fair, and Pro-Growth: Proposals to Fix America's Tax System.* Nov. 2005.

Reuben, Kim. "The Impact of Repealing State and Local Tax Deductibility." *State Tax Notes* (Aug. 15, 2005): 497–513.

Stark, Kirk J. "The Federal Role in State Tax Reform." *Virginia Tax Review* (Fall 2010): 407–44.

Stark, Kirk J. "Fiscal Federalism and Tax Progressivity: Should the Federal Income Tax Encourage State and Local Redistribution?" *UCLA Law Review* (June 2004): 1389–434.

Tax Foundation. "PEP and Pease: Repealed for 2010 but Preparing for a Comeback." Special Report No. 178 (Apr. 2010).

Turnier, William J. "Evaluating Personal Deductions in an Income Tax—The Ideal." *Cornell Law Review* (Jan. 1981): 262–96.

U.S. Treasury Department. *Tax Reform for Fairness, Simplicity, and Economic Growth: The Treasury Department Report to the President,* Vol. 1. 1984.

Chapter 14

The Problem of Charitable Contributions

The deduction for charitable contributions is a large tax expenditure. Its size is a bit confusing because the Treasury Department lists it separately under three different categories: those for education, those for health care, and all others. The total revenue loss was $53 billion in 2012. It will undoubtedly be an issue in tax reform if only because the incentive to make charitable contributions is to a large extent a function of one's marginal tax rate: those in the top bracket save 35 cents for every $1 they contribute. If the top rate is reduced, therefore, the tax saving for every $1 contributed will necessarily fall. Every time tax reform comes up, the large and politically powerful nonprofit sector issues warnings about the effect on contributions.

Another perennial issue is fairness. A vast amount of charitable contributions cannot be deducted because they are made by those who do not itemize and take the standard deduction instead. Most of the money thrown into the collection plate each week is probably never deducted on tax returns. In 2009, 55 percent of the tax saving from the charitable contributions deduction went to those making more than $200,000; another 26 percent went to those making between $100,000 and $200,000. Less than 5 percent went to those making less than $50,000 (see Table 14.1).

Table 14.1 Taxpayers Who Itemized, 2010

Statutory Tax Rate	Percentage Who Itemized	Percentage of Total
0	3.9	4.1
10	16.2	8.8
15	37.0	39.6
25	65.5	32.7
25 (AMT)	97.9	3.8
28	79.6	5.0
28 (AMT)	98.6	4.9
33	70.9	0.3
35	89.4	0.8
All	30.1	100.0

Source: Tax Policy Center.

PRIORITIES OF THE WEALTHY OVERREPRESENTED

Because the incentives for giving are so much greater for the wealthy, the priorities of the wealthy tend to be overrepresented among nonprofit institutions. According to surveys, 66 percent of contributions by those with incomes below $100,000 goes to religious institutions; only 7 percent goes to organizations focusing on health, education, or the arts. By contrast, among those with incomes over $1 million, 66 percent of contributions goes to health, education, or the arts; only 17 percent goes to religious organizations.

And because the tax code permits a full deduction for the fair market value of assets contributed to charity, this system also tends to primarily benefit the well-to-do. Consider a rich woman who bought some stock for $10 that is now worth $100. If she sold the stock and realized a capital gain, she would pay $13.50 in taxes (15 percent of $90). Donating the balance to charity would save $30 in taxes (35 percent of $85). When the capital gains tax is subtracted, she saves $17 in taxes on net. But if she donates the stock without first selling it, she can deduct the full $100 and save $35 in taxes—twice the tax saving. Since those with modest incomes are less likely to be able to donate appreciated property to charity, they don't benefit from this tax provision to the same extent.

Of course, the tax saving for the rich is potentially even greater in the case of assets such as art or real estate for which it may not be possible to calculate the true market value without a sale. It's easy enough to find some expert who will say that a painting is worth $1 million—saving the donor as much as $350,000 in taxes—when its market value may be a fraction of the assessed value. And it's in the interest of recipients to assist in exaggerating the value of such contributions to facilitate gift-giving.

THEORETICAL JUSTIFICATION

The justification for the charitable contributions deduction has been a continuing issue of debate among tax theorists. While the First Amendment provides solid ground for it in the case of gifts to religious institutions, allowing a deduction for donations to art museums or public television is much more problematic. Some theorists argue that such contributions are just a form of consumption from which the giver benefits in various ways, such as having his or her name prominently displayed on a building or exhibition.

In other cases, deductible contributions to think tanks and related organizations are substitutes for nondeductible political contributions. I once talked to a wealthy contributor to a think tank where I was working. I was curious about the extent to which our tax-exempt status affected his giving. He said it had no impact at all. He said that he had a certain budget for political and public policy giving, and contributions to political candidates, think tanks, and similar organizations were lumped together in that budget, with no distinction between those that were tax-exempt and those that weren't.

I was shocked by this revelation. There isn't any way a think tank can compete with a political party in promising legislative action on some policy question. Theoretically think tanks aren't even supposed to endorse legislation, although all of them do. They meet the letter of the law by adding a disclaimer at the end of their reports saying that nothing in the report should be taken as an effort to affect the passage of legislation.

To the extent that rich people saw contributions to candidates and political parties, on the one hand, and those to think tanks, on the other, as fungible, it would put inexorable pressure on the latter to produce immediate political results on the contributor's agenda. Think tanks have responded by setting up sister organizations for which contributions are not tax deductible but which are permitted to be openly partisan, endorsing candidates, running advertisements, making campaign contributions, and so on.

For example, in 2010 the conservative Heritage Foundation, which is tax exempt under section 501(c)(3) of the tax code, set up a parallel organization called Heritage Action for America, which is not tax exempt and is organized under section 501(c)(4) of the tax code. This reorganization permits Heritage to be more active politically on the issues of concern to its contributors without jeopardizing its tax-exempt status. Conversely, many political groups and trade associations have 501(c)(3) affiliates for those that need tax-exempt status to receive funds from a foundation, an estate, or someone in need of the tax deduction.

THINK TANK CORRUPTION

It's hard to know to what extent this trend has corrupted the original idea of the think tank as an academic institution not unlike a university department that simply doesn't hold classes. Instead think tanks view members of Congress, administration officials, and the media as their students, so to speak. Unfortunately the pressure to deliver immediate political results has corrupted this ideal. It is not uncommon these days for Washington think tanks to fire analysts for partisan reasons unrelated to the quality of their work, and research that runs afoul of a think tank's political agenda has disappeared down the memory hole. This practice would be a scandal in academia, but is considered standard practice among think tanks.

Many think tanks now pay their leaders salaries equivalent to those earned by the CEOs of major corporations, who occupy most of the positions on think tank boards, and they are inclined to view their president as a peer who should be paid equivalently. Academics, who used to be common on think tank boards, have almost entirely disappeared from them. In my observation, they had an "annoying" tendency to view a think tank's success more by the quality of its work than by the growth of its contributions. As long as its contributions continue to rise, a think tank considers itself successful even if its agenda goes nowhere, the major media ignore its work, and its research fails to pass a basic test of competence in the academic sphere.

REFORM OPTIONS

A number of reforms have been suggested over the years for improving the operation and effectiveness of the nonprofit sector, as well as the fairness of the deduction for charitable contributions. Here are a few.

CHANGE THE DEDUCTION TO A CREDIT. Instead of making the tax saving a function of one's marginal tax rate, so that savings are greater for those with high incomes, allow a tax credit of, say, 15 percent of a contribution. That way the tax saving would be the same for everyone. Nonprofit organizations would be less intent on currying favor with the well-to-do, and those addressing the concerns of average people would benefit. We would probably see less money go to art museums and more to groups such as the Salvation Army that aid those in need.

ALLOW ONLY DEDUCTIONS ABOVE A FLOOR. Another idea would be to limit the deduction for charitable contributions that exceed 2 percent of adjusted gross income. The idea is to reward marginal contributions rather than those that would be made anyway. While it would reduce contributions somewhat, it would raise tax revenue that could perhaps be better targeted in some other way.

ALLOW A DEDUCTION FOR NONITEMIZERS. As noted earlier, those taking the standard deduction cannot deduct charitable contributions. Allowing them to do so would increase charitable contributions, but also reduce tax revenue, increase tax complexity, and open the door to allowing the deductibility of other expenses that the standard deduction is in lieu of. Permitting a deduction for nonitemizers above a floor, however, would prevent rewarding people for something they would do anyway, and this would increase contributions while limiting the loss of revenue.

LIMIT THE DEDUCTIBILITY OF CHARITABLE CONTRIBUTIONS TO INSTITUTIONS GENUINELY ENGAGED IN PUBLIC SERVICE. The test for becoming a 501(c)(3) organization is rather loose, and few organizations are ever audited. Far too many devote excessive resources to fundraising and little to programs. There ought to be some reasonable test of effectiveness that can weed out groups with impressive-sounding names but nonexistent accomplishments.

TAX THE INVESTMENT INCOME OF CHARITIES. The Harvard law professor Daniel Halperin argues that even if a deduction for charitable contributions is justified, it doesn't follow that the investment income of charities should be tax-free. He believes that this tax treatment is an unjustified subsidy. In recent years some policymakers have questioned the propensity of some colleges to accumulate vast endowments that compound tax-free without offering any apparent benefits to students.

RESTRICT THE BUSINESS ACTIVITIES OF NONPROFITS. More and more nonprofits engage in business activities that directly compete with commercial businesses. Nonprofit credit unions compete with banks, electrical and telephone cooperatives compete with public utilities, nonprofit hospitals compete with for-profit hospitals, and so on. Among nonprofits providing private goods and services, three-quarters of their revenue derives from such provision. Many commercial businesses complain that they are suffering from unfair competition.

Some scholars suggest getting rid of the charitable contributions deduction altogether. Many countries do not allow such a deduction and don't appear to suffer as a result. These include Austria, Finland, Ireland, Italy, Sweden, and Switzerland. Some scholars argue that the efficiency of nonprofits would increase if they weren't given a tax subsidy and that it is inherently unfair for taxpayers to subsidize the giving of others just because the recipient has 501(c)(3) status.

If I give a poor person $10 to buy some food, I get no deduction. My donation must be channeled through a tax-exempt organization that provides food to the poor. This discourages spontaneous relief efforts and the creation of commercial enterprises that might be more effective at improving the lot of the poor.

Although it is unlikely that Congress will ever abolish the charitable contributions deduction, it can be improved in terms of fairness and efficiency in ways that wouldn't increase the revenue cost. The debate on tax reform should examine charitable giving.

FURTHER READINGS

Altman, Daniel. "If the I.R.S. Gets Less, Does Charity Get More?" *New York Times* (May 8, 2005).

Andrews, William D. "Personal Deductions in an Ideal Income Tax." *Harvard Law Review* (Dec. 1972): 309–85.

Auten, Gerald E., James M. Cilke, and William C. Randolph. "The Effects of Tax Reform on Charitable Contributions." *National Tax Journal* (Sept. 1992): 267–90.

Bittker, Boris I., and George K. Rahdert. "The Exemption of Nonprofit Organizations from Federal Income Taxation." *Yale Law Journal* (Jan. 1976): 299–358.

Buettner, Russ. "Reaping Millions in Nonprofit Care for the Disabled." *New York Times* (Aug. 2, 2011).

Chamberlain, Andrew, and Mark Sussman. "Charities and Public Goods: The Case for Reforming the Federal Income Tax Deduction for Charitable Gifts." Tax Foundation Special Report No. 137 (Nov. 2005).

Clotfelter, Charles T. *Federal Tax Policy and Charitable Giving*. University of Chicago Press, 1985.

Clotfelter, Charles T. "Tax-Induced Distortions in the Voluntary Sector." *Case Western Reserve Law Review* (1988–89): 663–94.

Clotfelter, Charles T., and Richard L. Schmalbeck. "The Impact of Fundamental Tax Reform on Nonprofit Organizations." In *The Economic Effects of Fundamental Tax Reform*, ed. Henry Aaron and William G. Gale, 211–46. Brookings Institution, 1996.

Congressional Budget Office. *Effects of Allowing Nonitemizers to Deduct Charitable Contributions*. Dec. 2002.

Congressional Budget Office. *Options for Changing the Tax Treatment of Charitable Giving*. May 2011.

Congressional Budget Office. *Taxing the Untaxed Business Sector*. July 2005.

Congressional Research Service. "An Overview of the Nonprofit and Charitable Sector." Report No. R40919 (Nov. 17, 2009).

Congressional Research Service. "Tax Issues Relating to Charitable Contributions and Organizations." Report No. RL34608 (Aug. 5, 2008).

Feldstein, Martin. "A Deduction from Charity." *Washington Post* (Mar. 25, 2009).

Gergen, Mark P. "The Case for a Charitable Contributions Deduction." *Virginia Law Review* (Nov. 1988): 1393–450.

Greene, Pamela, and Robert McClelland. "Taxes and Charitable Giving." *National Tax Journal* (Sept. 2001): 433–53.

Halperin, Daniel. "Is Income Tax Exemption for Charities a Subsidy?" *Tax Law Review* (2011): 283–312.

Harris, Benjamin H., and Daniel Baneman. "Who Itemizes Deductions?" *Tax Notes* (Jan. 17, 2011): 345.

Hechinger, John. "College Endowment Tax Is Studied." *Wall Street Journal* (May 9, 2008).

Hochman, Harold M., and James D. Rogers. "The Optimal Tax Treatment of Charitable Contributions." *National Tax Journal* (Mar. 1977): 1–18.

Izzo, Todd. "A Full Spectrum of Light: Rethinking the Charitable Contributions Deduction." *University of Pennsylvania Law Review* (June 1993): 2371–402.

Joint Committee on Taxation. "Description and Analysis of Present Law and Proposals to Expand Federal Tax Incentives for Charitable Giving." Report No. JCX-13–01 (Mar. 13, 2001).

Joint Committee on Taxation. "Historical Development and Present Law of the Federal Tax Exemption for Charities and Other Tax-Exempt Organizations." Report No. JCX-29–05 (Apr. 19, 2005).

Joint Committee on Taxation. "Present Law and Background Relating to the Federal Tax Treatment of Charitable Contributions." Report No. JCX-55–11 (Oct. 14, 2011).

Kahn, Jeffrey H. "Personal Deductions—A Tax Ideal or Just Another Deal?" *Michigan State Law Review* (2002): 1–55.

Kelman, Mark G. "Personal Deductions Revisited: Why They Fit Poorly in an 'Ideal' Income Tax and Why They Fit Worse in a Far from Ideal World." *Stanford Law Review* (May 1979): 831–83.

List, John A. "The Market for Charitable Giving." *Journal of Economic Perspectives* (Spring 2011): 157–80.

Madoff, Ray D. "Dog Eat Your Taxes?" *New York Times* (July 9, 2008).

McCormack, Shannon W. "Taking the Good with the Bad: Recognizing the Negative Externalities Created by Charities and Their Implications for the Charitable Deduction." *Arizona Law Review* (2010): 977–1026.

Randolph, William C. "Dynamic Income, Progressive Taxes, and the Timing of Charitable Contributions." *Journal of Political Economy* (Aug. 1995): 709–38.

Reich, Robert B. "Is Harvard a Charity?" *Los Angeles Times* (Oct. 1, 2007).

Roberts, Russell. "A Positive Model of Private Charity and Public Transfers." *Journal of Political Economy* (Feb. 1984): 136–48.

Steuerle, Eugene. "When Nonprofits Conduct Exempt Activities as Taxable Enterprises." Urban Institute (May 1, 2001).

Stokeld, Fred. "Charities Fear Loss of Deduction under Flat Tax Proposals." *Tax Notes* (Feb. 19, 1996): 935–38.

Strom, Stephanie. "Grab Bag of Charities Grows, Along with U.S. Tax Breaks." *New York Times* (Dec. 6, 2009).

Strom, Stephanie. "Nonprofits Fear Losing Tax Benefit." *New York Times* (Dec. 3, 2010).

Thaler, Richard H. "It's Time to Rethink the Charity Deduction." *New York Times* (Dec. 19, 2010).

Valentine, Paul. "A Lay Word for a Legal Term: How the Popular Definition of Charity Has Muddled the Perception of the Charitable Deduction." *Nebraska Law Review* (2010): 997–1045.

Chapter 15

The Problem of Taxing Capital Gains

apital gains have long presented special problems for tax policy. The key quandary is that capital gains are not taxed until an asset is sold and the gain is realized. Thus the taxpayer decides if, when, and how to be taxed. Another is that unrealized capital gains held until death never pay the capital gains tax. When heirs sell assets, they are taxed as if the assets were purchased on the day they were inherited insofar as the capital gains tax is concerned. The third major problem is that capital gains are not indexed for inflation. Research shows that a substantial portion of realized gains represent only inflation, but are taxed as if they were real.

ARE CAPITAL GAINS INCOME?

When Congress created the modern income tax in 1913, there were a great many tax issues not thought through or not addressed legislatively. Among these was the taxation of capital gains. When the Civil War income tax was in effect, capital gains were taxed like any other form of income. But after the war, in the case of *Gray v. Darlington* (1872), the Supreme Court ruled that because capital gains might represent income earned over many years, taxing capital gains as if all the income had been earned in the year in which gains were realized was unconstitutional.

The decision had no practical effect, as the Civil War income tax was allowed to lapse the same year the case was decided. But when the income tax was revived in 1913, many commentators assumed that the ruling in *Darlington* would hold. The Internal Revenue

Service, however, ignored it and taxed capital gains as ordinary income. This led to a number of confusing court decisions.

Economists at the time generally supported the idea that capital gains were not a form of income independent from the income generated by capital: interest, rent, and dividends. If the income from capital was taxed, taxing capital gains as well was in effect a double tax on the same income. Economists noted that this was the long-standing view in Britain, where capital gains were tax-free except for professional traders.

The analogy, one often heard at the time, was that capital is like a fruit-bearing tree. Income is like the annual fruit harvest. To the extent that the tree grew larger and could produce more fruit, this growth represented a capital gain. But the additional fruit resulting from the growth would also raise income. Therefore taxing both the fruit and the growth of the tree was a double tax that would diminish the tree's productive capacity and reduce fruit production.

In the case of *Merchants Loan and Trust Co. v. Smietanka* (1921), the Supreme Court overruled itself and decided that capital gains were indeed taxable. Commentators have speculated that the Court might have ruled otherwise if the government hadn't been under such intense pressure to raise revenue wherever it could be found, to meet the fiscal demands of World War I.

With the capital gains question having been resolved as a constitutional matter, Congress was left to decide how capital gains should be taxed. Historically the factor that has been of primary concern is revenue and the extreme sensitivity of capital gains tax receipts to changes in the tax rate, the holding period, and the treatment of capital losses. Considerations of fairness and the impact on economic growth have tended to be secondary, although they are often invoked by politicians seeking to change the taxation of capital gains.

TAX HISTORY

It is difficult to summarize the historical tax treatment of capital gains. A recent effort by the Joint Committee on Taxation required a five-page table to do so, and a 2006 report by the Congressional Research Service found at least twenty major legislative acts affecting capital gains since 1913. The important thing to know is that except for a couple of brief periods, long-term capital gains have been taxed at preferential rates well below the tax rate on ordinary income. This differential was especially important during periods when the top statutory income tax rate was particularly high. During the 1940s and 1950s, when the top income tax rate was over 90 percent, there was an alternative rate of just 25 percent on long-term capital gains.

Normally assets needed to be held six months to get long-term treatment; short-term gains were taxed as ordinary income. The purpose of the holding period, apparently, was to suppress the volatility of stock prices.

In the early years of the income tax, capital gains were taxed as ordinary income, but capital losses were fully deductible against ordinary income. As a consequence the government suffered a net loss of revenue. In 1921 Congress instituted the first preference for capital gains, taxing them at a rate of just 12.5 percent. But since losses were still deductible against ordinary income, which could be taxed at rates as high as 73 percent, little net revenue was raised. If gains had not been taxed at all there would have been no reason to allow losses to be deductible. The government would have gained revenue.

Congress enacted a limit on the deductibility of losses against ordinary income of $1,000 in 1942. Since 1978 taxpayers have been allowed to deduct only $3,000 of capital losses against ordinary income. (Realized capital losses are deductible against realized gains.) Economists believe that this is a severe impediment to risk-taking. In effect, the government gets a share of all realized gains, but does not share when there are losses. Had deductible losses kept pace with inflation since 1978, taxpayers would be able to deduct more than $10,000 against ordinary income today.

An even bigger problem, insofar as inflation affects capital gains, is that the taxes apply to those gains that simply represent inflation as well as those that are real. In principle, taxation should apply only to real gains. During periods of high inflation, it is not uncommon for the capital gains tax to exceed 100 percent of real gains, thus imposing a confiscatory burden on investors that impedes capital formation.

Over the years a number of proposals have been made to index capital gains so that taxes would apply only to real gains. Unfortunately there are serious administrative problems with doing so, such as determining what measure of inflation is appropriate and indexing losses so that they can be used to offset gains appropriately. Although these problems are not insurmountable, indexing capital gains would add enormous complexity to an already complex tax system. Historically Congress has felt that excluding a portion of gains from taxation or taxing capital gains at a lower rate is a better way to deal with the problem of inflation.

REVENUE CONSIDERATIONS DOMINATE

In recent years revenue considerations have dominated the capital gains debate. The Tax Reform Act of 1969 raised the maximum tax rate on long-term capital gains from 25 percent to 35 percent, phased in over three years. Subsequently, realized gains and capital gains revenues fell, rather than rising as expected. Revenues fell from $5.9 billion in 1968 to $3.2 billion in 1970. Some of this was just a timing effect—people realized gains they planned to realize later—and some was due to the recession. But nominal revenues didn't get back to their 1968 level until 1976, with inflation being the principal factor. In real terms they were still below their 1968 level. Aggregate gains fell from almost 4 percent of GDP in 1968 to just 1.9 percent in 1975.

In the late 1970s a number of economists, especially Martin Feldstein of Harvard, argued that a high capital gains tax combined with inflation created a powerful lock-in effect. People held on to their assets or borrowed against them rather than selling them. This tendency both deprived the government of revenue and created economic inefficiency. Old and underperforming assets were protected from market forces, while new business start-ups and those with more growth potential were deprived of capital. Feldstein argued that a cut in the capital gains tax rate would pay for itself by increasing realizations.

The Feldstein argument was so powerful that a Democratic Congress enacted a reduction in the long-term capital gains rate to 28 percent in 1978. Although Treasury Secretary Michael Blumenthal objected to this legislation, President Carter signed it into law. A 1985 study by the Treasury Department concluded that the rate cut did raise revenue initially, but probably not in the longer run.

Aggregate capital gains realizations rose from 2.2 percent of GDP in 1978 to 2.9 percent in 1979 before falling to 2.7 percent in 1980 and 2.6 percent in 1981.

At that time the effective capital gains tax was reduced by allowing taxpayers to exclude 60 percent of gains from taxation, with ordinary income tax rates applying to the balance. Thus on a $100 gain, only $40 would be taxed. With the top income tax rate being 70 percent, a 60 percent exclusion therefore yielded a maximum effective capital gains rate of 28 percent (70 percent of 40 percent). Consequently when Congress reduced the top income tax rate to 50 percent in 1981, this automatically reduced the top capital gains rate to 20 percent. Realized capital gains rose from 2.6 percent of GDP in 1981 to 4.1 percent of GDP in 1985. Capital gains revenues went from $12.8 billion in 1981 to $26.5 billion in 1985 despite the lower rate.

CAPITAL GAINS AS REGULAR INCOME

In 1986 Congress and the Reagan administration agreed to a reform that reduced the top income tax rate to just 28 percent. Liberals insisted that the preference for capital gains be eliminated as a matter of fairness. They have long objected to the special treatment of capital gains as an unjustified tax loophole. Reagan reasoned that raising the maximum capital gains rate to what it was after the 1978 legislation was a reasonable price to pay for getting the top rate on all income down to its lowest level since the 1920s.

There was a burst of capital gains realizations before the rate went up. Aggregate realizations jumped to 7.35 percent of GDP in 1986 and revenues doubled to $53 billion from the year before. But revenues and realizations fell sharply thereafter. Realizations fell steadily to 1.9 percent of GDP in 1991 and revenues dropped to $25 billion. The George H.W. Bush administration pushed hard for a cut in the capital gains rate to stimulate investment and growth, and argued that it would pay for itself in terms of increased capital gains realizations. The Democratic Congress would not go along.

After Republicans gained control of Congress in 1994, they succeeded in getting President Clinton to agree to a cut in the maximum capital gains rate to 20 percent in 1997. Revenues rose from $66 billion in 1996 to $127 billion in 2000. Realizations as a share of GDP rose from 3.3 percent to 6.5 percent. Of course, the tech bubble of the late 1990s contributed heavily to the rise in realizations and revenues, but the capital gains tax cut undoubtedly helped fuel the boom by making it easier for tech companies to raise capital.

In 2003 George W. Bush and a Republican Congress reduced the maximum capital gains rate to 15 percent, primarily as an economic stimulus measure. The stimulus was undermined, however, since this provision was in effect only temporarily due to congressional budget rules. It expired at the end of 2010. President Obama had proposed raising the maximum capital gains rate to 20 percent as a deficit reduction measure, but in December 2010 agreed to a two-year extension of the 15 percent rate. It will expire again at the end of 2012. Economists agree that temporary tax changes are less effective at modifying behavior than permanent ones.

While there is no question that changes in the capital gains tax rate can affect realizations and revenues, its impact on economic growth is ambiguous. A 2009 report by the Congressional Research Service found little evidence that the cut in the capital gains rate raised saving or investment. Consequently there is little reason to believe that it has increased economic growth. Supporters of a lower capital gains rate, however, point to its impact on the composition of investment and on innovation and risk-taking, factors difficult to quantify but potentially important.

In the debate on tax reform, the treatment of capital gains will be a major issue. Conservatives will insist that the tax rate not be raised lest it devastate the economy. Liberals will emphasize the highly unequal distribution of capital gains. A lower rate on capital gains benefits the wealthy almost exclusively, as Table 15.1 illustrates.

Table 15.1 Distribution of Capital Gains by Income, 2006

Adjusted Gross Income	Percentage of All Returns	Share of Total Income	Share of Capital Gains Realizations	Percentage of Returns Reporting Capital Gains	Capital Gains as a Share of Income
Under $75,000	80.3	36.8	6.2	8.5	1.8
$75,000–$200,000	16.8	32.0	11.2	27.1	3.6
$200,000–$1 million	2.7	16.1	22.0	53.9	13.5
$1 million and over	0.3	15.1	60.6	76.3	39.5

Source: Tax Policy Center.

Conservatives will respond that poor people do not create jobs and that many of those benefiting from the capital gains preference are entrepreneurs who start businesses or finance new start-ups. They will also argue that many of those with high incomes may have been in that group for only a single year, when they sold a farm or business and realized a large capital gain that may have represented a lifetime of small, unrealized annual gains.

REFORM OPTIONS

As noted earlier, the treatment of tax losses probably has more impact on entrepreneurship and risk-taking than does the capital gains rate. In principle, investors should be able to deduct all losses against ordinary income, but Congress is unlikely to ever enact such a proposal, as it would reduce tax revenues sharply. Investors would sell primarily assets that had fallen in value and realize their losses, which would reduce their taxable income. Meanwhile they would hold on to assets that had risen in value, which would be tax-free until realized. The only way a full loss offset would be feasible is if Congress moved toward taxing unrealized gains annually, a move that some tax theorists favor. But politically there is zero chance that this change will ever happen.

Since a lower capital gains rate is to a large extent compensation for the failure to index capital gains for inflation, one possible trade-off might be to raise the capital gains rate but apply the tax only to real gains.

Another issue that comes up with the capital gains tax is that most gains are reinvested, making it more of a transactions tax than one on income. If gains are rolled over into another investment, the thinking goes, taxpayers should be permitted to delay paying a tax on any gain. Again, this might be a reasonable trade-off for raising the rate.

A related problem that Congress may wish to address is the tax treatment of mutual funds. When fund managers realize capital gains or losses, these pass through to the fund's investors. Thus someone who never sold his or her mutual fund shares may nevertheless be forced to report gains and pay taxes on them. A number of proposals have been put forward over the years to allow mutual fund investors to defer taxes until they sell their shares.

Should Congress consider reform of capital gains taxes it will certainly visit the issue of hedge funds, a type of private equity investment limited to the wealthy that has more risk and reward potential than mutual funds. At present, hedge fund managers are taxed on their profits, often called "carried interest," at the capital gains tax rate of 15 percent. But many people argue that such profits are management fees that ought to be taxed as ordinary income at rates as high as 35 percent. The argument is complicated, but as a matter of politics and fairness, the current policy appears untenable.

It would be desirable in principle to get rid of the step-up basis on assets held until death. As long as people can have in effect a zero capital gains rate if they hold an asset until death, there will always be a capital gains lock-in effect, no matter how low the rate. It's also unfair because two people with the same capital gains will pay significantly different taxes if one realizes those gains before death while the other does not.

FURTHER READINGS

Auerbach, Alan J. "Capital Gains Taxation and Tax Reform." *National Tax Journal* (Sept. 1989): 391–401.

Bartlett, Bruce. "Inflation and Capital Gains." *Tax Notes* (June 2, 1997): 1263–66.

Blum, Walter J. "A Handy Summary of the Capital Gains Arguments." *Taxes—The Tax Magazine* (April 1957): 247–66.

Burman, Leonard. *The Labyrinth of Capital Gains Tax Policy*. Brookings Institution, 1999.

Congressional Budget Office. *Indexing Capital Gains*. Aug. 1990.

Congressional Research Service. "The Economic Effects of Capital Gains Taxation." Report No. R40411 (Mar. 4, 2009).

Congressional Research Service. "Individual Capital Gains Income: Legislative History." Report No. 98–473 (May 18, 2006).

Dickson, Joel M., and John B. Shoven. "Taxation and Mutual Funds: An Investor Perspective." *Tax Policy and the Economy* 9 (1995): 151–80.

Domar, Evsey D., and Richard A. Musgrave. "Proportional Income Taxation and Risk-Taking." *Quarterly Journal of Economics* (May 1944): 388–422.

Fleischer, Victor. "Two and Twenty: Taxing Partnership Profits in Private Equity Funds." *New York University Law Review* (Apr. 2008): 1–59.

Johnson, Calvin H. "Taxing the Consumption of Capital Gains." *Virginia Tax Review* (Winter 2009): 477–529.

Joint Committee on Taxation. "Present Law and Historical Overview of the Federal Tax System." Report No. JCX-1–11 (Jan. 18, 2011).

Kornhauser, Marjorie E. "The Origins of Capital Gains Taxation: What's Law Got to Do with It?" *Southwestern Law Journal* (Nov. 1985): 869–928.

Mayhall, Van. "Capital Gains Taxation—The First 100 Years." *Louisiana Law Review* (Fall 1980): 81–99.

Organization for Economic Cooperation and Development. *Taxation of Capital Gains of Individuals*. Tax Policy Study No. 14 (2006).

Paschall, C. Thomas. "U.S. Capital Gains Taxes: Arbitrary Holding Periods, Debatable Tax Rates." *Southern California Law Review* (May 2000): 843–78.

Repetti, James R. "The Use of Tax Law to Stabilize the Stock Market: The Efficacy of Holding Period Requirements." *Virginia Tax Review* (Winter 1989): 591–637.

Seltzer, Lawrence H. *The Nature and Tax Treatment of Capital Gains and Losses*. National Bureau of Economic Research, 1951.

Somers, Harold M. "Capital Gains Tax: Significance of Changes in Holding Period and Long Term Rate." *Vanderbilt Law Review* (June 1963): 509–33.

Surrey, Stanley S. "Definitional Problems in Capital Gains Taxation." *Harvard Law Review* (Apr. 1956): 985–1019.

U.S. Treasury Department. *Report to Congress on the Capital Gains Tax Reductions of 1978*. 1985.

Viard, Alan D. "The Taxation of Carried Interest: Understanding the Issues." *National Tax Journal* (Sept. 2008): 445–60.

Warren, Alvin C. "The Deductibility by Individuals of Capital Losses under the Federal Income Tax." *University of Chicago Law Review* (Winter 1973): 291–326.

Weisbach, David A. "The Taxation of Carried Interests in Private Equity." *Virginia Law Review* (May 2008): 715–64.

Chapter 16

Some Unresolved Issues in the Taxation of Corporations

Corporations present special problems for taxation, as they are entities separate and distinct from their owners, who are taxed as well, leading to double taxation of income earned in the corporate sector. For sole proprietorships or partnerships, only one layer of taxation exists, but there are two layers on what are called "C corporations," which are publicly traded firms owned by one group of people, the shareholders, but controlled by another group, the managers. Corporations pay taxes, and the owners pay taxes on exactly the same income when it is paid out as dividends.

Economists have long known that there is a fundamental problem of control between the shareholders and the managers. Because their ownership is diffused and may be indirect through pensions or mutual funds, shareholders don't have the time or ability or access to information necessary to prevent them from being exploited by managers, who may grossly overpay themselves or undertake investments that may advance their power and influence without adding to shareholder value. Economists call this the "agency problem."

The corporate income tax contributes to this problem by creating a sort of veil between owners and managers. Excessive pay and perks enjoyed by managers may not be as thoroughly scrutinized by shareholders as they should be, because they are viewed as deductible business expenses. Thus they come at least partially at the government's expense rather than the shareholders'. And the higher the corporate tax rate, the more the government shares. By contrast, when a business is run as a sole proprietorship or partnership, the owners tend to be much more cost-conscious.

DOUBLE TAXATION

More important, the double taxation of income earned in the corporate sector discourages the payment of dividends. Since profits retained at the corporate level pay only the corporate tax, while dividends pay the individual income tax as well, shareholders don't pressure managers to pay them all the profits to which they are entitled. To some extent, shareholders know that even if profit remains in the firm, it will raise share prices and allow the shareholders to get some of that profit in the form of capital gains, which have long been taxed at preferential rates. Managers may also use profits to buy back shares, and this will also raise share prices.

Unfortunately, retained earnings are sometimes treated as free money that managers can invest in ways that don't enhance shareholder value. In early 2011, for example, News Corporation's chairman Rupert Murdoch was widely criticized by shareholders for using company assets to buy his daughter's company for $675 million. In the 1980s economists argued that many corporate takeovers and mergers were motivated less by the opportunities for profit than by a desire to build little empires that enhanced managerial power and prestige.

Another critical consequence of the double taxation of corporate profits is that corporate financial structures are distorted. In particular, corporations have a strong incentive to raise capital through borrowing rather than issuing new shares. Interest payments are a deductible business expense that reduces taxes; dividend payments are not. Many economists believe that the favored treatment of debt has led corporations to become overleveraged, contributing to bankruptcies during economic slowdowns. While dividend payments can be suspended when corporate income falls, interest payments must be made on schedule regardless of circumstances.

The double taxation of corporate profits also raises the cost of capital and reduces investment in the corporate sector. It distorts capital allocation within the business sector by encouraging excessive investment in certain sectors that may be better able to mitigate the effects of double taxation than others. Thus we see that effective tax rates vary throughout the business sector, depending on the type of investment and the nature of its financing. Table

16.1, produced by the Treasury Department in 2007, illustrates the variance in business tax rates.

Table 16.1 Marginal Effective Tax Rates on New Investment Vary Substantially by Sector

Investment	Tax Rate
Business	25.5
Corporate business	29.4
Asset type	
Equipment	25.3
Structures	34.2
Land	32.9
Inventories	32.9
Financing	
Debt financed	-2.2
Equity financed	39.7
Noncorporate business	20.0
Owner-occupied housing	3.5
Economywide	17.3

Source: Treasury Department.

Another consequence of the impact of the corporate tax on the cost of capital is that the burden of the tax is shifted onto workers. If investors don't get an adequate after-tax rate of return, they will reduce their investment until, through supply and demand, the rate of return rises to where the after-tax rate of return is sufficient. The capital stock will be lower, and this circumstance will reduce productivity and, eventually, wages. Many economists now believe that the ultimate burden of the corporate income tax actually falls largely on labor.

For these reasons, economists and policymakers across the political spectrum have long advocated the elimination of double taxation. The main question is how. Ideally it would be desirable to treat corporations like partnerships, with all profits and losses, whether distributed or not, attributed to the owners. Economists call this "full integration." Unfortunately Congress has never seriously considered the idea. Instead it has adopted a variety of measures to mitigate, but not eliminate, double taxation. Most recently, in 2003, it reduced the tax rate on dividends for individuals to 15 percent. However, studies have shown that this action did little to spur corporate investment or even increase dividend payouts.

One important constraint on reform is revenue. For many years the top individual income tax rate was well above the corporate rate. Until 1981 the top individual rate was 70 percent, while the corporate rate was 46 percent. This differential gave wealthy individuals an incentive to incorporate and take their income in the form of salary or benefits rather than dividends. Integration would have raised revenue by subjecting more income to higher individual income tax rates, and this was one reason liberals supported the idea. But in the Tax Reform Act of 1986 the top individual rate fell to 28 percent, while the corporate rate fell only to 34 percent. This change created the opposite effect: people had an incentive to disincorporate and take all their income on the individual rate schedule. That is one reason measured income inequality, which is based largely on tax data, increased. Income that used to be reported on corporate returns was now reported on individual tax returns.

The magnitude of this effect can be seen in the changed distribution of business forms. In 1986 there were 2.6 million C corporations in the United States. By 2008 that number had fallen to 1.8 million. At the same time the number of S corporations quintupled, from 400,000 to over 4 million. These are a special type of corporation with a limited number of shareholders that are not double-taxed at the corporate and shareholder level. Sole proprietorships increased from 12 million in 1986 to 23 million in 2008, and the number of partnerships rose from 1.7 million to 3.1 million. Economists call businesses that are not double-taxed "pass-through" or "flow-through" entities, since all their taxable income passes through to the owners.

Over the years any number of proposals have been put forward to eliminate the double taxation problem. Because they would all have different political and economic implications, no single approach has ever emerged as a consensus position. Approaches to mitigating double taxation also vary from one country to another. Obviously, coming up with a permanent solution to this problem would be desirable as part of tax reform.

DEPRECIATION

The corporation first emerged as the dominant form of business organization in the nineteenth century. At that time the federal government did not have a tax on any form of income, except briefly during the Civil War, so corporations did not consider the tax implications of their structure. Their main purpose was financial. Corporations could raise larger amounts of capital than any individual or partnership by tapping a broader ownership base. Railroads were the primary spur to development of the corporation, as they required more capital than any previous private undertaking in history.

Railroads created a special problem of accounting that would later have enormous implications for tax policy. Historically businesses operated more or less on a cash-flow basis. If there was more inflow than outflow during a year, most businesses considered that their profit. Since they had little in the way of tangible capital, this crude accounting worked well enough most of the time.

But a huge part of a railroad's expenses was not operational but long-lived fixed assets: locomotives, land, rails, stations, and so on. If outlays for capital were treated in the way expenses historically had been treated, every railroad would show a loss for many, many years. On the other hand, profits would be overstated if they didn't account for the wearing out of plants and equipment that would eventually have to be replaced. Hence the railroads developed the idea of depreciation to properly account for the annual expense represented by the wearing out of tangible capital.

By the time the federal corporate income tax came into existence in 1909, the concept of depreciation was still in its infancy, as was the development of modern accounting. Accounting, such as it was, existed primarily so that managers could control costs and investors could know whether or not they were making money, rather than for tax purposes. Much early accounting was developed by engineers to suit their needs and lacked an economic basis, so it led to confusion about the true nature of profit and loss that continues to the present day.

The corporate income tax clearly contemplated taxing only profits, that is, revenue minus legitimate business expenses such as wages, raw materials, and so on. The Internal Revenue Service accepted that the wearing out of plants and equipment, although not mentioned in the law, was a valid deductible cost. But the IRS was keen to make sure that depreciation was calculated in a systematic way that could be audited and could not be easily manipulated for tax avoidance.

The IRS decided that the right way to account for depreciation was to calculate the useful life of an asset. If an asset was expected to last twenty years, the IRS would allow a business to deduct one-twentieth of the purchase price each year for twenty years. This treatment is known as "straight-line" depreciation. For many years the IRS expended vast resources calculating the useful lives of various assets; the results were published in a document called Bulletin F.

Needless to say, there has been a constant struggle between the IRS and the business community over what is the useful life of an asset for depreciation purposes, as well as the definition of a depreciable asset. In general the IRS favors calculating useful lives over a much greater number of years than businesses would prefer, thus reducing the annual deduction for depreciation. It also tries to force businesses to capitalize as many major purchases as possible rather than treating them as current expenses that may be deducted immediately. The preferred IRS methods reduce deductible business costs and therefore raise taxable profits, increasing business taxes.

Over the years there have been many changes to depreciation schedules, with Congress often shortening them and increasing opportunities for businesses to "expense" or write off spending for machinery and equipment immediately to encourage capital investment. At times Congress has also allowed businesses to have an Investment Tax Credit equal to some percentage, usually 10 percent, of an outlay for machinery or equipment that could be subtracted directly from a firm's tax liability in addition to depreciation allowances.

In the 1970s inflation distorted the accounting for depreciation. In theory depreciation allowances should be large enough to pay for replacement of a piece of equipment when it is no longer usable. But inflation increased the cost of replacing equipment, while depreciation allowances were based on the original purchase price of an asset rather than its replacement cost. Many economists believed that the failure of capital consumption allowances to take inflation into account led to underinvestment by businesses that contributed to slow growth during that decade.

The biggest problem today is that a growing share of business investment is in the form of intangible capital: research and development, licenses, human capital, patents, trademarks, copyrights, and other forms of capital that can't be depreciated. A related problem is that even in the case of tangible capital such as computers, the old idea of depreciation as a physical wearing out of equipment is meaningless. The real problem is obsolescence, which almost always happens long before high-tech equipment wears out in the same sort of way that a lathe or drill press or another piece of industrial equipment eventually becomes unusable.

Indeed an interesting argument has been made by the economist Maurice Scott that the concept of depreciation as a physical wearing out of equipment never made any sense in the first place. To the extent that tangible capital decayed physically, the cost of maintenance, which has always been deductible as a normal business expense, compensated for it. The only real depreciation is and always has been obsolescence, he argues.

This theory suggests that the only rational tax treatment of capital is full expensing, an immediate write-off just like any other routine business expense. Alternatively firms should be permitted to increase their unused depreciation allowances by the rate of interest so that they get the economic equivalent of expensing even if they continue to depreciate assets over a period of years. But even that won't help in cases where the real problem is obsolescence, which these days can occur in a period of months.

In recent years there has been movement toward expensing. The George W. Bush administration got Congress to enact a "bonus" depreciation deduction of 50 percent for certain investments as a stimulus measure. The Obama administration had this raised to 100 percent—that is, an immediate write-off—for investments made in late 2010 and 2011. It is debatable whether temporary changes in depreciation policy are stimulative or a good idea for the long run. One goal of tax reform ought to be to rationalize and update depreciation policy for an economy in which the nature of capital has changed dramatically from the railroad era.

WHERE TO TAX A CORPORATION

The biggest administrative problem in taxing corporations these days is how to determine where they exist for tax purposes. A business may be incorporated in one state or country, have its headquarters in another, and have subsidiaries and production facilities in many others. Since corporations have a great deal of flexibility in moving around income and assets, it is difficult for governments everywhere, at all levels, to tax corporate income.

For a long time the Organization for Economic Cooperation and Development, which represents the economic interests of all major countries, has been working hard to make it more difficult for corporations to move income around to minimize their tax liability. Conservatives decry these efforts, believing that there should be as much competition among governments as possible in order to drive down tax rates. In general they tend to focus on the statutory corporate tax rate. However, economists focus more on the effective tax rate, taking account of various tax preferences and tax rates on shareholders, as well as measures to relieve double taxation. As Table 16.2 demonstrates, although the United States has the highest statutory rate, the combined rate when followed through to shareholders is not far out of line with our most important international competitors.

Table 16.2 Overall Statutory Tax Rates on Dividend Income, 2010

Country	CIT[1]	PIT[2]	Combined[3]	Country	CIT	PIT	Combined
Denmark	25.0	42.0	56.5	Spain	30.0	18.0	42.6
France	34.4	48.7	55.9	Luxembourg	28.6	39.0	42.5
U.K.	28.0	42.5	54.0	Portugal	26.5	20.0	41.2
U.S.	39.2	17.0	49.5	Finland	26.0	28.0	40.5
Germany	30.2	26.4	48.6	Chile	17.0	40.0	40.0
Ireland	12.5	41.0	48.4	Hungary	19.0	25.0	39.3
Sweden	26.3	30.0	48.4	New Zealand	30.0	38.0	38.0
Norway	28.0	28.0	48.2	Switzerland	21.2	20.0	36.9
Canada	29.5	46.4	48.2	Italy	27.5	12.5	36.6
Korea	24.2	38.5	47.8	Poland	19.0	19.0	34.4
Australia	30.0	46.5	46.5	Turkey	20.0	35.0	34.0
Japan	39.5	10.0	45.6	Greece	24.0	10.0	32.5
Netherlands	25.5	25.0	44.1	Czech Republic	19.0	15.0	31.2
Belgium	34.0	15.0	43.9	Mexico	30.0	30.0	30.0
Austria	25.0	25.0	43.8	Iceland	15.0	10.0	23.5

1. Statutory corporate tax rate, including state or provincial taxes.
2. Statutory rate on dividends, including state or provincial taxes.
3. Combined tax rate on dividends received, including other provisions not listed.

Source: OECD.

Of course, effective tax rates on particular corporations or industries depend on a variety of factors, such as whether an investment is debt- or equity-financed, that are impossible to summarize. It is simplistic to look solely at the statutory rate on corporations, as many conservatives tend to do, without taking into account other tax factors that may be far more important in determining corporate investment and location decisions.

A complicating factor as far as the United States is concerned is that many countries tax their businesses only on income earned within their borders. These countries include Canada, France, Germany, and Switzerland. But the United States taxes corporations based in the United States on their worldwide income. Thus if a Canadian company earns income in the United States, it pays U.S. taxes on that income but does not owe taxes in Canada on that same income. A U.S.-based multinational, however, would pay taxes in Canada on income earned there, plus U.S. taxes as well, although it would receive a credit against its tax liability in the United States for taxes paid in Canada. However, U.S. taxes are paid only when foreign income is repatriated to the United States. As long as companies leave their profits in foreign countries, U.S. taxes are deferred.

Liberals tend to view deferral as an unjustified tax loophole, while conservatives believe that the United States should adopt a territorial tax system such as Canada has. Both conservatives and liberals have at times supported the idea of a tax holiday that would temporarily lower the tax rate on repatriated earnings to raise revenue. However, many tax experts fear that corporations will be encouraged to leave even more of their profits abroad than they otherwise would in the expectation that another tax holiday will come along eventually.

THE COST OF REFORM

It is not hard to make the case that there should be no corporate income tax at all. Over the years many tax reformers on both the left and the right have done so. The main constraint is revenue. In 2010 the corporate income tax raised about $200 billion, revenue that would be hard to replace if the corporate income tax were abolished. But it has been a declining revenue source for many years. In the early 1950s taxes on corporations constituted 33 percent of federal revenue. In 2010 the figure was less than 10 percent.

The main reason, historically, for the decline in corporate tax revenue is that debt, with its tax-deductible interest payments, has replaced equity as the major source of corporate finance. When I worked at the Treasury Department during the George H. W. Bush administration, we referred to this trend as "privatization of the corporate income tax." But another reason is the growth of tax preferences enacted by Congress. According to the IRS, after enactment of the Tax Reform Act of 1986 taxable corporate profits equaled 98 percent of gross corporate profits. By 2007 taxable profits were down to just 72 percent of gross profits; this suggests that broadening the corporate tax base could raise at least some of the revenue to compensate for lowering the corporate tax rate to make it more internationally competitive.

In the longer run, policymakers will have to address whether it is possible to tax corporate income in a world of increasing globalization. Finding its nexus is just too difficult when capital is relatively free to seek the highest after-tax return. For this reason, both liberal and conservative economists have suggested replacing the corporate tax with a broad-based consumption tax, since consumption is relatively immobile internationally. This change would improve competitiveness, eliminate many problems inherent in the nature of the corporate tax, and give the government a more stable source of revenue.

FURTHER READINGS

Aizcorbe, Ana M., Carol E. Moylan, and Carol Robbins. "Toward Better Measurement of Innovation and Intangibles." *Survey of Current Business* (Jan. 2009): 10–23.

Arlen, Jennifer, and Deborah M. Weiss. "A Political Theory of Corporate Taxation." *Yale Law Journal* (Nov. 1995): 325–91.

Bank, Steven A. "Entity Theory as Myth in the Origins of the Corporate Income Tax." *William and Mary Law Review* (Dec. 2001): 447–537.

Borden, Bradley T. "Three Cheers for Passthrough Taxation." *Tax Notes* (June 27, 2011): 1353–61.

Doran, Michael. "Managers, Shareholders, and the Corporate Double Tax." *Virginia Law Review* (May 2009): 517–95.

Congressional Research Service. "International Corporate Tax Rate Comparisons and Policy Implications." Report No. R41743 (Mar. 31, 2011).

Hines, James R., and Lawrence H. Summers. "How Globalization Affects Tax Design." *Tax Policy and the Economy* 23 (2009): 123–57.

Hubbard, R. Glenn. "Corporate Tax Integration: A View from the Treasury Department." *Journal of Economic Perspectives* (Winter 1993): 115–32.

Jensen, Matthew H., and Aparna Mathur. "Corporate Tax Burden on Labor: Theory and Empirical Evidence." *Tax Notes* (June 6, 2011): 1083–89.

Joint Committee on Taxation. "Present Law and Background Relating to Tax Treatment of Business Debt." Report No. JCX-41–11 (July 11, 2011).

Kaplan, Robert S. "The Evolution of Management Accounting." *Accounting Review* (July 1984): 390–418.

Knoll, Michael S. "Taxing Prometheus: How the Corporate Interest Deduction Discourages Innovation and Risk-Taking." *Villanova Law Review* (1993): 1461–1516.

Kwall, Jeffrey L. "The Uncertain Case Against the Double Taxation of Corporate Income." *North Carolina Law Review* (Apr. 1990): 613–57.

Littleton, A. C. *Accounting Evolution to 1900.* Russell & Russell, 1966 (1933).

Organization for Economic Cooperation and Development. *Fundamental Reform of Corporate Income Tax.* Tax Policy Study No. 16 (2007).

Scott, Maurice F. *A New View of Economic Growth.* Oxford University Press, 1989.

U.S. Treasury Department. "Approaches to Improve the Competitiveness of the U.S. Business Tax System for the 21st Century." Office of Tax Policy (Dec. 20, 2007).

U.S. Treasury Department. "The Case for Temporary 100 Percent Expensing: Encouraging Business to Expand Now by Lowering the Cost of Investment." Office of Tax Policy (Oct. 29, 2010).

U.S. Treasury Department. *The Deferral of Income Earned through U.S. Controlled Foreign Corporations.* Dec. 2000.

U.S. Treasury Department. "A History of Federal Tax Depreciation Policy." Office of Tax Analysis Working Paper No. 64 (May 1989).

U.S. Treasury Department. *Report of the Department of the Treasury on Integration of the Individual and Corporate Tax Systems: Taxing Business Income Once.* 1992.

U.S. Treasury Department. *Report to Congress on Depreciation Recovery Periods and Methods.* July 2000.

U.S. Treasury Department. "Treasury Conference on Business Taxation and Global Competitiveness: Background Paper." Office of Tax Policy (July 23, 2007).

World Bank. *Where Is the Wealth of Nations? Measuring Capital in the 21st Century.* 2006.

Chapter 17

The Problem of Tax Administration

A critical goal of tax reform must be to improve the tax collection system. Too many businesses and individuals do not pay the taxes they owe, the Internal Revenue Service increasingly lacks the resources to do its job properly, and tax complexity has become so severe that even tax professionals have difficulty interpreting the law. Radical simplification would aid both taxpayers and tax collectors. But while everyone supports simplification in principle, meaningful simplification seldom attracts significant political support.

TAX COLLECTION

Problems with tax collection date back to the origins of the state. No one has ever liked paying taxes even when they were low, at least by today's standards. Kings and emperors long employed harsh methods to get taxpayers to pay what they owed. The philosopher Philo, who lived during the time of Christ, tells us about a certain tax collector known to carry off the wives, children, and even parents of those who had fled rather than pay their taxes. When these hostages couldn't or wouldn't reveal a fugitive's whereabouts, this tax collector employed sadistic methods to make them talk. In Philo's words:

> This tax-collector did not let them go till he had tortured their bodies with racks and wheels, so as to kill them with newly invented kinds of death, fastening a basket full of sand to their necks with cords, and suspending it there as a very heavy weight, and then placing them in the open air in the middle of the market place, that some of them, being tortured and being

overwhelmed by all these afflictions at once, the wind, and
the sun, and the mockery of the passers by, and the shame,
and the heavy burden attached to them, might faint miserably.

No doubt some today have a similar image of how the IRS oper-
ates. But the truth is that the tax collection machinery in the United
States today is light. According to the Organization for Economic
Cooperation and Development, the United States has the fewest tax
collectors per capita of any major country, with 1,680 workers for
each tax collector in 2009. By contrast, there were 744 workers per
tax collector in Italy, 482 in Canada, 441 in Britain, 392 in France,
and 371 in Germany. Not surprisingly, tax-phobic Switzerland had
the fewest tax collectors per capita, with one for every 4,794 workers—ten times fewer than most other European countries.

Few Americans are ever audited. The widespread use of tax
software has reduced the time and expertise needed to fill out
tax returns, while sharply reducing mistakes and identifying tax-
reducing provisions that taxpayers would otherwise overlook.
Many taxpayers today look forward to getting their taxes done
so that they can get a refund, which they view as "found money."
It's worth remembering that until 1943 there was no withholding
of taxes from wages, so taxpayers had to write a big check to the
government annually for all of their income taxes.

Some conservatives think it would be a good idea to get rid of
tax withholding so that people are more conscious of their tax liability. This idea is obviously not viable and will never be put into
practice. But on the other hand, all tax advisers tell their clients
that they should avoid overwithholding and make arrangements
with their employers so that their withheld taxes come as close as
possible to their actual tax liability. This step will eliminate large
refunds, but also stop giving the Treasury an interest-free loan for
much of the year.

Withholding and reporting are the IRS's first lines of defense
against tax cheating. But they are losing their effectiveness as the
amount of taxable income not reported or with no withholding
requirement has risen over time. Most tax evasion takes the form
of not being declared on tax returns, rather than people claiming
deductions or credits for which they are not entitled. Those who

do are usually just making an honest mistake, not consciously evading taxes.

DETERIORATING COMPLIANCE

The deterioration in tax compliance can be seen by comparing the Commerce Department's estimate of adjusted gross income from business and employer sources with adjusted gross income reported on tax returns. In 2005 this gap was estimated at $1.3 trillion, up from $400 billion in 1990. As Table 17.1 indicates, in percentage terms, the gap has risen by about a third, from 10.3 to 14.8 percent. Not surprisingly, forms of income for which there is no withholding and which have weak reporting requirements are more likely to be undeclared on tax returns.

Table 17.1 Adjusted Gross Income Gap (percentage)

Type of Income	1990	2005
Wages and salaries	3.9	7.3
Proprietors' income (farm)	96.1	182.7
Proprietors' income (nonfarm)	44.0	56.8
Personal rental income	38.5	11.3
Personal dividend income	35.8	34.0
Personal interest income	6.0	30.4
Taxable pensions and annuities	25.5	22.2
Taxable unemployment benefits	15.5	8.0
Taxable Social Security benefits	13.2	6.9
Total	**10.3**	**14.8**
Income other than wages subject to reporting requirements	19.2	24.2
Income not subject to reporting requirements	48.1	56.6

Source: Commerce Department.

The IRS has studied the tax gap for years and put forward a variety of proposals for reducing it. But they all depend on funding. The IRS needs more staff and resources to pursue unreported income and unpaid taxes. Since the mid-1990s Republicans in Congress have consciously used the IRS as a whipping boy to justify cuts in its budget and deny requests for new laws to increase and improve reporting requirements.

One consequence of the political war against the IRS has been a rise in the number of people making frivolous arguments to avoid paying the taxes they owe. The IRS now encounters these arguments on a regular basis: that tax filing and tax payments are voluntary, that only foreign-source income is taxable, that Federal Reserve notes are not income, that the "United States" consists only of the District of Columbia and federal territories, that only those employed by the federal government are subject to taxation, that the First Amendment to the Constitution allows taxpayers to avoid taxation on religious grounds, that income taxation violates the Fifth and Thirteenth Amendments to the Constitution, that the Sixteenth Amendment was not properly ratified and does not authorize the taxation of nonapportioned taxes, and many others.

One often sees advertisements on late-night television shows for seminars that will explain how anyone can legally avoid paying income taxes. Among those taken in by such schemes was the well-known actor Wesley Snipes, who was misled by a group called American Rights Litigators. This group convinced him not to file tax returns despite the fact that he was making millions of dollars from Hollywood films. He was sentenced to three years in jail for tax evasion. In 2008 one of the top tax defiers, Irwin Schiff, was convicted of fifteen criminal contempt charges as well as conspiring to defraud the United States, filing false tax returns, aiding and assisting the preparation of false income tax returns, and evading the payment of millions of dollars in back taxes.

On various radio shows where I have been a guest I have often encountered callers making frivolous tax arguments. Most do not sound as if they hold the sort of job that would put them much above the lowest tax bracket, but they insist that the income tax is confiscatory and ought to be abolished. I like to ask them whether they have an Individual Retirement Account or 401(k) account and, if so, whether they have contributed the maximum amount. I also ask whether they have checked to see whether they qualify for the Earned Income Tax Credit and whether they have their savings invested in tax-free municipal bonds. In most cases the callers have no idea what I am talking about. They know the legislative history of the Sixteenth Amendment by heart, but have never made any effort to learn about the many legal tax-avoidance opportunities available to all taxpayers. Utilizing them would more than likely have eliminated the bulk of their tax liability.

TAX COMPLEXITY

It's hard to know to what extent tax complexity contributes to taxpayers' frustration and makes them susceptible to criminal schemes. However, the political evidence suggests that people are primarily motivated by taxation itself and will happily jump through hoops if doing so reduces their taxes.

Various plans have been put forward over the years that would exempt most people from having to file returns, but they have never gained political traction. One idea, developed by the Treasury Department in 2003, would have shifted the burden of tax compliance more toward employers and financial institutions to match tax withholding to actual tax liabilities, thus creating a return-free tax system for most taxpayers. Some thirty-five countries already have such a system. Another proposal has been put forward by the Columbia University law professor Michael Graetz: it would essentially abolish the income tax except for the wealthy and replace the revenue with a value-added tax on goods and services.

Neither plan has gone anywhere. People resist increased withholding and income-reporting requirements as intrusions on their privacy; businesses don't want the additional compliance burden; politicians fear losing the ability to buy votes with targeted tax cuts; and everyone fears paying more under whatever system replaces the one we have now. Also, a return-free system like the Treasury's plan would require radical simplification of the tax law to be viable.

One option for improving taxpayer compliance would be to combine a tax amnesty with any measures that would increase compliance. Once taxpayers have started to engage in some tax-evasion activity, such as not filing returns, it is hard for them to go back when they know it increases their odds of being caught. And the threat of interest and penalties that may exceed the tax evaded, not to mention criminal penalties, may also act as a constraint on compliance once a taxpayer has engaged in tax evasion.

Under an amnesty, if a taxpayer voluntarily steps forward and pays the back taxes and interest owed, the tax authorities will waive the penalties and criminal charges. This allows the taxpayer to start with a clean slate while putting money into the government's coffers that might not otherwise have been collected, or that could be collected only at great cost. The experience at the state level and in foreign countries shows that combining tax amnesty with increased enforcement can be an effective combination for raising tax compliance. The main negative effect is that once an amnesty happens, taxpayers may figure that another one will come along in the future, and this belief may increase the incentive for tax evasion.

IRS RESOURCES

One question that always arises in terms of improving taxpayer compliance is where the IRS should target its limited resources. Among individual taxpayers, the greatest number of those misreporting income are at the low end of the distribution. A key reason is that the EITC gives them a powerful incentive to report fictitious income to get an undeserved refund from the government. But the amount of money involved is obviously going to be low, and it's not cost-effective to subject the poor to a rigorous tax audit. In percentage terms, the greatest underreporting of income occurs among farmers, but again the amount of money involved is low and doesn't justify the commitment of major IRS resources.

The two places where there are major compliance problems and significant amounts of money are among the self-employed and big corporations that aggressively push the boundary between legal tax avoidance and illegal tax evasion. One suggestion for dealing with the latter is to require large public corporations to release their tax returns publicly. It's possible that allowing people to see the returns would exert some pressure through public opinion for compliance and for less aggressive tax avoidance. Another suggestion comes from the University of Texas law professor Calvin Johnson, who suggests replacing the corporate income tax for publicly traded companies with a small tax on firms' market capitalization, easily determined from public sources.

Whatever is done to improve tax compliance, it is reasonable to assume that it will be unpopular. Public opinion polls consistently show that people hate doing their taxes and abhor the IRS. A 1997 Fox News poll found that 57 percent of people would abolish the IRS and replace it with a new tax collection agency. And a 2000 Fox News poll found that people would prefer root canal dental surgery to an IRS audit by a margin of 51 to 34 percent.

Nevertheless the case for improved compliance is strong. Not only does the Treasury need the money at a time when resistance to explicit tax increases is overwhelming, but it's unfair for the dishonest to shift their tax burden onto those who pay the taxes they owe willingly, if not happily. And we know that there are threshold effects in illegal behavior. Once the view becomes widespread that certain behavior is tolerated by society and is not likely to be punished by the authorities, it tends to grow.

To the extent that tax complexity encourages tax evasion by fundamentally honest taxpayers who simply throw up their hands at the incomprehensibility of the tax law, simplification will improve compliance. It will also reduce the belief that others avoid paying their fair share of taxes because they are better at exploiting obscure tax loopholes. But at the end of the day, no one likes paying taxes. Some degree of coercion will always be necessary.

FURTHER READINGS

Aaron, Henry J., and Joel Slemrod. *The Crisis in Tax Administration.* Brookings Institution, 2004.

Alm, James. "Administrative Options to Close the Tax Gap." *Tax Notes* (Oct. 29, 2007): 495–531.

Alm, James, and William Beck. "Tax Amnesties and Tax Revenues." *Public Finance Quarterly* (Oct. 1990): 433–53.

Barlett, Donald L., and James B. Steele. *The Great American Tax Dodge.* Little, Brown, 2000.

Blank, Joshua D., and Daniel Z. Levin. "When Is Tax Enforcement Publicized?" *Virginia Tax Review* (Summer 2010): 1–37.

Bowman, Karlyn, and Andrew Rugg. *Public Opinion on Taxes.* American Enterprise Institute, 2010.

Broder, John M. "Demonizing the I.R.S." *New York Times* (Sept. 20, 1997).

Cowell, Frank A. *Cheating the Government: The Economics of Evasion.* MIT Press, 1990.

Doernberg, Richard L. "The Case against Withholding." *Texas Law Review* (Dec. 1982): 595–653.

Graetz, Michael J. *100 Million Unnecessary Returns.* Yale University Press, 2008.

Guyton, John L., et al. "Estimating the Compliance Cost of the U.S. Individual Income Tax." *National Tax Journal* (Sept. 2003): 673–88.

Hibbs, Douglas A., and Violeta Piculescu. "Tax Toleration and Tax Compliance: How Government Affects the Propensity of Firms to Enter the Unofficial Economy." *American Journal of Political Science* (Jan. 2010): 18–33.

Internal Revenue Service. *Compliance Estimates for Earned Income Tax Credit Claimed on 1999 Returns.* Feb. 28, 2002.

Internal Revenue Service. *The Truth about Frivolous Tax Arguments.* Jan. 1, 2011.

Jackson, Christopher S. "The Inane Gospel of Tax Protest: Resist Rendering unto Caesar—Whatever His Demands." *Gonzaga Law Review* (1996–97): 291–329.

Johns, Andrew, and Joel Slemrod. "The Distribution of Income Tax Noncompliance." *National Tax Journal* (Sept. 2010): 397–418.

Johnson, Calvin H. "Taxing GE and Other Masters of the Universe." *Tax Notes* (July 11, 2011): 175–85.

Johnston, David Cay. *Perfectly Legal: The Covert Campaign to Rig Our Tax System to Benefit the Super Rich—and Cheat Everybody Else.* Portfolio, 2003.

Joint Committee on Taxation. "Options to Improve Tax Compliance and Reform Tax Expenditures." Report No. JCS-02–05 (Jan. 27, 2005).

Joint Committee on Taxation. *Study of the Overall State of the Federal Tax System and Recommendations for Simplification, Pursuant to Section 8022(3)(B) of the Internal Revenue Code of 1986,* 3 vols. Report No. JCS-3–01 (Apr. 2001).

Joint Committee on Taxation. "Tax Amnesty." Report No. JCS-2–08 (Jan. 30, 1998).

Ledbetter, Mark. "Comparison of BEA Estimates of Personal Income and IRS Estimates of Adjusted Gross Income." *Survey of Current Business* (Nov. 2007): 35–41.

Lederman, Leandra. "Reducing Information Gaps to Reduce the Tax Gap: When Is Information Reporting Warranted?" *Fordham Law Review* (Mar. 2010): 1733–59.

Lenter, David, Joel Slemrod, and Douglas Shackelford. "Public Disclosure of Corporate Tax Return Information: Accounting, Economics, and Legal Perspectives." *National Tax Journal* (Dec. 2003): 803–30.

Logue, Kyle D., and Gustavo G. Vettori. "Narrowing the Tax Gap through Presumptive Taxation." *Columbia Journal of Tax Law* (2011): 100–149.

Martinez, Leo P. "Federal Tax Amnesty: Crime and Punishment Revisited." *Virginia Tax Review* (Winter 1991): 535–85.

Organization for Economic Cooperation and Development. *Tax Administration in OECD and Selected Non-OECD Countries: Comparative Information Series.* Mar. 3, 2011.

Rossotti, Charles O. *Many Unhappy Returns.* Harvard Business School Press, 2005. Rossotti was IRS commissioner from 1997 to 2002.

Roth, Jeffrey A., John T. Scholz, and Ann D. Witte. *Taxpayer Compliance,* 2 vols. University of Pennsylvania Press, 1989.

Sawicky, Max B. *Bridging the Tax Gap: Addressing the Crisis in Federal Tax Administration.* Economic Policy Institute, 2005.

Senate Finance Committee. *Practices and Procedures of the Internal Revenue Service.* 1997.

Slemrod, Joel. "Cheating Ourselves: The Economics of Tax Evasion." *Journal of Economic Perspectives* (Winter 2007): 25–48.

Slemrod, Joel. *Why People Pay Taxes: Tax Compliance and Enforcement.* University of Michigan Press, 1992.

Toder, Eric. "What Is the Tax Gap?" *Tax Notes* (Oct. 22, 2007): 367–88.

Turnier, William J., and Scott L. Little. "Is It Time for an American PAYE?" *Tax Notes* (May 3, 2004): 559–75.

U.S. Government Accountability Office. *Complexity and Taxpayer Compliance.* Report No. GAO-11–747T (June 28, 2011).

U.S. Treasury Department. *A Comprehensive Strategy for Reducing the Tax Gap.* 2006.

U.S. Treasury Department. *Return-Free Tax Systems: Tax Simplification Is a Prerequisite.* 2003.

Young, Marilyn, Michael Reksulak, and William F. Shughart II. "The Political Economy of the IRS." *Economics and Politics* (July 2001): 201–20.

Zelenak, Lawrence. "Tax or Welfare? The Administration of the Earned Income Tax Credit." *UCLA Law Review* (Aug. 2005): 1867–916.

Zengerle, Jason. "Hell Nay, We Won't Pay!" *New York Times Magazine* (Mar. 29, 2009): 40–45.

Part III

THE FUTURE

Chapter 18

The History of Tax Reform

The history of tax reform starts with liberal reformers in the 1960s concerned that the rich could easily escape high statutory tax rates by taking advantage of various tax loopholes. From 1954 to 1963 the top rate on individuals was 91 percent, and from 1965 to 1981 it was 70 percent. But the effective rates paid by the wealthy were much lower because of easily available exclusions, deductions, and other legal methods of reducing income subject to tax at high nominal rates.

Liberals wanted to bring effective rates much closer to statutory rates by getting rid of tax shelters. But they were frustrated by conservative control of the Senate Finance Committee and House Ways and Means Committee. Over the years the members of these committees had largely been responsible for creation of the very loopholes that were the targets of reformers. High statutory rates eased their creation because on the surface it looked as if the rich were being soaked.

When John F. Kennedy became president he set in motion the modern tax reform movement by appointing the Harvard law professor Stanley Surrey as assistant secretary of the Treasury for tax policy. Kennedy even put forward a number of significant tax reform proposals in 1963. But Congress jettisoned them in favor of tax cuts.

CREATION OF THE TAX EXPENDITURES BUDGET

Surrey thought that part of the reason Congress and the public were so blasé about tax loopholes was that they didn't know just how many there were or how much revenue was being sacrificed. He had the Treasury staff compile a list and calculate their revenue effect. They became known as "tax expenditures." The first compilation appeared in the last days of the Johnson administration.

The Treasury investigation revealed that 155 tax filers with adjusted gross incomes above $200,000 ($1.3 million in today's dollars), including twenty-one with AGIs above $1 million ($6.5 million today), paid no federal income taxes in 1967. This fact was revealed in testimony before the Joint Economic Committee on January 17, 1969, by Treasury Secretary Joseph W. Barr. The ensuing outcry forced Congress and the Nixon administration to enact the Tax Reform Act of 1969, a Treasury-drafted effort to restrict some of the most conspicuous tax loopholes.

The success of the Tax Reform Act of 1969 inspired liberal activists and think tanks to pressure Congress to enact further reforms. In spite of Republican control of the White House, the liberals made significant headway. The Congressional Budget and Impoundment Control Act of 1974 required Treasury to publish an annual list of tax expenditures. Gerald Ford signed into law the Tax Reform Act of 1976, extending the loophole brush-cleaning effort started by the 1969 act.

Although liberals felt that there was still considerable work to do, the slow economic growth of the late 1970s threw cold water on their efforts. Inflation pushed average people up into high tax brackets, forced investors to pay taxes on illusory capital gains, and raised corporate taxes by eroding the real value of depreciation allowances.

Even as the 1976 act made its way through Congress, conservatives mounted a counterattack. Treasury Secretary William Simon brought the Princeton economist David Bradford to Washington to serve as deputy assistant secretary for tax analysis. He developed a conservative tax reform plan based on shifting to a consumption base. Their report didn't appear until the last day of the Ford administration, but it was extremely important in showing that conservatives could also play the tax reform game.

Conservatives have supported consumption-based taxation for centuries. The seventeenth-century political philosopher Thomas Hobbes was an early advocate. A key constraint, however, was a widespread view that it was impractical. As the economist John Maynard Keynes put it, "An expenditure tax, though perhaps theoretically sound, is practically impossible." The Treasury "Blueprints" study, largely written by Bradford, addressed the practical problems of implementing a consumption-based tax system. Another important contribution was a pathbreaking article by the Harvard law professor William D. Andrews published in 1974.

The Carter administration made an effort to keep the liberal tax reform effort alive by throwing in the sweetener of lower statutory rates, something that had been missing from the 1969 and 1976 efforts. (The 1969 act lowered the top rate to 50 percent on earned income, but raised the basic tax rate on long-term capital gains from 25 to 35 percent.) Treasury Secretary Michael Blumenthal signaled a desire to reduce the top statutory rate to 50 percent, while eliminating the special treatment of capital gains and the double taxation of corporate profits.

TAX CUTS, NOT TAX REFORM

But by late 1977 it was clear that there was little appetite in Congress for another big tax reform. The desire to cut taxes was overwhelming. As Blumenthal put it in October, "There is a big constituency in the country for tax reduction but not for tax reform, except as reform is used as a code word for reduction."

Although the Carter administration nevertheless put forward a fairly liberal tax reform proposal in 1978, it died immediately. By mid-1978 the passage of Proposition 13 in California marked the beginning of a new era in tax policy. Tax cuts, rather than tax reform, would dominate the agenda. When Congress acted on a tax bill later that year, almost all of the reforms were gone. Its hallmark features were a cut in the tax rate on long-term capital gains to 28 percent and the creation of the 401(k) account. Although Blumenthal threatened a presidential veto, Carter nevertheless signed the legislation into law.

The Republicans' ability to force a Democratic president and Congress to enact what was essentially a conservative tax bill emboldened them. They pressed forward with more radical tax reduction efforts, the principal one being the tax bill introduced in 1977 by Rep. Jack Kemp (R-NY) and Sen. Bill Roth (R-DE). It would have reduced the top statutory rate from 70 percent to 50 percent and the bottom rate from 14 percent to 8 percent.

As a member of Kemp's staff, I had much to do with the development of this legislation. I remember too well how slow the progress was in getting Republicans to cosponsor the legislation at a time when inflation was a growing problem and the GOP still cared about a balanced federal budget. Republican House members repeatedly told me that it would be irresponsible to cut taxes without cutting spending by the same amount—something that would have doomed our effort, as there was not the slightest chance of cutting spending.

Prop. 13, however, showed that voters were less concerned about deficits—there was no spending offset in the initiative—and just wanted lower taxes. In effect, people were saying that if the politicians cared about deficits, let them worry about cutting spending. Thus was born the starve-the-beast theory, which soon replaced the balanced budget as Republican dogma.

CONSERVATIVE TAX REFORM

For the next several years conservatives were mainly concerned with cutting tax rates, achieving victory with the election of Ronald Reagan and passage of the Kemp-Roth–based Economic Recovery Tax Act in August 1981. The emergence of large federal budget deficits, however, halted further tax-cutting efforts. But conservatives were still determined to get tax rates down further. This led to renewed interest in the flat tax.

The earliest reference I have been able to find to Republican support for a flat tax is from Rep. Ogden Mills (R-NY) in 1921. During congressional debate on reducing the high World War I tax rates, Mills argued that the ideal should be a flat-rate consumption-based tax system. "Money saved and reinvested in productive enterprises of the country should be taxed at a flat rate," he said.

In the modern era, the conservative columnist William F. Buckley appears to have been the first one to propose a flat-rate tax system in his 1973 book, *Four Reforms*. He proposed eliminating all tax exemptions and deductions except those related to the cost of acquiring income. Buckley would also have abolished the corporate income tax and the special tax treatment of capital gains, which he would have taxed on an accrual basis, without realization. He proposed a single rate of 15 percent and a tax credit for any taxes paid by those below the poverty line.

The first and most important contribution to the new flat-tax focus was a *Wall Street Journal* op-ed on December 10, 1981, by the Hoover Institution scholars Robert Hall and Alvin Rabushka. They laid out an extraordinarily simple proposal whose hallmark was that the tax return of every individual, family, or business would fit on a postcard. In essence, the tax base was pure consumption less a large personal exemption. Hall and Rabushka estimated that a single rate of 19 percent would equal the revenues being raised from both the individual and the corporate income taxes at that time.

In early 1982 the conservative economist David Hale published an article in the Heritage Foundation's journal arguing that Republicans had to turn their attention away from tax cutting in light of rising budget deficits. Building on "supply-side economics," he suggested that a flat tax that was revenue-neutral on a static basis was actually a revenue-raiser on a dynamic basis because it would increase growth and therefore broaden the tax base. This was a better way to raise new revenue than raising taxes directly, Hale said. Since Congress was already beginning to think about raising taxes to close the deficit—an idea that would result in enactment of the Tax Equity and Fiscal Responsibility Act later in the year—his approach got a lot of attention among conservatives who feared Reagan's backsliding on taxes.

SUPPORT FOR THE FLAT TAX

By the middle of 1982 the Reagan administration was cautiously supportive of legislative efforts to enact a flat tax. David Stockman, the director of the Office of Management and Budget, suggested that it might be included in the FY1984 budget message. On July 6 President Reagan said the flat tax "does look tempting" and was "something worth looking at." On July 27 the Joint Economic Committee held the first of two days of hearings on the flat tax, and in September the Senate Finance Committee held three days of hearings on the topic.

A pure flat tax wasn't a politically doable tax reform option. But interest in it spurred Kemp and Sen. Bob Kasten (R-WI) to draft a conservative tax reform plan and Sen. Bill Bradley (D-NJ) and

Rep. Dick Gephardt (D-MO) to draft a liberal proposal. The overall similarity in their approaches did a lot to convince people that some sort of bipartisan compromise might be within reach.

In his January 1984 State of the Union address, Reagan asked the Treasury Department to draft a tax reform proposal that would simplify the tax code, improve fairness, and provide incentives for growth. The Treasury reported back on November 27 with a three-volume report. The White House sent a revised version of the proposal to Congress in May 1985. A year of hearings and debate followed, with passage of the Tax Reform Act of 1986 in the summer of that year. It was signed into law by President Reagan on October 22, 1986.

Since then there has been relatively little discussion of tax reform on either side of the aisle, except for a brief flat-tax boomlet in the mid-1990s, when the publisher Steve Forbes came from nowhere to be a contender for the Republican presidential nomination in 1996. The cornerstone of his campaign was the flat tax. For a time House Ways and Means Committee Chairman Bill Archer (R-TX) was enamored with the so-called FairTax, which would have replaced federal taxes with a national retail sales tax, but it went nowhere, although former Arkansas governor Mike Huckabee supported it in his race for the Republican presidential nomination in 2008.

The most recent effort to gin up interest in tax reform was a commission appointed by George W. Bush in 2005, but he declined to support its recommendations and the effort fizzled. In the 2000s Republicans have been preoccupied with cutting taxes without regard for the deficit or the impact on the tax structure. Democrats have been ineffectual in challenging them, even abandoning their opposition to extending lower rates on the wealthy due to expire at the end of 2010.

FURTHER READINGS

Andrews, William D. "A Consumption-Type or Cash Flow Personal Income Tax." *Harvard Law Review* (Apr. 1974): 1113–88.

Averett, Susan L., Edward N. Gamber, and Sheila A. Handy. "William E. Simon's Contribution to Tax Policy." *Atlantic Economic Journal* (Sept. 2003): 233–41.

Bartlett, Bruce. *Reaganomics: Supply-Side Economics in Action.* Arlington House, 1981.

Birnbaum, Jeffrey, and Alan Murray. *Showdown at Gucci Gulch.* Random House, 1987.

Bradford, David F. *Taxation, Wealth, and Saving.* MIT Press, 2000.

Bradford, David F. *Untangling the Income Tax.* Harvard University Press, 1986.

Broder, David S. "Stockman: President May Seek a Flat-Rate Income Tax for All." *Washington Post* (June 22, 1982).

Hale, David. "Rescuing Reaganomics." *Policy Review* (Spring 1982): 57–69.

Hall, Robert, and Alvin Rabushka. "A Proposal to Simplify Our Tax System." *Wall Street Journal* (Dec. 10, 1981).

Jackson, Dudley. "Thomas Hobbes' Theory of Taxation." *Political Studies* (June 1973): 175–82.

Joint Economic Committee. *The Flat Rate Tax.* 1982.

Levine, Richard. "Delay in Unveiling of Carter's Tax Plan Leaves Final Shape of Revisions in Doubt." *Wall Street Journal* (Oct. 31, 1977).

McLure, Charles E., and George R. Zodrow. "Treasury I and the Tax Reform Act of 1986: The Economics and Politics of Tax Reform." *Journal of Economic Perspectives* (Summer 1987): 37–58.

Mills, Ogden. *Congressional Record* (Aug. 17, 1921): 5137–39.

President's Advisory Panel on Federal Tax Reform. *Simple, Fair, and Pro-Growth: Proposals to Fix America's Tax System.* Nov. 2005.

Reagan, Ronald. "Remarks and a Question-and-Answer Session at a Briefing on Federalism for State and Local Officials in Los Angeles, California." American Presidency Project (July 6, 1982).

Rowen, Hobart. "Treasury Chief Favors Uniform, Lower Income Tax Rate." *Washington Post* (Jan. 23, 1977).

Senate Finance Committee. *Flat-Rate Tax,* 2 parts. 1982.

Stern, Philip M. *The Great Treasury Raid.* Random House, 1964.

Stern, Philip M. *The Rape of the Taxpayer: Why You Pay More While the Rich Pay Less.* Random House, 1973.

Surrey, Stanley. "Complexity and the Internal Revenue Code: The Problem of the Management of Tax Detail." *Law and Contemporary Problems* (Autumn 1969): 673–710.

Surrey, Stanley. *Pathways to Tax Reform.* Harvard University Press, 1973.

Surrey, Stanley S., and Paul R. McDaniel. *Tax Expenditures.* Harvard University Press, 1985.

U.S. Treasury Department. *Blueprints for Basic Tax Reform.* Jan. 1977.

U.S. Treasury Department. *The President's 1978 Tax Program.* Jan. 1978.

U.S. Treasury Department. *Tax Reform for Fairness, Simplicity, and Economic Growth,* 3 vols. Nov. 1984.

White House. *The President's Tax Proposals to the Congress for Fairness, Growth, and Simplicity.* May 1985.

Chapter 19

The Pros and Cons of Popular Tax Reform Proposals

Ideas and proposals, some of which involved enormous amounts of time and effort to devise, litter the tax reform landscape. Nevertheless some contain elements that may be worth recycling, while others will almost certainly have support in their original form, as they have never been completely abandoned. Following is a brief summary of the more substantive fundamental tax reform proposals of recent years.

THE FLAT TAX

Many people call any tax system with a single statutory tax rate a flat tax. While there may be some benefits to such a tax system, the benefits tend to be overrated. The important problems with the tax system relate primarily to the tax base—what is being taxed—rather than to the number of tax rates. Moreover although it appears on the surface that a single rate would simplify the tax code, the simplification achieved would be minimal for the vast bulk of taxpayers, most of whom have no idea what their tax bracket is. The bulk of complexity comes from defining the tax base, not from the rate structure. Moreover simply establishing a single rate without making significant changes to the tax base would inevitably involve a massive tax increase for those in a lower tax bracket and a massive tax cut for those in a higher bracket.

In my discussion of the flat-rate tax, I will refer exclusively to the proposal devised by the economist Robert Hall and the political scientist Alvin Rabushka, both of the Hoover Institution, in 1981. Theirs was the first detailed flat-tax proposal and the one upon which almost all subsequent flat-tax proposals are based.

The tax rate in their plan has always been set at 19 percent, but Hall and Rabushka's intention has been to implement their plan in a revenue-neutral manner, neither raising nor lowering aggregate income tax revenues. Their plan does not deal with the payroll tax.

In principle it doesn't matter what the rate is. Its level is more a function of the size of the personal exemption and what achieves the most political support. Polls and experience have shown that support is sensitive to the tax rate. Once it gets above 20 percent, support declines rapidly with each additional percentage point. Once it gets above 23 percent, support largely vanishes.

Hall and Rabushka would start by eliminating all deductions, exclusions, and credits, including popular ones such as the deduction for mortgage interest and the exclusion for employer-provided health insurance. The corporate and individual income taxes would be fully integrated, with business cash flow and wages taxed at the same rate. All business receipts would be taxed, less only purchases from other businesses for supplies and such. Only cash wages would be taxed on the individual side, less a large personal allowance.

In the most recent version of the Hall-Rabushka plan, the allowance would be set at $9,500 per person, $14,000 for single heads of households, and $16,500 for married couples filing jointly. Dependent children would receive an allowance of $4,500. Thus a married couple with two children would receive a total allowance of $25,500 and would pay 19 percent on cash wages above that level. Therefore if this family had total wage income of $50,000, it would pay tax on only $24,500, which yields a tax of $4,655. This works out to an effective tax rate of a little over 9 percent.

It's important to note that for individuals, only cash wages are taxed. There would be no tax at all on so-called unearned income such as interest, dividends, rent, or capital gains. In effect, these sources of income would be taxed at the business level. Businesses would report all receipts, including those from rent, dividends, and interest. The only allowable deduction would be purchases from other businesses, which become taxable receipts for them, and for cash wages, which are taxed at the individual level. This means no deduction for interest or depreciation. But purchases of capital equipment would be fully deductible, just as current operating expenses are now.

In theory you have a closed loop in which all income is taxed, including a lot of income that currently escapes taxation. Businesses would get no deduction for fringe benefits paid to employees; they would deduct only cash wages. Thus health insurance would be brought into the tax base. The only leakage is through the personal allowance. Its purpose is to relieve regressivity and make the tax visible to individuals. Without it, individuals wouldn't have to be taxed at all. The deduction for cash wages could simply be eliminated and 100 percent of taxes collected by businesses.

In effect, the Hall-Rabushka plan is what is called a "subtraction-method value-added tax" on the business side. It's mathematically identical to the credit-invoice VAT used in every country except Japan, but it doesn't require businesses to keep any records they don't keep at present. The problem is that it requires a single rate and a comprehensive tax base to work, and this is why it hasn't been adopted more widely. Politicians like being able to exempt certain items and reduce rates on others, which is possible under a credit-invoice style of VAT.

The Hall-Rabushka plan is so simple that every individual or business, no matter how large, could theoretically file its tax return on a postcard. But the flat tax has always suffered from at least three problems that are difficult to overcome.

First, unless the personal allowance is high enough to exempt everyone not currently paying income taxes, some people who are now paying nothing or who are in the 10 or 15 percent bracket would see a large tax increase. This problem is exacerbated by the Hall-Rabushka plan's elimination of all tax credits, which give some people a negative tax liability. In effect, a zero tax rate would constitute a tax increase for some people. At the same time, those now in tax brackets above 19 percent would get an enormous tax cut, especially if they have large amounts of unearned income, on which they would pay no tax directly.

Second, politicians have been loath to support a pure version of the flat tax. They always feel compelled to retain a couple of favored deductions, especially for mortgage interest and charitable contributions. This creates two problems: it shrinks the tax base, thus requiring a higher rate to equal current revenues; also, once any exception is made for one popular deduction, it becomes difficult to say no to the next most popular deduction. Soon you are right back where you started.

Third, there are technical problems with getting from where we are now to a flat-tax system. Businesses, for example, complain that since there is no deduction for depreciation, they will be stuck with large depreciation allowances that they could use under current law but that would have no value under a flat tax. There's also a problem with banks because there is no deduction for interest in the flat tax, but interest is the banks' basic cost of doing business. Obviously special provisions would have to be developed for the financial sector. There would need to be transition rules for other businesses.

THE FAIRTAX

The FairTax would abolish all federal taxes, including the payroll tax and the income tax, and replace them with a 23 percent retail sales tax like those levied by the states. Indeed the states would be required to collect the tax for the federal government, thus allowing for abolition of the Internal Revenue Service. To relieve the burden on the poor, everyone would receive a monthly rebate on the tax equal to the tax on a poverty-level income.

FairTax supporters are fervent and well financed by a group of Texas millionaires. They are evangelical in the belief that their plan would bring forth a vast amount of economic growth and that it would be an enormous blessing for Americans not to have to file income tax returns or keep all the associated financial records. As Gov. Huckabee put it, "When the FairTax becomes law, it will be like waving a magic wand releasing us from pain and unfairness."

Tax experts, however, are nearly unanimous in their belief that while the FairTax may look good on paper, it is completely unworkable in practice. Although most economists believe it would probably be a good idea to move toward a consumption-based tax system, there are many administrative problems with collecting all federal revenue on retail sales. The incentive and opportunities for evasion are simply too great. That is why no country has ever adopted a system remotely like the FairTax. Those that have looked into the idea have always concluded that at a rate much above 10 percent, the collection system will break down.

There are also a number of oddities in the FairTax to which its supporters seldom call attention. One is that the true rate is not 23 percent. Thought of the way people think of state retail sales taxes, the rate is actually 30 percent. The 23 percent figure is derived this way: On a $1 purchase, the tax would be 30 cents, for a total price of $1.30. Since the 30 cent tax is 23 percent of $1.30, FairTax supporters argue that the true tax rate is 23 percent. Nonsupporters are more inclined to think that this is just a trick to make the tax rate appear lower than it really is, so as to increase support for it.

Another oddity is that the FairTax would apply to all government spending, including federal spending, as well as private spending. This will undoubtedly force state and local governments to raise their taxes, since the cost of all their expenses, including wages for their workers, will rise by the FairTax rate. And it serves no logical purpose for the federal government to tax itself.

FairTax supporters argue that the prices of all goods and services will fall by about as much as the 23 percent tax that would be imposed because of the elimination of existing federal taxes. It is all a wash, they say. What FairTax supporters don't mention is that all workers will have to cut their real wages by the amount of the tax for this wash to happen. But there is nothing in their proposal to compel workers to take a pay cut and no reason to think that they won't resist doing so.

Finally, FairTax supporters have always maintained that their plan would neither raise nor lower aggregate federal revenues. Yet revenues have fluctuated between 14.9 percent of GDP and 20.6 percent of GDP over the time the FairTax has been under consideration without any change in the proposed 23 percent rate. In any case, every serious effort to score the FairTax by the Treasury Department, the Joint Committee on Taxation, and the Brookings Institution has concluded that a rate significantly higher than 23 percent would be necessary for it to be revenue-neutral.

There are many other technical problems with the FairTax as well, such as the interaction between a national retail sales tax and state and local sales taxes collected on different goods and services; the problem of exempting sales between businesses so that taxes aren't levied on top of taxes, a problem economists call "cascading"; how the states will be compelled to collect federal sales taxes, especially in states with no sales tax; that state income taxes will still require people to file returns and keep the necessary records; and how to prevent people from collecting rebates fraudulently.

Every serious study of imposing some sort of national consumption tax in the United States has concluded that a value-added tax would work much better. That is because it was designed to overcome the administrative problems inherent in the nature of the FairTax. In other words, if the FairTax is a good idea, the VAT is a far better idea.

OTHER PROPOSALS

In the mid-1990s Sens. Sam Nunn (D-GA) and Pete Domenici (R-NM) put together a tax reform plan designed to tax only consumption by allowing an unlimited deduction for saving, rather than taxing consumption directly as the VAT or FairTax would. Hence it was dubbed the USA Tax, with USA standing for "unlimited savings allowance." While an impressive amount of research went into the development of this plan, the authors wanted to mirror the existing distribution of taxation and neither burden the poor nor excessively benefit the rich. This required a top tax rate of 40 percent, which proved to be unattractive politically. When Nunn and Domenici retired from the Senate, their plan died.

In 1995 the Republican leaders of Congress, Senate Majority Leader Bob Dole and Speaker of the House Newt Gingrich, asked former representative Jack Kemp to head up a commission that would examine the tax system and make some recommendations for reform. (I assisted Kemp in a voluntary capacity.) In early 1996 the commission issued a report that failed to propose a specific tax reform plan, opting instead to state certain principles that ought to guide any tax reform effort. These include a single, low tax rate; a generous personal exemption and reduction in the tax burden on working families; deductibility of the payroll tax; and others. It did not lead to any legislative action, in large part because the emergence of budget surpluses shifted the attention of Republicans away from tax reform and toward tax cutting.

The tax reform commission appointed by George W. Bush in 2005 proposed two tax reform options. The first would have eliminated a variety of tax preferences and lowered tax rates along the lines of the Tax Reform Act of 1986. The second option was a hybrid income tax/consumption tax designed to move toward a consumption base while retaining a degree of progressivity. In the end President Bush chose not to endorse either option, preferring to focus his attention instead on Social Security reform. The report, however, remains an excellent discussion of various issues relating to tax reform, including good chapters on the VAT and national retail sales tax.

In 2010 Sen. Ron Wyden (D-OR) and Sen. Judd Gregg (R-NH) introduced a tax reform bill that would establish three individual income tax rates of 15, 25, and 35 percent and establish a single rate of 24 percent on corporations. It would also triple the standard deduction, repeal the Alternative Minimum Tax, and make numerous other changes. The Tax Policy Center found that it would be revenue-neutral over a ten-year period and would slightly increase the overall progressivity of the tax system.

In 2010 and 2011 a number of deficit-reduction plans were put forward by various individuals and organizations, including Rep. Paul Ryan (R-WI) and a bipartisan commission cochaired by Republican Alan Simpson and Democrat Erskine Bowles that included tax reform elements. In general they propose sharp reductions in tax rates, even though their stated purpose is deficit reduction; the reduced rates would be paid for with base broadening, loophole closing, and other changes. However, none of these plans ever specified any actual tax-raising provisions. Rep. Ryan, for example, simply ordered the Congressional Budget Office to assume that his plan would raise revenues equal to 19 percent of GDP when it was scored, thus allowing him to both raise taxes and cut them at the same time without those whose taxes would be raised ever knowing it.

In October 2011, businessman Herman Cain, a contender for the Republican presidential nomination, put forward something he called the 9–9–9 plan because it would establish a 9 percent tax rate on individuals, a 9 percent rate on corporations, and a 9 percent national sales tax. However, the corporate and individual tax bases would be quite different from what they are under current law. Individuals would be taxed on all of their wages without even receiving a personal exemption or standard deduction. Businesses would be taxed on all of their receipts except for purchases from other firms. With no deduction for wages, the business side of the Cain plan is essentially a subtraction-method VAT. USC law professor Edward Kleinbard concluded that the 9–9–9 plan was equivalent to a 27 percent tax on wage income, which would raise taxes for all except the rich.

There are, of course, many other tax reform plans besides those discussed here. Curiously missing, however, are any plans that are forthrightly liberal, moving in the direction of a comprehensive income tax base using a Haig-Simons definition of income. In practice conservatives have completely dominated the tax reform debate since the 1980s.

Consequently virtually all major tax proposals of the past twenty or so years—especially those with the deepest support, the flat tax and the FairTax—have proposed moving in the direction of a consumption-based tax system. Keep in mind that consumption need not be taxed directly to have a consumption-based tax system; since the only two things people can do with income is either save it or spend it, eliminating taxes on saving and investment necessarily moves in the direction of a tax on spending.

It may be that there is a consensus around the idea that taxing consumption is preferable to taxing income. What no one has yet figured out is how to get from here to there.

FURTHER READINGS

Adler, Hank, and Hugh Hewitt. *The FairTax Fantasy: An Honest Look at a Very, Very Bad Idea*. Townhall Press, 2009.

Bankman, Joseph, and Barbara H. Fried. "Winners and Losers in the Shift to a Consumption Tax." *Georgetown Law Journal* (Jan. 1998): 539–68.

Bartlett, Bruce. "The Ryan Tax Plan: Assume a Can Opener." *Tax Notes* (Apr. 18, 2011): 321–24.

Bartlett, Bruce. "Why the FairTax Won't Work." *Tax Notes* (Dec. 24, 2007): 1241–54.

Boortz, Neal, and John Linder. *The FairTax Book*. Regan Books, 2005.

Boortz, Neal, and John Linder. *FairTax: The Truth*. HarperCollins, 2008.

Bradford, David. "What's in a Name? Income, Consumption, and the Sources of Tax Complexity." *North Carolina Law Review* (Nov. 1997): 222–31.

Cnossen, Sijbren. "Evaluating the National Retail Sales Tax from a VAT Perspective." In *United States Tax Reform in the 21st Century,* ed. George R. Zodrow and Peter Mieszkowski, 215–44. Cambridge University Press, 2002.

Congressional Budget Office. *Comparing Income and Consumption Tax Bases.* July 1997.

Congressional Research Service. "Flat Tax Proposals and Fundamental Tax Reform: An Overview." Report No. IB95060 (Mar. 23, 2005).

Congressional Research Service. "The Flat Tax, Value-Added Tax, and National Retail Sales Tax: Overview of the Issues." Report No. RL32603 (Dec. 14, 2004).

Congressional Research Service. "A Value-Added Tax Contrasted with a National Sales Tax." Report No. IB92069 (Sept. 30, 2004).

Doernberg, Richard L. "A Workable Flat Rate Consumption Tax." *Iowa Law Review* (Jan. 1985): 425–85.

Gale, William G. "The Kemp Commission and the Future of Tax Reform." *Tax Notes* (Feb. 5, 1996): 717–29.

Gale, William. "The National Retail Sales Tax: What Would the Rate Have to Be?" *Tax Notes* (May 16, 2005): 889–911.

Gale, William, et al. "Taxing Government in a National Retail Sales Tax." *Tax Notes* (Oct. 5, 1998): 97–109.

Ginsburg, Martin D. "Life under a Personal Consumption Tax: Some Thoughts on Working, Saving, and Consuming in Nunn-Domenici's Tax World." *National Tax Journal* (Dec. 1995): 585–602.

Hall, Robert E. "Potential Disruption from the Move to a Consumption Tax." *American Economic Review* (May 1997): 147–49.

Hall, Robert E., and Alvin Rabushka. *The Flat Tax,* 3rd ed. Hoover Institution Press, 2007.

Hubbard, R. Glenn. "How Different Are Income and Consumption Taxes?" *American Economic Review* (May 1997): 138–42.

Kleinbard, Edward D. "Herman Cain's 9-9-9 Tax Plan." University of Southern California Center in Law, Economics and Organization (Oct. 10, 2011).

McCaffery, Edward J. *Fair Not Flat.* University of Chicago Press, 2002.

Murray, Matthew N. "Would Tax Evasion and Tax Avoidance Undermine a National Retail Sales Tax?" *National Tax Journal* (Mar. 1997): 167–82.

National Commission on Economic Growth and Tax Reform. *Unleashing America's Potential: A Pro-Growth, Pro-Family Tax System for the Twenty-First Century.* St. Martin's Press, 1996.

President's Advisory Panel on Federal Tax Reform. *Simple, Fair, and Pro-Growth: Proposals to Fix America's Tax System*. Nov. 2005.

Schenk, Alan. "The Plethora of Consumption Tax Proposals: Putting the Value Added Tax, Flat Tax, Retail Sales Tax, and USA Tax into Perspective." *San Diego Law Review* (Fall 1996): 1281–328.

Sease, Douglas R., and Tom Herman. *The Flat-Tax Primer*. Viking, 1996.

Seidman, Laurence S. *The USA Tax: A Progressive Consumption Tax*. MIT Press, 1997.

Slemrod, Joel. "Deconstructing the Income Tax." *American Economic Review* (May 1997): 151–55.

Warren, Alvin C. "The Proposal for an 'Unlimited Savings Allowance.'" *Tax Notes* (Aug. 28, 1995): 1103–8.

Weisbach, David A. "Ironing Out the Flat Tax." *Stanford Law Review* (Feb. 2000): 599–664.

Wyden, Ron, and Judd Gregg. "A Bipartisan Plan for Tax Fairness." *Wall Street Journal* (Feb. 23, 2010).

Yin, George K. "Is the Tax System beyond Reform?" *Florida Law Review* (Dec. 2006): 977–1041.

Zelenak, Lawrence. "The Selling of the Flat Tax: The Dubious Link between Rate and Base." *Chapman Law Review* (Spring 1999): 197–232.

Chapter 20

The Need for More Revenue

Republicans and Democrats don't agree on much when it comes to taxes, but at least in principle they both believe that the government should raise enough revenue to cover its legitimate functions. The question is, of course, what are the legitimate functions of government?

In a sense it doesn't matter, because we aren't starting from scratch with no government and deciding what a government should or shouldn't do. We have a vast governmental system that does a great many things, and as a practical matter all of the debate between the two parties is really around the edges.

MANDATORY SPENDING

The central problem is that a large and growing share of spending is classified as "mandatory." This spending includes programs such as Social Security and Medicare, as well as interest on the debt, that in effect have permanent appropriations. Spending is automatic unless Congress changes the law governing eligibility. The percentage of the budget that Congress has meaningful control over, which economists call "discretionary" and which includes national defense and homeland security, fell from three-fifths of all spending in 1971 to just two-fifths in 2010.

According to long-term budget forecasts by the Congressional Budget Office (CBO), the U.S. Government Accountability Office, and others, the mandatory portion of the budget will continue to grow in coming years as the giant baby-boom generation retires and becomes eligible for Social Security and Medicare. The CBO's alternative fiscal scenario estimates that spending for Social Security will rise about 30 percent, from 4.8 percent of the gross domestic product in 2011 to 5.3 percent in 2021 and 6.1 percent in 2035.

Medicare spending will rise from 3.7 percent of GDP in 2011 to 4.3 percent in 2020 and 6.7 percent in 2035.

CBO assumes that revenues as a share of GDP will be allowed to rise from 14.8 percent of GDP in 2011 to 18.4 percent in 2021 and stay there indefinitely, as economic growth increases tax receipts but the Bush tax cuts are extended. It also assumes that the discretionary portion of the budget will fall about 25 percent, from 12.3 percent of GDP in 2011 to 9.1 percent in 2021 and 8.5 percent in 2035, as stimulus spending expires and the wars in Iraq and Afghanistan wind down. Nevertheless the rise in mandatory spending is so great that the national debt is projected to rise from 69 percent of GDP in 2011 to 101 percent in 2021 and 187 percent in 2035.

Economic theory and historical research tell us that when national debt hits 100 percent of GDP an important threshold is reached. Since the long-term real interest rate is approximately equal to the long-term rate of real growth in the economy, once debt is more than 100 percent of GDP, a nation can no longer grow its way out of it. Interest on the debt will increase the debt/GDP ratio until it simply can't be paid and there is some sort of default unless drastic actions are taken to reduce the debt.

Of course, in practice a crisis would be likely to occur well in advance of that point. Financial markets are, after all, forward-looking. In particular the companies that rate sovereign debt, such as Standard & Poor's and Moody's, will warn bond investors that a crisis is looming. This will add a risk premium to interest rates and hasten the onset of a point at which debts can no longer be paid and default looms.

HOW MARKETS VIEW DEBT RISK

Although policymakers and most economists look at the debt/GDP ratio as the principal determinant of whether a nation's debts are sustainable, market analysts use a different metric. To them the key measure of whether a nation's debts are sustainable is interest on the debt as a share of revenues. The Morgan Stanley economist Arnaud Marès explained this perspective in a 2010 investment report:

Whatever the size of a government's liabilities, what matters ultimately is how they compare to the resources available to service them. One benefit of sovereignty is that governments can unilaterally increase their income by raising taxes, but they will only ever be able to acquire in this way a *fraction* of GDP. Debt/GDP therefore provides a flattering image of government finances. A better approach is to scale debt against actual government revenues. An even better approach would be to scale debt against the maximum level of revenues that governments can realistically obtain from using their tax-raising power to the full. This is, *inter alia,* a function of the people's tolerance for taxation and government interference.

Simon Johnson, a former chief economist at the International Monetary Fund, put it a little differently. "The key to debt sustainability isn't how much revenue the government can raise relative to gross domestic product or some other characteristic," he wrote in late 2010. "It's whether a country has the political will to raise taxes or cut spending when under pressure from the financial markets."

Precisely what level of interest spending as a share of revenues is the tipping point is a judgment call. In a May 2010 interview, Pierre Cailleteau, managing director of Moody's, said that 18 to 20 percent is the limit of interest outlays as a share of revenues, in his firm's opinion. According to CBO, that should occur in the United States in approximately 2020.

If, as Johnson suggests, a willingness to raise taxes is an important signal to financial markets on debt sustainability, failure to allow the Bush tax cuts to expire on schedule at the end of 2012 may be seen as a serious failure of will by both Congress and the White House, as all that is necessary for the revenue rise to take effect is do nothing and let the law take effect as written. According to CBO, permitting the Bush tax cuts to expire would allow revenues to rise to 20.8 percent of GDP in 2021 and 23.2 percent in 2035. Almost by itself, that is enough to stabilize the debt/GDP ratio. Instead of rising to 187 percent of GDP in 2035, it would rise only to 84 percent.

INFLATION

Another factor that may hasten the day of reckoning is if inflation rises faster than CBO anticipates. Inflation raises the market rate of interest by approximately the same amount. Thus inflation 1 percent higher than expected will cause long-term interest rates to rise by 1 percent more than forecast.

Of course, higher inflation will erode the real value of the debt to some degree. This is essentially how the nation paid off the debts accumulated during World War II. Some people believe that another round of inflation is in the pipeline because of all the money created by the Federal Reserve since 2008 to maintain liquidity in financial markets and prevent a collapse. Higher inflation, they may think, will obviate the necessity of raising additional revenue to pay the nation's debts. However, the problem with using inflation as a backdoor default is that the debt must have a fixed maturity for this to work. At the end of World War II close to 50 percent of all marketable Treasury securities were in the form of long-term bonds. At the end of 2010 this figure was less than 10 percent.

With so much of the debt being of relatively short duration—most of it consists of Treasury bills that turn over every three months—inflation has little effect in reducing the real value of the debt. Inflation adds an inflation premium to interest rates, so the government's cost of borrowing and its outlays for interest on the debt rise as fast as or even faster than inflation pays it down, thus maintaining the real value of the debt. According to the Office of Management and Budget, if interest rates are just 1 percent higher than expected over the next ten years, this will add approximately $1 trillion to the debt.

Moreover for inflation to aid in reducing the debt burden, it must be largely owned domestically. At the end of World War II almost all the debt was owned by Americans; we owed it to ourselves. But today about half of the national debt is owned by foreigners, such as the Chinese. If inflation should rise in the United States, it would cause the exchange value of the dollar to fall, discouraging foreigners from rolling over their lending unless we began to issue securities denominated in foreign currencies.

One factor that has prevented a debt crisis so far is that the U.S. national debt is denominated 100 percent in dollars. Historically, severe international debt crises have arisen primarily because a nation could not obtain the foreign currency to service its external debt. If the United States should ever reach the point where its currency is so weak from inflation that foreigners will not buy our bonds unless protected from exchange risk, we would then be close to the point of defaulting.

Some conservatives believe that default is preferable to raising taxes enough to service the debt. Indeed they rejoice at the thought that no one would ever be foolish enough to lend money to the U.S. government ever again, and that this would force the nation to balance its budget once and for all. However, the cost of default would be enormous. Untold numbers of individuals, retirees, pension funds, and insurance companies and other institutions would face devastating losses. Default would constitute a grossly immoral theft of trillions of dollars from those who loaned money to the federal government in good faith so others could enjoy the benefits of what that money bought without having to pay for it.

During a debate on raising the debt limit in 2011, more than a few Republicans in Congress said they would never support a higher debt limit regardless of the consequences. Although a last-minute deal was reached to raise the debt limit, Standard & Poor's lowered the Treasury's bond rating from AAA to AA+, largely because of increased political risk. S&P is less worried about America's ability to pay its debts than about its willingness to do so. Since all future debt limit increases are likely to be held hostage to political demands, such concerns are not unreasonable.

As Sen. Mitch McConnell (R-KY) put it at the end of the 2011 debt limit debate, "Some of our members may have thought the default issue was a hostage you might take a chance at shooting. Most of us didn't think that. What we did learn is this—it's a hostage that's worth ransoming."

SPENDING CAN'T BE CUT ENOUGH

The reality is that the debt will be paid, and there are no easy ways to do that. Either spending must be slashed or taxes must be raised. Many conservatives think that the answer is obvious: cut spending as much as necessary. But as noted earlier, that's easier said than done when the main sources of the deficit are mandatory programs such as Social Security and Medicare, not to mention interest on the debt.

The elderly, who are the principal beneficiaries of these programs, are a large and growing percentage of the voting population. They are not likely to support any significant cuts in programs that benefit them. According to the Census Bureau, the proportion of the population age sixty-five and older will grow from 13 percent in 2010 to 16.1 percent in 2020, and 19.3 percent in 2030. In political terms, the clout of the elderly will grow even more because the percentage of those over sixty-five who vote is the highest of any age group. In 2008, 70.3 percent of those sixty-five and older voted, while only 48.5 of those age eighteen to twenty-four did.

According to Standard & Poor's, age-related spending in the United States is expected to rise from 10.8 percent of GDP in 2010 to 12.5 percent in 2020, 15.1 percent in 2030, 17.1 percent in 2040, and 18.5 percent in 2050. These estimates may even be conservative if longevity rises as much as some researchers expect. One estimate projected cumulative outlays for Social Security and Medicare that could be between $3.2 trillion and $8.3 trillion above current government forecasts by 2050 due to higher than expected longevity.

Moreover even if the political support existed to cut spending enough to forestall a debt crisis, it is hard to cut spending on mandatory programs quickly. It's difficult to imagine reducing Social Security benefits for current beneficiaries, and if Medicare reimbursement rates are slashed, doctors will simply refuse to treat those on Medicare. As a practical matter, therefore, major cuts in such programs have to be phased in over a long period of time. It's worth remembering that when Social Security ran into financing problems in the early 1980s, the only benefit cut that Congress would consider was a rise in the retirement age twenty-five years in the future. In the short run, the way it solved the Social Security problem was with higher taxes.

It's also worth remembering that when inflation became a problem in the 1960s, people saw budget deficits as the primary cause. This made them more sympathetic to tax increases, such as the 1968 surtax. As painful as they might be, insofar as they were a plausible way of reducing the cause of inflation, higher taxes were the lesser of the potential evils.

Some conservative economists deny any direct relationship between budget deficits and inflation, viewing inflation as resulting solely from a loose monetary policy. But one thing that happens in a debt crisis is that the central bank essentially loses control of monetary policy. As people shun a nation's bonds, the central bank has no choice but to monetize the debt, essentially printing money to buy bonds. Should this scenario arise, it won't be difficult to convince people that higher taxes are preferable to hyperinflation.

Inflation isn't the only thing that tends to make people sympathetic to higher taxes. High interest rates do so as well. The connection is that deficits are a factor in crowding out private borrowers from financial markets, and this crowding out will reduce home buying, business investment, productivity, and jobs. The federal government preempts the available supply of saving because, unlike private borrowers, it will pay any interest rate, no matter how high. When this drives up rates that businesses and consumers must pay, it won't be hard to convince people that higher taxes may be preferable to high interest rates.

Some economists also argue that tax increases will be less burdensome to growth than spending cuts. The economist Christina Romer, of the University of California, Berkeley, for example, estimates that a tax increase equivalent to 1 percent of GDP will reduce GDP about 1 percent after eighteen months. But a spending cut of 1 percent of GDP will reduce GDP by 1.5 percent.

Waiting to cut spending, however, may be a bad idea. Higher interest rates, whether caused by crowding out, inflation, or Fed tightening, will raise the federal government's spending on interest payments rapidly. It's easy to imagine circumstances in which the budget cannot be cut fast enough to compensate for rising interest costs. At that point the only options will be higher taxes or default.

Incidentally, default doesn't mean only a failure to pay a debt. It may involve changing the terms of repayment. Economists have speculated that "financial repression" may be one way that the government will cope with a debt crisis. Such repression may involve forced purchases of Treasury securities, caps on interest rates, and controls on the ability to move capital out of the United States.

POLITICAL OPPOSITION

At the present time conservative opposition to higher taxes is overwhelming and probably insurmountable. But attitudes can change. Back in the 1980s the conservative commentator George Will repeatedly argued that America was "undertaxed." At least a few conservatives make similar arguments today. In April 2011 Reagan's budget director David Stockman was asked about the deficit. He said, "I think the biggest problem is revenues. It is simply unrealistic to say that raising revenue isn't part of the solution." In August 2011 the University of Chicago law professor Richard Posner said that growth of the deficit "cannot be arrested without more tax revenues."

It should also be noted that public opinion polls have consistently shown that to get the deficit under control the American people support some increase in taxation versus cutting spending alone by a 2-to-1 margin (see Table 20.1).

Table 20.1 Can/Should the Budget Deficit Be Reduced with Spending Cuts Alone or Should There Be an Increase in Taxes? (percentage)

Poll	Date	Some/All Taxes	No Taxes/ All Spending Cuts
Time	10-13-11	69	29
National Journal	9-19-11	62	28
New York Times/CBS News	9-16-11	74	21
Associated Press	8-26-11	69	29
Gallup	8-10-11	66	33
CNN	8-10-11	63	36
McClatchy/Marist	8-9-11	68	29
New York Times/CBS News	8-4-11	63	34
CNN	8-2-11	60	40
Ipsos/Reuters	7-26-11	68	19
Rasmussen	7-25-11	56	34
CNN	7-21-11	64	34
Washington Post/ABC News	7-19-11	66	32
NBC News/Wall Street Journal	7-19-11	62	27
CBS News	7-18-11	69	28
Quinnipiac	7-14-11	67	25
Gallup	7-13-11	73	20
Washington Post/ABC News	6-9-11	61	37
Ipsos/Reuters	6-9-11	59	26
Bloomberg	5-13-11	64	33

Poll	Date	Some/All Taxes	No Taxes/ All Spending Cuts
Ipsos/Reuters	5-12-11	61	27
Gallup	4-29-11	76	20
USC/*Los Angeles Times*	4-25-11	62	33
New York Times/CBS News	4-22-11	66	19
Washington Post/ABC News	4-20-11	62	36
Washington Post/ABC News	3-15-11	67	31
Washington Post/ABC News	12-12-10	62	36
Associated Press/CNBC	11-26-10	65	33
Average		65	30

Source: Author's research.

Many conservatives would have us believe that there is nothing worse than higher taxes. This is nonsense. Failure to reduce growth of the debt can lead to consequences far worse than higher taxes: inflation, double-digit interest rates, debt default, financial repression, slower growth resulting from all of the above, and more. While spending should be reduced to the greatest extent possible, I believe that higher revenues will be necessary to stabilize the nation's finances. One of the goals of tax reform should be to make that higher tax burden more bearable.

Higher tax rates are unnecessary to raise the revenue needed. Tax expenditures can be curtailed. Should Congress be unwilling to tackle them directly, a number of economists have suggested restricting tax expenditures indirectly by, for example, disallowing some portion of a taxpayer's tax preferences or allowing only those that exceed some percentage of income. Others have proposed integrating tax expenditures more fully into the budget process so that people can more easily see that these are oftentimes simply a different way of spending public funds.

FURTHER READINGS

Aizenman, Joshua, and Nancy Marion. "Using Inflation to Erode the U.S. Public Debt." National Bureau of Economic Research Working Paper No. 15562 (Dec. 2009).

Burman, Leonard E., and Marvin Phaup. "Tax Expenditures, the Size and Efficiency of Government, and Implications for Budget Reform." National Bureau of Economic Research Working Paper No. 17268 (Aug. 2011).

Burman, Leonard E., et al., "Catastrophic Budget Failure." *National Tax Journal* (Sept. 2010): 561–84.

Census Bureau. "The Older Population in the United States: 2010 to 2050." Report No. P25–1138 (May 2010).

Census Bureau. "Voting and Registration in the Election of November 2008." Report No. P20–562 (May 2010).

Congressional Budget Office. *CBO's Long-Term Budget Outlook*. June 2011.

Congressional Budget Office. *Federal Debt and Interest Costs*. Dec. 2010.

Congressional Research Service. "The Federal Government Debt: Its Size and Economic Significance." Report No. RL31590 (Feb. 3, 2010).

Congressional Research Service. "Reducing the Budget Deficit: Tax Policy Options." Report No. R41641 (July 13, 2011).

Congressional Research Service. "Sovereign Debt in Advanced Economies: Overview and Issues for Congress." Report No. R41838 (May 26, 2011).

Congressional Research Service. "Standard & Poor's Downgrade of U.S. Government Long-Term Debt." Report No. R41955 (Aug. 9, 2011).

Congressional Research Service. "The Sustainability of the Federal Budget Deficit: Market Confidence and Economic Effects." Report No. R40770 (June 28, 2011).

Feldstein, Martin, Daniel Feenberg, and Maya MacGuineas. "Capping Individual Tax Expenditure Benefits." National Bureau of Economic Research Working Paper No. 16921 (Apr. 2011).

International Monetary Fund. "Default in Today's Advanced Economies: Unnecessary, Undesirable, and Unlikely." Staff Position Note No. SPN/10/12 (Sept. 1, 2010).

Leeper, Eric M., and Todd B. Walker. "Fiscal Limits in Advanced Economies." National Bureau of Economic Research Working Paper No. 16819 (Feb. 2011).

Marès, Arnaud. "Ask Not *Whether* Governments Will Default, but *How*." Morgan Stanley Global Economic Forum (Aug. 26, 2010).

Olshansky, S. Jay, et al. "Aging in America in the Twenty-first Century: Demographic Forecasts from the MacArthur Foundation Research Network on an Aging Society." *Milbank Quarterly* (Dec. 2009): 842–62.

Reinhart, Carmen M., Jacob F. Kirkegaard, and M. Belen Sbrancia. "Financial Repression Redux." *Finance & Development* (June 2011): 22–26.

Reinhart, Carmen M., and Kenneth S. Rogoff. "A Decade of Debt." National Bureau of Economic Research Working Paper No. 16827 (Feb. 2011).

Reinhart, Carmen M., and Kenneth S. Rogoff. *This Time Is Different: Eight Centuries of Financial Folly.* Princeton University Press, 2009.

Reinhart, Carmen M., and M. Belen Sbrancia. "The Liquidation of Government Debt." National Bureau of Economic Research Working Paper No. 16893 (Mar. 2011).

Romer, Christina. "The Rock and the Hard Place on the Deficit." *New York Times* (July 3, 2011).

Standard & Poor's. *Global Aging 2010: An Irreversible Truth.* Oct. 7, 2010.

Standard & Poor's. *In the Long Run, We Are All Debt: Aging Societies and Sovereign Ratings.* June 28, 2005.

Standard & Poor's. *Sovereign Credit Ratings: A Primer.* Oct. 19, 2006.

Standard & Poor's. *United States of America Long-Term Rating Lowered to "AA+" on Political Risks and Rising Debt Burden; Outlook Negative.* Aug. 5, 2011.

Story, Louise. "Deal May Avert Default, but Some Ask If That's Good." *New York Times* (Aug. 1, 2011).

Will, George. "Money for Adult Toys, but Not for Children." *Washington Post* (Jan. 24, 1982).

Chapter 21

The Case for a Value-Added Tax

T he value-added tax, or VAT, is a type of consumption tax widely used in every major country except the United States. From the point of view of efficiency, it is generally considered to be the best tax ever invented. It raises more revenue at less economic cost than any other tax. For this reason, many conservatives oppose it. They think taxes should be painful and burdensome, to keep them as low as possible. But as long as taxes are necessary to fund government, it's foolish to impose a large extra burden on the economy by raising revenue inefficiently.

DEADWEIGHT COST

It's important to understand that all taxes have what economists call a "deadweight" or "welfare" cost over and above the tax itself in the form of output discouraged by the form of the tax rather than its amount. In other words, output would be higher if the same revenue were raised in a less burdensome way. It is estimated that the deadweight cost of the federal tax system is equal to about one-third of revenue raised or about 5 percent of the gross domestic product. Thus the economy bears a total tax burden some 5 percent of GDP higher than is shown simply by measuring revenues as a share of GDP.

Economists have long known that taxes on consumption, such as excise taxes and retail sales taxes, have a lower deadweight cost than taxes on incomes or profits. Political philosophers have also long argued that taxes on consumption are morally preferable to taxes on saving or the return to saving. Thomas Hobbes, for example, argued that consumption is what people take out of society, while saving is what they put in. Therefore it is best to tax only consumption while exempting saving.

Alexander Hamilton, the first secretary of the Treasury, argued further that the taxation of consumption is more consistent with freedom than taxes on incomes because people can more easily reduce their consumption than their income if taxes become excessively burdensome. As he wrote in *Federalist* 21:

> It is a signal advantage of taxes on articles of consumption, that they contain in their own nature a security against excess. They prescribe their own limit; which cannot be exceeded without defeating the end proposed, that is, an extension of the revenue. When applied to this object, the saying is as just as it is witty, that, "in political arithmetic, two and two do not always make four." If duties are too high, they lessen the consumption; the collection is eluded; and the product to the treasury is not so great as when they are confined within proper and moderate bounds. This forms a complete barrier against any material oppression of the citizens by taxes of this class, and is itself a natural limitation of the power of imposing them.

One problem with consumption taxes, however, is that evasion is relatively easy. Both buyer and seller have an incentive to collude in cutting the tax collector out of a sale. The higher sales tax rates are, the greater the incentive for evasion. Consequently economists have long observed that retail sales taxes such as those in the states become too difficult to collect above a rate of about 10 percent.

Another problem with retail sales taxes is called "cascading," and it occurs when taxes are levied on taxes rather than on goods and services. For example, a contractor may buy some construction materials at retail, pay a sales tax, and then have another sales tax applied to the final bill that includes the taxes on the materials. Thus the final tax is partially a tax on a tax. Cascading needs to be eliminated to the greatest extent possible for reasons of both efficiency and fairness.

HISTORY OF THE VAT

The VAT was created in Europe after World War I to deal with the problem of cascading. The idea was to levy a tax at each stage of production or distribution while giving a credit for taxes previously paid. Moreover collecting the tax at many points in the production-distribution process, rather than just at the point of final sale, improved compliance. Sellers had an incentive to pay taxes; otherwise, they would be unable to claim credits on the taxes they paid on raw materials or goods purchased for resale.

Here's a simple example of how a VAT works. The farmer grows wheat, and a tax is assessed when it is sold to the miller to make flour. When the miller sells the flour to the baker to make bread, the tax is assessed again, but the miller gets credit for the taxes he paid when he bought the wheat. When the baker sells the bread to the grocer, the tax is assessed again, with the baker getting credit for the taxes paid by both the farmer and the miller. When the grocer sells the bread to a consumer, the tax is assessed once again, but the grocer gets credit for all of the previous taxes paid by the farmer, the miller, and the baker. In practice the consumer pays all the tax.

Note that even if the grocer fails to collect his share of the tax from the consumer, most of the tax will still be paid because it was already collected from the farmer, the miller, and the baker. The grocer paid those taxes when he bought the bread from the baker. The government would lose only the tax that would have been collected on the final price markup charged by the grocer.

Thus what is being taxed at each stage is the value being added to the original raw materials. The miller added value to the wheat by converting it into flour, the baker added more value by converting the flour into bread, and the grocer added still more value by making the bread available for consumption. Since the vast bulk of the value added is the labor of the miller, baker, and grocer, a VAT is essentially a tax on labor.

Another advantage of a VAT is that it can be assessed on imports and rebated on exports. While this sounds like a trick to levy a tariff on imports and provide a subsidy to exports, as many businesspeople believe, that is not the case at all. The purpose is to provide neutrality, so that goods traveling through different countries bear only the tax imposed in the country of final sale.

This aspect of the VAT became attractive to Europeans as they began the process of full economic integration in the 1960s. When formal trade barriers were abolished, countries did not want them replaced by domestic taxes that had the same effect. Therefore every member of the European Union was required to replace its national sales taxes with VATs so that goods could travel freely from one country to another without being burdened by taxes that could cascade as the goods moved.

People often wonder why it isn't possible to rebate other taxes, such as the corporate income tax, at the border so as to improve the competitiveness of American businesses. The reason is that world trade law prohibits rebating taxes at the border unless the precise amount of tax contained in the price of a good or service is known. And unfortunately economists have never figured out to what extent, if any, the corporate income tax is passed on to consumers. With a VAT, however, the amount is known to the penny because it is documented by the invoice trail that allows producers and sellers to claim credits for the VAT they pay.

In the 1970s and early 1980s many conservatives—such as Norman Ture, undersecretary of the Treasury for tax and economic policy; and Murray Weidenbaum, chairman of the Council of Economic Advisers, both for President Reagan—supported an American VAT. The conservative columnist George Will favored one, and Richard Nixon was strongly tempted by it. But in the end conservatives concluded that its liabilities outweighed its virtues. They feared that it would become a "money machine" that would raise revenue too easily, too painlessly, and thus would both raise the tax burden and increase government spending. At a press conference on February 21, 1985, Reagan cemented conservative opposition to the VAT, saying it "gives government a chance to grow in stature and size."

I myself long opposed the VAT on "money machine" grounds, but I changed my mind in 2004, when I realized that there was no longer any hope of controlling entitlement spending before the baby-boom deluge hit. The United States needs a money machine, I concluded.

THE POLITICS OF A VAT

Although some liberals have periodically been attracted by the VAT's revenue potential, none has made a serious effort to enact one since House Ways and Means Committee Chairman Al Ullman (D-OR) floated the idea in 1979 and was defeated in his reelection bid the following year—a loss widely attributed to his support for the VAT. Since then, Ullman's name has been invoked as proof that a VAT is politically suicidal. In the words of Congressman (later Sen.) Byron Dorgan (D-ND), "The last guy to push a VAT isn't working here anymore."

Politicians are also mindful that foreign leaders imposing VATs often suffered electoral defeat as a consequence. After enacting a VAT in Japan in 1986, Prime Minister Yasuhiro Nakasone was defeated the following year largely because of it. Prime Minister Brian Mulroney imposed a VAT in Canada in 1991, and it was considered the major factor in his 1993 defeat. Although Prime Minister John Howard survived enactment of a VAT in Australia in 1998, his party suffered major losses as a consequence.

Today several factors may have changed that could make a VAT viable in the United States. First, the magnitude of the fiscal crisis will have to be addressed soon. Spending for Social Security and Medicare alone will require a tax increase equivalent to about 80 percent of current individual income tax revenue in today's dollars over coming decades, according to the trustees' reports of those systems.

Second, the recent explosion of stimulus spending has made the fiscal problem worse. The United States is not immune from the debt problems that countries like Greece and Portugal have lately suffered. Economists of all political stripes worry that unchecked budget deficits could cause inflation and interest rates to skyrocket, at which point a large tax increase will be politically inevitable. The only question will be how taxes will be raised.

It would be advisable to raise taxes in a way least likely to impede economic growth, assuming taxes have to rise. It would be silly to raise taxes in a way that will cause saving to fall if the main purpose of a tax increase is to reduce interest rates that have risen because the budget deficit is crowding private borrowers out of financial markets. The conservative notion that taxes should be as painful as possible would, under such circumstances, be masochistic.

Concerns about the competitiveness of American industry may also make a VAT more palatable. If a tax that is rebatable at the border replaced a tax that is not, this would give exporters an advantage over what they have now. And since the tax would also apply at the border on goods and services that now enter the country tax-free, it would shift the tax burden partly onto foreigners, given that the United States runs a large trade deficit. Thus the taxes levied on imports would exceed rebates on exports.

And a VAT would address a growing conservative concern about the large percentage of the population that pays no federal income taxes. In 2011, 47 percent of all returns had no federal income tax liability. It's unrealistic to think that income taxes will be imposed on such people once they have become exempt. A VAT, by contrast, would get all Americans to pay for the federal government's general operations.

Of course, a VAT would be highly regressive, taking more in percentage terms out of the pockets of the poor than the well-to-do. Regressivity is the principal liberal objection to a VAT. Historically governments have tried to mitigate the burden on the poor by exempting things such as food from the VAT. But this creates a lot of complexity that increases the deadweight cost of the tax. Economists prefer to avoid exemptions and address regressivity, perhaps by cutting the payroll tax, which, as noted, has roughly the same incidence as a VAT because it is also a tax on labor.

Back in 1988 the Harvard economist and later Treasury secretary Larry Summers quipped that the reason the United States doesn't have a VAT is that liberals think it's regressive and conservatives think it's a money machine. We'll get a VAT, he said, when they reverse their positions.

REVENUE POTENTIAL

Estimates of how much an American VAT could raise depend a lot on what assumptions are made about the tax base. Economists would prefer that coverage be as broad as possible to avoid distortion and to keep the rate as low as possible. Although VATs can work at rates well above those that would cause a retail sales tax to break down, research shows that they start to have serious compliance problems at rates above 20 percent.

The Congressional Budget Office has looked at the revenue potential of a VAT. It believes that a broad base would cover about a third of GDP. This is consistent with the experience of other major countries. I estimate that the VAT covers 37 percent of GDP in the United Kingdom and France, 33 percent in Canada, and 30 percent in both Italy and Germany. Therefore a 20 percent VAT—the average for the European Union—could raise $1 trillion per year of new revenue.

Obviously it would be politically impossible to enact a 20 percent VAT all at once. On the other hand, it wouldn't make sense to impose one at a rate of less than 5 percent. The start-up costs are large; the IRS would need a new bureaucracy to administer the tax; and businesses would need extensive training. A 1993 IRS study estimated that it would need close to 30,000 additional staff members and two full years to implement a VAT before it could begin to collect any revenue from this tax.

A consequence of the long lead time needed to implement a VAT is that it cannot fill the revenue hole in the event of a debt crisis. Should one occur, we will need revenue immediately, and this means that it will have to be collected by raising the rates of existing taxes. It would be better to put in place the mechanism for the VAT well in advance of a crisis that would lead to higher taxes.

One obvious option would be to use VAT revenues to finance tax reform in a revenue-neutral manner. A 6 percent VAT would raise about as much revenue as the corporate income tax. Another percentage point could finance abolition of the Alternative Minimum Tax. The Columbia University law professor Michael Graetz has suggested using a VAT to abolish the individual income tax for the vast bulk of Americans. With a fully phased-in VAT capable of raising about $50 billion per percentage point in 2011 dollars, there are many worse taxes that could be reduced or abolished, thereby improving the efficiency of the tax system by raising the same revenue at a lower deadweight cost.

FURTHER READINGS

Bartlett, Bruce. "A New Money Machine for the U.S." *Los Angeles Times* (Aug. 29, 2004).

Bartlett, Bruce. "Not VAT Again!" *Wall Street Journal* (Apr. 16, 1993).

Bartlett, Bruce. "Revenue-Raising Redux: It's VAT Time Again." *Wall Street Journal* (Aug. 2, 1984).

Congressional Budget Office. *Effects of Adopting a Value-Added Tax*. Feb. 1992.

Congressional Research Service. "Consumption and Wage Tax Equivalency: A Brief Exposition." Report No. 95–1063E (Oct. 25, 1995).

Dresch, Stephen P., An-lo Lin, and David K. Stout. *Substituting a Value-Added Tax for the Corporate Income Tax*. National Bureau of Economic Research, 1977.

Ebrill, Liam, et al. *The Modern VAT*. International Monetary Fund, 2001.

Graetz, Michael J. *100 Million Unnecessary Returns*. Yale University Press, 2008.

Internal Revenue Service. *A Study of Administrative Issues in Implementing a Federal Value Added Tax*. Office of the Assistant Commissioner for Planning and Research (May 1993).

Keen, Michael, and Ben Lockwood. "The Value-Added Tax: Its Causes and Consequences." International Monetary Fund Working Paper No. WP/07/183 (July 2007).

Matthews, Kent, and Jean Lloyd-Williams. "Have VAT Rates Reached Their Limit? An Empirical Note." *Applied Economics Letters* (Feb. 2000): 111–15.

Nicholson, Michael W. "Value-Added Taxes and U.S. Trade Competitiveness." Forum for Research in Empirical International Trade Working Paper No. 186 (July 2010).

Rosen, Jan M. "Tax Watch: The Likely Forms of New Taxes." *New York Times* (Dec. 19, 1988).

Schenck, Alan, and Oliver Oldman. *Value Added Tax: A Comprehensive Approach*. Cambridge University Press, 2007.

Sullivan, Clara K. *The Tax on Value Added*. Columbia University Press, 1965.

Ture, Norman. *The Value Added Tax: Facts and Fancies*. Heritage Foundation and Institute for Research on the Economics of Taxation, 1979.

U.S. Government Accountability Office. *Summary Estimates of the Costs of the Federal Tax System.* Report No. GAO-05–878 (Aug. 2005).

Weidenbaum, Murray, David G. Raboy, and Ernest S. Christian Jr. *The Value-Added Tax: Orthodoxy and New Thinking.* Kluwer Academic, 1989.

Will, George. "The Retreat on Defense." *Washington Post* (Sept. 14, 1981).

Chapter 22

The Case Against a Value-Added Tax

I n the previous chapter, I explained why I think it would be desirable for the United States to adopt a value-added tax: I don't
think it's possible to cut spending enough to forestall a fiscal
crisis; taxes will eventually rise a lot; it will be economically debili-
tating to raise income tax rates as high as would be necessary to
get the necessary revenue; and a broad-based consumption tax such
as a VAT would be much less damaging to the economy than large
budget deficits.

Now I want to look at some of the arguments against my view.
Some are serious, but many are not. The latter are just straw men
created solely for the purpose of obfuscating the issue. I will try to
deal with them in order of seriousness, from least to most serious.

1. We must repeal the Sixteenth Amendment to avoid having both a VAT and an income tax.

In its 2008 platform the Republican Party made this point, and
in his column in 2010 George Will made it the centerpiece of his
case against the VAT. But it's not a serious argument. Contrary to
popular belief, Congress was not prohibited from taxing incomes
prior to the Sixteenth Amendment. As the historian David Levenstam wrote in the libertarian magazine *Reason,* in the case of
Pollack v. Farmers Loan (1895) the Supreme Court struck down
an income tax enacted in 1894 on narrow grounds and did not find
the taxation of incomes to be unconstitutional per se.

Even without the 16th Amendment, *Pollack* would allow
Congress to impose a tax on a broad range of income. The
Supreme Court clarified the point in a series of cases, includ-

ing *Brushaber v. Union Pacific Railroad* (1915), *Stanton v. Baltic Mining Company* (1916), and *Eisner v. Macomber* (1920). In these cases, the Court ruled that the 16th Amendment granted Congress no new power to tax; the 16th Amendment simply reclassified an income tax on tangible property as an indirect tax. . . .

Fourteen years after *Pollack,* Congress imposed a 1 percent flat tax on corporate net income in excess of $5,000 ($95,000 in 1998 dollars). By taxing corporations on dividends from other corporations, the 1909 act began the practice of double taxing corporate income. Opponents challenged the 1909 act in court, too. In 1911—two years before the adoption of the 16th Amendment—the Supreme Court ruled in *Flint v. Stone Tracy Company* that the tax on corporations was constitutional as "an excise upon the particular privilege of doing business in a corporate capacity." In other words, according to the Court's reasoning in 1911, just because the corporation tax was a tax on income didn't mean it was an income tax.

So even before the 16th Amendment, the *Pollack, Spreckles,* and *Flint* decisions gave a clear signal to Congress that it could impose a tax on wages, salaries, professional service fees, interest, dividends, royalties from intellectual property, estates, gifts, gross receipts, and any income earned by corporations. Congress could even double tax corporate income.

It would be hard to find a competent legal expert who thinks the Supreme Court would find the income tax unconstitutional today even if the Sixteenth Amendment was repealed.

While it is reasonable to say that it might be a bad idea to tax both consumption and incomes, repealing the Sixteenth Amendment would provide no guarantee against this. We would have to both get rid of the Sixteenth Amendment and enact another amendment that unambiguously prohibited the federal government from taxing incomes. This is probably impossible if only because the definition of income is so elastic.

2. The VAT is a hidden tax.

This argument is silly because the VAT is no more hidden than any other tax. Ask yourself: Do you really know what the sales tax rate is in your state, or the property tax rate in your community, or even what your effective federal income tax rate was last year? (Guess and then check; more than likely you overestimated all of them.) According to polls, most people have no idea. The chances are far better that those who pay the VAT in other countries can tell you precisely what the rate is because it covers such a wide array of goods and services and is consistent throughout the country.

Moreover even if the VAT were an especially hidden tax, the only grounds for being concerned would be if there is reason to believe that hidden taxes are more easily increased than more visible taxes. But there is no support for this belief. The University of Chicago economist Casey Mulligan, an opponent of the VAT, looked for evidence and could find none. He concluded that "tax visibility is empirically unrelated to the amount of taxation and government spending."

3. The VAT is too complicated and will be riddled with exemptions.

This argument is weak because all taxes are complicated. They're complicated because people dislike paying them, requiring governments to plug new loopholes and combat evasion tactics that are always being discovered, and because Congress continually meddles with the tax code to buy votes and redress legitimate grievances.

While a VAT would indeed be complicated to implement, once in place it is not especially complicated in operation, certainly no more so than the retail sales taxes that exist in almost every state. And since so many other countries have a VAT we can learn from their experience and avoid making ours unnecessarily complicated.

4. The VAT is inflationary.

While it is true that imposition of a VAT will be more than likely to raise the price level by about the amount of the tax, economists don't think of this as inflation. That would be a continuing rise in the price level year after year, resulting primarily from excessive money creation by the central bank. Any rise in prices resulting from a VAT would be a onetime event with no effect on the general inflation trend.

5. The VAT is a money machine.

This concern is probably the biggest one most conservatives have about a VAT. In their minds, its primary virtue—the ability to raise large amounts of revenue at low deadweight cost—is also its primary vice. If taxes are insufficiently burdensome, conservatives reckon, they will be too easy to raise. To keep taxes low, they believe we should raise them in the most painful and burdensome manner possible.

First, we will enact a VAT only if we really need a lot of new revenue; hence it is considered a money machine. While it is theoretically possible to reduce spending enough to avoid the necessity of higher taxes, I don't believe it is politically possible to do so. It may take a few years before this reality is accepted by Congress, but I think it is inevitable that taxes will rise significantly and we will need a VAT to raise revenue.

Second, the data don't really support the "money machine" argument. While it is often implied that the trend of the VAT is continuously upward, this is wrong. According to the OECD, eight of the thirty countries with a VAT have lower rates today than they had previously: Canada, Chile, the Czech Republic, France, Ireland, the Netherlands, Portugal, and the Slovak Republic. And several countries have never increased their VAT rates: Australia, Finland, Korea, and Poland. The average VAT rate in OECD countries was exactly the same in 2010 as it was in 1984: 17.9 percent.

Another problem with the money-machine argument is that it fails to note the critical impact of inflation on fueling higher VAT rates. When the general price level was rising rapidly it was easy for governments to raise VAT rates because they were hardly noticed. What was another 1 percent rise in prices due to a higher VAT when inflation was at double-digit rates? Moreover, to the extent that inflation was a function of budget deficits, higher taxes were seen as a plausible means of reducing it. In the Keynesian model, higher taxes are anti-inflationary because they reduce purchasing power.

I think it is critical that any money-machine analysis distinguish between those countries that adopted VATs before the great inflation of the 1970s and those adopting VATs in the era of relative price stability since then. I have done so in Table 22.1. It shows that to the extent that there is a valid money-machine argument, it is only for the countries able to piggyback on inflation to ratchet up their rates in the 1970s. VAT rates show little evidence of a ratchet effect during the era of price stability.

Table 22.1 VAT Rates in OECD Countries (ranked by year of establishment)

Country	Initial Rate	Year	2010 Rate	Percent Change
Established in the Inflationary Era (before 1974)				
Denmark	10	1967	25	+150
France	16.66	1968	19.6	+17.6
Germany	10	1968	19	+90
Netherlands	12	1969	19	+58.3
Sweden	11.11	1969	25	+125
Luxembourg	8	1970	15	+87.5
Norway	20	1970	25	+25
Belgium	18	1971	21	+16.7
Ireland	16.37	1972	21	+28.3
Austria	16	1973	20	+25
Italy	12	1973	20	+66.7
U.K.	10	1973	17.5	+75
Average	**13.3**	—	**20.6**	**+54.9**
Established in the Era of Price Stability (after 1974)				
Chile	20	1975	19	-5
Korea	10	1977	10	0
Mexico	10	1980	16	+60
Turkey	10	1985	18	+80
New Zealand	10	1986	12.5	+25
Portugal	17	1986	20	+17.6
Spain	12	1986	16	+33.3
Greece	16	1987	19	+18.75
Hungary	25	1988	25	0
Iceland	22	1989	25.5	+15.9
Japan	3	1989	5	+66.7
Canada	7	1991	5	-28.6
Czech Republic	23	1993	20	-13
Poland	22	1993	22	0
Slovak Republic	25	1993	19	-24
Finland	22	1994	22	0
Switzerland	6.5	1995	7.6	+16.9
Australia	10	2000	10	0
Average	**14.7**	—	**16.2**	**+10.2**

Source: OECD.

Finally, it should be noted that VATs often replaced other taxes when implemented. Many countries previously had manufacturers' excise taxes that had many economic and administrative problems. The VAT allowed them to be abolished. In other cases, the VAT provided revenue to implement various tax reforms that improved the economy and offset the burden on lower income groups. Therefore even in cases where the VAT rate has risen, it doesn't prove the money-machine argument unless it can be shown to have raised the overall level of taxation.

6. The VAT is regressive, taking more out of the pockets of the poor.

This is probably the strongest argument against the VAT. Since the poor consume a higher percentage of their income than the well-to-do, they are necessarily going to pay more VAT as a percentage of their income than the well-to-do are. It is certainly something that would have to be addressed if we were to adopt a VAT.

That said, one important benefit of a VAT is that everyone would be contributing to the general cost of government. We all benefit from homeland security, the justice system, and so on, and everyone ought to pay something for it. But as it is, 47 percent of those filing federal income tax returns have either a zero or a negative tax liability. The latter pay nothing but still get a tax refund.

When this point is brought up, liberals always cite all the payroll taxes low-income workers pay. But they seldom note that the negative income tax liability comes mainly from the Earned Income Tax Credit (EITC), which was established to indirectly offset the payroll tax of low-income workers. For a substantial number of taxpayers the EITC offsets all of their payroll tax liability as well as their income tax liability. Furthermore the payroll tax does not support the government's general operations. It funds specific benefit programs, Social Security and Medicare, from which the vast majority of beneficiaries get back far more than they ever pay in (see Table 22.2).

Table 22.2 Percentage of Tax Units with a Zero or Negative Federal Tax Liability, 2010

Cash Income Level	Income Tax Only	Income Plus Payroll Tax
Less than $20,000	89.9	51.6
$20,000–$50,000	48.2	22.2
$50,000–$100,000	12.5	2.0
Over $100,000	2.0	0.6
All tax units	45.0	22.9

Source: Tax Policy Center.

Oddly, conservatives are the ones most likely to complain that the poor aren't pulling their weight. Yet they refuse to see that a VAT is probably the only way of getting the poor to help finance the general cost of government. It's extremely unlikely that we will ever impose income taxes on very many of those now paying nothing.

It should be noted as well that viewing the VAT over a lifetime rather than in single-year snapshots reduces its regressivity considerably. Economists now generally accept that consumption taxes are roughly proportional to income over a lifetime because consumption itself is roughly proportional to income.

OTHER OBJECTIONS

Of course, there are any number of other reasons people oppose a federal VAT. One key constituency is state governments, which view consumption as a tax base that belongs exclusively to them. But they could easily piggyback onto a federal VAT, which would also be able to tax things like Internet and mail-order sales that the states have struggled to collect sales taxes on.

Finally, we would never impose a VAT until well after the economy had returned to reasonable health. And a VAT would have a heavy economic cost even if that cost would be far less than the cost of an equivalent income tax rate increase. But, as noted earlier, a VAT is never going to be seriously considered unless the need is overwhelming. That will be when large deficits impose on the American people costs that are even worse in the form of inflation, high interest rates, and economic instability.

If, as former vice president Dick Cheney used to say, deficits don't matter, we have nothing to worry about. But anyone who believes that deficits have economic costs has to accept that at some point those costs may be greater than the cost of raising taxes to reduce them, if, as I believe, spending will never be cut enough to keep deficits from rising to economically disastrous levels.

FURTHER READINGS

Becker, Gary, and Casey B. Mulligan. "Deadweight Costs and the Size of Government." *Journal of Law and Economics* (Oct. 2003): 293–340.

Caspersen, Erik, and Gilbert Metcalf. "Is a Value Added Tax Regressive? Annual versus Lifetime Incidence Measures." *National Tax Journal* (Dec. 1994): 731–46.

Cnossen, Sijbren. "Administrative and Compliance Costs of the VAT: A Review of the Evidence." *Tax Notes* (June 20, 1994): 1609–26.

Duncan, Harley. "VATs in a Federal System." *Tax Notes* (Mar. 29, 2010): 1643–53.

Duncan, Harley, and Jon Sedon. "Coordinating a Federal VAT with State and Local Sales Taxes." *Tax Notes* (May 31, 2010): 1029–38.

Keen, Michael, and Ben Lockwood. "Is the VAT a Money Machine?" *National Tax Journal* (Dec. 2006): 905–28.

Levenstam, David B. "Repealing the 16th Amendment Wouldn't Kill the Income Tax." *Reason* (Jan. 1999): 53–54.

Metcalf, Gilbert E. "Life Cycle versus Annual Perspectives on the Incidence of a Value Added Tax." *Tax Policy and the Economy* 8 (1994): 45–64.

Stockfisch, J. A. "Value-Added Taxes and the Size of Government: Some Evidence." *National Tax Journal* (Dec. 1985): 547–52.

Tait, Alan. "Is the Introduction of a Value-Added Tax Inflationary?" *Finance & Development* (June 1981): 38–42.

Turnier, William J. "VAT: Minimizing Administration and Compliance Costs." *Tax Notes* (Mar. 14, 1988): 1257–68.

U.S. Government Accountability Office. "Value-Added Taxes: Potential Lessons for the United States from Other Countries' Experiences." Report No. GAO-11-867T (July 26, 2011).

Will, George. "The Perils of the Value-Added Tax." *Washington Post* (Apr. 18, 2010).

Yin, George K. "Accommodating the 'Low-Income' in a Cash-Flow or Consumed Income Tax World." *Florida Tax Review* (1995): 445–91.

Chapter 23

What Should Be Done About the Bush Tax Cuts?

The central driver for tax reform in 2012 will be the expiration on December 31 of all the tax cuts enacted during the George W. Bush administration. Originally enacted with an expiration date of December 31, 2010, they were extended for two additional years at the last minute by President Obama. It is in the interest of both parties to use this leverage to come up with alternative tax changes so that they are not faced with the same choice that arose in late 2010, of either extending the Bush tax cuts in toto or allowing a large tax increase to take effect.

When we talk about the Bush tax cuts, it's important to acknowledge that there were many of them. According to a Treasury Department study, there were more major tax cuts during the Bush II administration than any other administration in history. And the aggregate revenue loss was the largest of any administration as a percentage of GDP (see Table 23.1). Both Harry Truman and Ronald Reagan passed larger individual tax cuts, but both took back about half of them with subsequent tax increases. Bush is remarkable for having never enacted a single tax increase. Reagan, by contrast, signed eleven major tax increases into law.

Table 23.1 Average Annual Revenue Loss from Bush-Era Tax Cuts

Legislation	Percent of GDP
Economic Growth and Tax Relief Reconciliation Act of 2001	0.68
Job Creation and Worker Assistance Act of 2002	0.26
Jobs and Growth Tax Relief Reconciliation Act of 2003	0.59
Working Families Tax Relief Act of 2004	0.20
Tax Increase Prevention and Reconciliation Act of 2005	0.16
Economic Stimulus Act of 2008	0.24
Bank Bailout Bill of 2008	0.19

Source: Treasury Department.

ORIGINS OF THE 2001 TAX CUT

On June 7, 2001, Bush signed into law the first major tax cut of his administration. Although sold as a way of stimulating the economy, raising growth, and reducing unemployment, it did none of that.

To understand why the 2001 Bush tax cut failed to achieve its purpose, it's important to recall its genesis. It grew out of a tax plan developed in mid-1999 by Bush's principal economic adviser, Lawrence Lindsey. Other contributors included the economists Michael Boskin, John Cogan, Martin Feldstein, and John Taylor.

In 1999 the last thing the economy needed was a stimulus. Real GDP grew 4.2 percent that year, well above its postwar trend of about 2.5 percent, and the unemployment rate was just 4.2 percent. Growth was so rapid that revenues poured into the Treasury. The federal government was on track to run a healthy budget surplus of $126 billion.

The Bush tax plan was announced on December 1, 1999. Since it was clearly implausible to argue that the economy needed a stimulus, Bush, at Lindsey's urging, defended his tax cut as "insurance against economic recession." Lindsey was bearish on the economy, and he anticipated a sharp economic slowdown—thus he was an outlier among economic forecasters, the bulk of whom were expecting a continuation of robust economic growth.

Of course, Bush's tax cut was designed as well for an explicit political purpose. He was running for the Republican presidential nomination against two strong opponents, Sen. John McCain of Arizona and the publisher Steve Forbes. Forbes in particular was running hard on the flat tax, which had propelled him from out of nowhere into contention for the Republican nomination in 1996. Bush also had to contend with the widespread Republican view that his father had made a dreadful mistake, both substantively and politically, by backing a tax increase in 1990.

Bush recognized that he could not compete with Forbes for the hearts of the party's supply-siders. He chose instead to emphasize the "compassionate conservatism" of his proposal, which reduced the top rate only modestly (by Republican standards) to 33 percent from 39.6 percent. The top rate at the end of his father's administration had been 31 percent, and it was 28 percent at the end of Reagan's. Other tax provisions in the Bush plan included doubling the child credit to $1,000, reducing the marriage penalty, allowing nonitemizers to deduct charitable contributions, and phasing out the estate tax. Liberal economists praised it as being more distributionally fair than congressional Republican tax proposals. They were also cautiously optimistic that there would be further improvements in the Bush plan because as governor of Texas he had shown an admirable willingness to work with Democrats on a bipartisan basis.

DISSIPATING THE BUDGET SURPLUS

Subsequently it became clear that another goal of the Bush tax cut was to dissipate the budget surplus. The Clinton administration had projected that by 2010 the national debt would effectively be paid off. Bush and his advisers were very wary of budget surpluses, fearing that they would put irresistible pressure on Congress to create new spending programs. Bush even criticized Federal Reserve Board Chairman Alan Greenspan for supporting budget surpluses.

On January 24, 2000, Bush said, "Mr. Greenspan believes that money around Washington, DC, will be spent on a single item— debt reduction. . . . I think it will be spent on greater government. He has got greater faith in the appropriators than I do."

In the end Bush won the Republican nomination and, eventually, the election. Unfortunately the long-drawn-out conclusion to the 2000 election, which wasn't resolved until the Supreme Court decided *Bush v. Gore* on December 12, deprived him of a third of his transition. One of the casualties may have been a rethinking of his campaign tax cut. In the year since it was first proposed, economic conditions had changed. Although few economists were forecasting a recession, almost all predicted a deceleration of growth. We now know that a recession began in March 2001.

The sensible thing for Bush to have done would have been to revise his tax plan and propose something more appropriate based on the economic deterioration. Nevertheless Bush told Congress to enact his campaign tax plan unchanged. His one concession to changed economic conditions was to support a one-shot $300 tax rebate, which was popular in Congress, to pump up aggregate demand—classic Keynesian economic policy, not the supply-side economics Republicans champion.

Passage of the Bush tax cut was ensured by Greenspan's endorsement in testimony before the Senate Budget Committee on January 25, 2001. His main argument was that large budget surpluses would be destabilizing. "Large deficits are bad. Large surpluses are bad," Greenspan said.

Work on the tax bill proceeded at an unusually rapid pace by Congress's usual standards. The members finished in late May. The final legislation had a number of provisions, but closely followed the Bush 1999 campaign proposal. Key elements included a new 10 percent tax bracket, a reduction in the top rate from 39.6 percent to 35 percent in 2006, an increase in the child credit from $500 to $1,000 over ten years, and elimination of the estate tax in 2010. Importantly, every provision of the 2001 law expired at the end of 2010 because budget rules prevented enactment of a permanent tax cut, and Republicans were unwilling to compromise with Democrats on a tax cut that could have been enacted permanently.

The Republican-leaning Heritage Foundation, pleased with the Bush tax cut, predicted that real GDP would rise by an average of 3.3 percent per year from 2001 to 2010. Actual growth was about half that, 1.7 percent per year. Heritage said the unemployment rate would average 4.7 percent over the same period. It actually averaged 6.1 percent.

ECONOMIC EFFECTS

By any measure the economic performance of the 2000s was dismal despite historically low taxes, which Republicans believe are the sine qua non of growth. Federal revenues averaged 17.6 percent of GDP from 2001 to 2008, compared with a postwar average of about 18.5 percent.

No comprehensive analysis of the impact of the 2001 tax cut exists. Even Republican economists seldom discuss it, preferring instead to focus on the 2003 tax cut, which reduced the maximum tax rate on dividends and capital gains to 15 percent—more classical supply-side tax policy. But it also failed to do much to stimulate growth or reduce unemployment (see Table 23.2).

Table 23.2 Economic Indicators before and after the Tax Cuts for Expansion Years (annual average)

Economic Indicator	1993–2000	2003–2007
Real GDP growth	3.9%	2.7%
Median real household income growth	1.7%	0.6%
Private employment growth	2.7%	1.2%
Weekly hours worked	34.4	33.8
Employment-population ratio	63.4%	62.7%
Unemployment rate	5.2%	5.2%
Personal saving rate	4.6%	2.6%
Business investment growth	10.3%	5.6%
Labor productivity growth	2.0%	2.2%

Source: Congressional Research Service.

The effect of the 2003 tax cut on dividends has been the subject of extensive economic analysis. The theory was that it would encourage corporations to pay out more dividends and raise the stock market. But there is little evidence that it did either. Studies show that dividend payouts on assets qualifying for a lower rate did not increase more than those that did not qualify. And stock indexes rose no faster in the United States following the tax cut than they rose in Europe. Insofar as dividends did increase, they were largely offset by lower share repurchases by corporations. In terms of paying out profits to shareholders, therefore, only the form changed, not the amount.

In 2011 the Congressional Budget Office (CBO) calculated that the Bush tax cuts increased the national debt by about $3 trillion, including debt service. As one can see, CBO was projecting about a $6 trillion surplus when Bush took office. Instead there was a $6 trillion deficit, for a fiscal turnaround of $12 trillion. Lower revenues accounted for about half and higher spending for half (see Table 23.3).

Table 23.3 Changes in CBO's Baseline Projections of the Surplus, 2001–2011

Change in Surplus	Billions of Dollars
Economic Growth and Tax Relief Reconciliation Act of 2001	–1,256
Jobs and Growth Tax Relief Reconciliation Act of 2002	–328
Working Families Tax Relief Act of 2004	–121
Economic Stimulus Act of 2008	–106
American Recovery and Reinvestment Act of 2009 (tax provisions)	–253
Tax Act of 2010	–354
Other	–461
Subtotal of legislated tax changes	–2,879
Subtotal of economic and technical effect on revenues	–3,484
Total revenue change	–6,363
Discretionary spending	–2,947
Mandatory spending	–1,403
Net interest	–1,376
Subtotal of legislated spending changes	–5,726
Subtotal of economic and technical effect on spending	+87%
Total spending change	–5,638
Projected surplus as of January 2001	+5,891
Actual deficit	–6,111
Total fiscal change	–12,002

Source: Congressional Budget Office.

FAILURE OF THE BUSH TAX CUTS

By the end of the Bush administration, it was hard to find an economist with anything good to say about its economic policies. The Harvard economist Dale Jorgenson, asked by the *New York Times* if he saw anything positive in the policies, replied, "I don't see any redeeming features, unfortunately." Even Douglas Holtz-Eakin of the Republican policy group the American Action Forum acknowledged that Bush's economic policy was a failure:

There was very little of the kind of saving and export-led growth that would be more sustainable. For a group that claims it wants to be judged by history, there is no evidence on the economic policy front that that was the view. It was all Band-Aids.

When the Congressional Research Service examined the economic consequences of allowing all the Bush tax cuts to expire at the end of 2010, it concluded that the impact would be slight because their impact on growth was virtually nonexistent. The report concluded:

> By almost any economic indicator, the economy performed better in the period before the tax cuts than after the tax cuts were enacted, regardless of whether recession years are omitted from the comparison. GDP growth, median real household income growth, weekly hours worked, the employment-population ratio, personal saving, and business investment growth were all lower in the period after the tax cuts were enacted.

Culprits for the ineffectiveness of the Bush tax cuts include a failure to control spending; the waste of revenue on tax rebates instead of more growth-oriented tax cuts in 2001 and 2008; the phasing in of many tax provisions, which caused investors and businesses to put off economic activity into the future; the expiration of all the Bush-era tax cuts at the end of 2010 in the original legislation, which discouraged long-term changes in behavior; and the tilting of the tax cuts too much toward the wealthy.

The CBO estimates that allowing all the Bush tax cuts to expire at the end of 2012 would raise aggregate revenues by about $3 trillion over the next decade—enough by itself to stabilize the debt-to-GDP ratio. Nevertheless despite widespread concern about the growing national debt on both sides of the aisle, there is no possibility that the Bush tax cuts will simply be ended. The prospect of such a large tax increase at a time when the economy will undoubtedly still be weak means, at a minimum, that they will be extended for another year or two, as they were at the end of 2010.

However, $3 trillion of higher revenue in the current law baseline forecast presents a potential win-win for both parties in which alternative tax cuts and reforms are substituted for the Bush tax cuts. In theory net revenues could be reduced a little less than $3 trillion, thus raising net revenue and reducing projected deficits, while tax reform would make a more meaningful contribution to economic growth than the Bush tax cuts ever did.

FURTHER READINGS

Amromin, Gene, et al. "How Did the 2003 Dividend Tax Cut Affect Stock Prices and Corporate Payout Policy?" Federal Reserve Board, Finance and Economics Discussion Series No. 2005–57 (Sept. 2005).

Auten, Gerald, Robert Carroll, and Geoffrey Gee. "The 2001 and 2003 Tax Rate Reductions: An Overview and Estimate of the Taxable Income Response." *National Tax Journal* (Sept. 2008): 345–64.

Bank, Steven A. "Dividends and Tax Policy in the Long Run." *University of Illinois Law Review* (2007): 533–74.

Bartlett, Bruce. "Explaining the Bush Tax Cuts." *Commentary* (June 2004): 23–27.

Brown, Jeffrey R., Nellie Liang, and Scott Weisbenner. "Executive Financial Incentives and Payout Policy: Firm Responses to the 2003 Dividend Tax Cut." Federal Reserve Board, Finance and Economics Discussion Series No. 2006–14 (Jan. 2006).

Burke, Karen C., and Grayson M. P. McCouch. "Turning Slogans into Tax Policy." *Virginia Tax Review* (Spring 2008): 747–81.

Carroll, Robert. "The Economic Effects of the Lower Tax Rate on Dividends." Tax Foundation Special Report No. 181 (June 2010).

Chetty, Raj, and Emmanuel Saez. "The Effects of the 2003 Dividend Tax Cut on Corporate Behavior: Interpreting the Evidence." *American Economic Review* (May 2006): 124–29.

Congressional Budget Office. *The Budget and Economic Outlook: An Update.* Aug. 2011.

Congressional Budget Office. *Changes in CBO's Baseline Projections since January 2001.* May 12, 2011.

Congressional Budget Office. *How CBO Analyzed the Macroeconomic Effects of the President's Budget.* July 2003.

Congressional Research Service. "The Budget Reconciliation Process: The Senate's 'Byrd Rule.'" Report No. RL30862 (Mar. 20, 2008).

Congressional Research Service. "The Bush Tax Cuts and the Economy." Report No. R41393 (Oct. 27, 2010).

Congressional Research Service. "The Impact of Major Legislation on Budget Deficits: 2001 to 2009." Report No. R41134 (Mar. 23, 2010).

Congressional Research Service. "The 2001 and 2003 Bush Tax Cuts and Deficit Reduction." Report No. R42020 (Sept. 23, 2011).

Congressional Research Service. "What Effects Would the Expiration of the 2001 and 2003 Tax Cuts Have on the Economy?" Report No. R41443 (Dec. 21, 2010).

Edgerton, Jesse. "Effects of the 2003 Dividend Tax Cut: Evidence from Real Estate Investment Trusts." Federal Reserve Board, Finance and Economics Discussion Series No. 2010–34 (June 2010).

Elmendorf, Douglas W., et al. "Distributional Effects of the 2001 and 2003 Tax Cuts: How Do Financing and Behavioral Responses Matter?" *National Tax Journal* (Sept. 2008): 365–80.

Fieldhouse, Andrew, and Ethan Pollack. "Tenth Anniversary of the Bush-Era Tax Cuts." Economic Policy Institute (June 1, 2011).

Gompers, Paul, Andrew Metrick, and Jeremy Siegel. "This Tax Cut Will Pay Dividends." *Wall Street Journal* (Aug. 13, 2002).

Gourio, François, and Jianjun Miao. "Transitional Dynamics of Dividend and Capital Gains Tax Cuts." National Bureau of Economic Research Working Paper No. 16157 (July 2010).

Graham, John D. *Bush on the Home Front.* Indiana University Press, 2010.

Hacker, Jacob S., and Paul Pierson. "Abandoning the Middle: The Bush Tax Cuts and the Limits of Democratic Control." *Perspectives on Politics* (Mar. 2005): 33–53.

House, Christopher L., and Matthew D. Shapiro. "Phased-In Tax Cuts and Economic Activity." *American Economic Review* (Dec. 2006): 1835–49.

Irwin, Neil, and Dan Eggen. "Economy Made Few Gains in Bush Years." *Washington Post* (Jan. 12, 2009).

Kawano, Laura. "Taxes and Financial Portfolio Choices: Evidence from the Tax Rate Reductions of the 2001 and 2003 Tax Acts." Social Science Research Network (Jan. 24, 2011).

Kopcke, Richard W. "The Taxation of Equity, Dividends, and Stock Prices." Federal Reserve Bank of Boston, Public Policy Discussion Paper No. 05–1 (Jan. 2005).

Leonhardt, David. "Partisan Economics in Action." *New York Times* (Oct. 7, 2009).

Lindsey, Lawrence. *What a President Should Know . . . but Most Learn Too Late.* Rowman and Littlefield, 2008.

Manning, Robert F., and David Windish. "Tax Analysts' Guide to the Economic Growth and Tax Relief Reconciliation Act of 2001." *Tax Notes* (June 11, 2001): 1777–811.

Poterba, James. "Taxation and Corporate Payout Policy." *American Economic Review* (May 2004): 171–75.

Sullivan, Martin A. "'Dubya's' Tax Plan: Realistic, Yes; Progressive, No." *Tax Notes* (Dec. 20, 1999): 1490–94.

Tempalski, Jerry. "Revenue Effects of Major Tax Bills." U.S. Treasury Department, Office of Tax Analysis (Sept. 2006).

Tempalski, Jerry. "Revenue Effects of Major Tax Bills: Updated Tables for All 2010 Bills." U.S. Treasury Department, Office of Tax Analysis (June 2011).

Wilson, D. Mark, and William W. Beach. "The Economic Impact of President Bush's Tax Relief Plan." Heritage Foundation Report No. CDA01–01Rev (Apr. 27, 2001).

Chapter 24

If Tax Reform Happens, It Will Be Because Grover Norquist Permits It

G rover Norquist is president of a group called Americans for Tax Reform (ATR), which was founded in 1985 to aid enactment of the Tax Reform Act of 1986 and continue the work of broadening the tax base and reducing marginal tax rates. Over the years he has become an influential power broker within the Republican Party, especially since the rise of the Tea Party and its obsessive opposition to taxes and to spending.

As part of his agenda, Norquist developed a "taxpayer protection pledge." Signers promise to "oppose any and all efforts to increase the marginal tax rates for individuals and/or businesses; and oppose any net reduction or elimination of deductions and credits, unless matched dollar for dollar by further reducing tax rates." In recent years only a handful of Republicans in Congress have not signed.

If one takes it literally, the pledge is not terribly objectionable. But in practice it has become a general prohibition on raising federal taxes in any way, for any reason, under any circumstances. Indeed this is the first sentence in Norquist's organization's description of itself: "Americans for Tax Reform opposes all tax increases as a matter of principle."

ANTI-VAT

Norquist has long treated the institution of any new tax as per se a tax increase even if it is coupled with tax cuts such that it doesn't raise net additional revenue. Consequently he opposes the value-added tax even as part of a revenue-neutral tax reform.

In 2010 Mitch Daniels, Republican governor of Indiana, suggested that a VAT might be part of a tax reform designed to raise saving and reduce consumption, which it clearly would do if coupled with a reduction in taxes on capital, such as a cut in the corporate tax rate. Norquist's opposition was swift, harsh, and unequivocal:

> This is outside the bounds of acceptable modern Republican thought, and it is only the zone of extremely left-wing Democrats who publicly talk about those things because all Democrats pretending to be moderates wouldn't touch it with a 10-foot pole. Absent some explanation, such as large quantities of crystal meth, this is disqualifying. This is beyond the pale.

Kevin Williamson, the economics editor of *National Review*, the nation's oldest and most respected conservative journal, came to Daniels's defense, noting, correctly, that the magnitude of the nation's budgetary problem is too great to be solved entirely on the spending side. He also criticized Norquist for focusing solely on holding down taxes, as if this were the one and only thing necessary to be fiscally responsible. Said Williamson, "Norquistism, by focusing on the taxing side of the ledger rather than on the spending side, has for decades enabled Republican spending shenanigans of the sort that helped put the party in the minority and ruined its reputation for fiscal sobriety."

STARVE THE BEAST

Norquist bases his uncompromising position on a popular conservative theory called "starve the beast," which argues that tax cuts will somehow or other automatically bring down the budget deficit. In early 2011 he criticized a group of conservative Republican senators—Saxby Chambliss of Georgia, Tom Coburn of Oklahoma, and Mike Crapo of Idaho—just for hinting at the possibility of supporting higher taxes as part of a grand budget deal that also cut entitlement spending. Norquist would have none of it, saying flatly,

"The only time the deficit comes down is when you refuse to raise taxes and you rein in spending." In a letter to the three senators on February 17, 2011, Norquist cited this history for his assertion:

> Back in 1982, President Reagan was promised $3 in spending cuts for every $1 in tax hikes. The tax hikes happened—and spending went up. In 1990, President George H. W. Bush was promised $2 in spending cuts for every $1 in tax hikes. The tax hikes happened—and spending came in above the CBO pre-deal baseline. In these bipartisan deals, Washington spenders are actually unharmed, and taxpayers are left holding the bag. This cannot be allowed to happen again.

Conspicuously absent from Norquist's letter are two powerful contrary examples. In 1993 Bill Clinton and a Democratic Congress raised taxes by about 0.6 percent of GDP. Starve-the-beast theory says that this should have fed the beast and led to higher spending. In fact spending fell from 22.1 percent of GDP in 1992 to 18.2 percent in Clinton's last year. And in 2001, 2002, 2003, 2004, and 2005 President George W. Bush and a Republican Congress cut taxes by just over 2 percent of GDP, from 20.6 percent of GDP in 2000 to 18.5 percent in 2007. Starve-the-beast theory holds that this cut should have led to a reduction in spending, but spending rose from 18.2 percent of GDP in 2000 to 19.6 percent in 2007. (The 2008 data are distorted by the recession.) And the vast bulk of this spending increase was legislated by the allegedly frugal Republicans. Indeed Republicans created an entirely new, unfunded entitlement program, Medicare Part D, which will add about $60 billion to the deficit in 2012.

On March 9, 2011, the *Washington Post*'s Ezra Klein questioned Norquist about the Clinton-era experience. His explanation was that the Republican Congress, which was elected in 1994, deserved all the credit because investors somehow or other knew that Republicans would cut the capital gains tax, as in fact they did in 1997, and this foreknowledge caused the stock market to rise as soon as they took control in 1995. As Norquist explained:

> Clinton is president for two years with a Democratic House and Senate. Stock market is flat. Employment is flat. Repub-

licans take House and Senate in 1994 and everything begins
shooting straight up because Republicans say we won't let
Clinton do any of the things he wanted to do, and we're cutting the capital gains tax.

Just to be clear, Klein questioned him further: "You're arguing
that the boom in the mid-1990s wasn't because of the Internet or
because we were snapping back from a recession, but because the
election of a Republican Congress had a major confidence effect."
Norquist replied, "Yes."

Norquist didn't explain how his logic related to the improvement in the budget, but he appears to imply an argument that other
Republicans have made: that the budget surpluses of the late 1990s
resulted primarily from a burst in revenues that came about not because of the 1993 tax increase but because of a Laffer Curve effect
from the 1997 cut in the capital gains tax. (The economist Arthur
Laffer hypothesized that since a 100 percent tax rate would raise
no revenue, it follows that tax rates may sometimes be too high to
maximize revenue and a rate cut would raise revenue.) As a former
speechwriter for Ronald Reagan, Clark Judge, explained in a *Wall
Street Journal* op-ed, "The surpluses of the late '90s were to a significant extent a product of the growth in revenues that came after
the capital gains tax was cut."

According to the Treasury Department, capital gains tax revenues rose by 0.6 percent of GDP between 1996 and 2000, from
$66.4 billion to $127.3 billion. While some of this increase may
have been due to an unlocking effect, as people realized gains that
may have accumulated over a period of years, it also occurred
during an enormous tech boom resulting from development of the
Internet, the roots of which long predate any change in the capital
gains tax. Either way, total federal revenues rose by 1.8 percent
of GDP between 1996 and 2000, and spending fell 2 percent of
GDP, for a total fiscal turnaround of 3.8 percent of GDP. Even if
we assume that all of the increase in capital gains revenues resulted
from the 1997 rate cut, it accounts for, at most, 15 percent of the
improvement over a four-year period.

Of course, even if Norquist is correct about the stock market
being the primary cause of higher revenues, this doesn't have any
bearing on the fact that spending fell after the 1993 tax increase.

His starve-the-beast model says that tax increases must lead to higher spending, and tax cuts must reduce spending. But the fact is that since at least 1993 there is not one iota of evidence supporting this idea, and there is considerable evidence that causation runs in the opposite direction. Arguably tax increases led to spending cuts and tax cuts led to spending increases.

One prominent conservative economist who has looked critically at starve-the-beast theory is William Niskanen of the Cato Institute, a member of the Council of Economic Advisers for Ronald Reagan. He argues that the actual impact of the theory has been perverse: by making it impossible to raise taxes to reduce deficits, starve-the-beast theory has reduced the tax cost of deficits. If people thought that higher spending would lead to higher taxes, they would be less supportive of it. But if higher spending never leads to higher taxes, something Norquist has guaranteed as long as Republicans have veto power over tax increases, higher spending is essentially a free lunch—all gain and no pain.

The impossibility of raising taxes also has macroeconomic implications. Many economists, such as Robert Barro of Harvard, believe in a theory called "Ricardian equivalence," which says that budget deficits are not stimulative because people implicitly discount the higher taxes that will be necessary to pay off the increase in debt. But when questioned about the effects of large budget deficits, people almost never say they expect higher taxes. According to a January 2011 *New York Times*/CBS News poll, only 4 percent of those who said they are very or somewhat concerned about the budget deficit said that they feared a tax increase.

Nevertheless the Norquist view is repeated dogmatically by Republicans. In a February 2011 floor speech, Sen. Orrin Hatch (R-UT) said, "If we raised taxes to eliminate the deficit, the current levels of spending would just cause a new deficit to arise." In March Rep. John Barrasso (R-WY) declared, "If you send more money to Washington, all they're going to do is spend it."

NORQUIST ON TAX REFORM

Unfortunately Norquist's philosophy, that tax cuts are the sum total of the Republican tax philosophy and that tax increases are not permitted under any circumstances, is a serious barrier to fundamental tax reform. The idea of *tax reform* has always meant ridding the tax code of unjustified preferences that bias individual and business behavior in ways that may not be optimal for them or the economy. In other cases, tax preferences simply waste money subsidizing people and businesses for no reason except that they belong to a politically favored group.

The goal of tax reform, which Republicans used to believe in, should be tax neutrality. People and businesses should make economic decisions based solely on the economics and not because the tax system subsidizes them to do one thing rather than another.

Perhaps the best example is the exclusion for employer-provided health insurance. It is clearly part of workers' compensation, but workers pay no taxes on it, and their employers deduct the cost. This makes $1 of health insurance far more valuable than $1 of cash wages, and it is a key reason health care costs have risen so much. Workers treat health care like something that's essentially free.

Once upon a time, long ago—2008, to be exact—Republicans like Sen. John McCain campaigned on getting rid of the health insurance exclusion as an essential element of health care reform. He argued, correctly, that there is little hope of getting health care costs under control unless the demand for health care is reduced. The best way of reducing demand is by encouraging people to be more cost-conscious, as they would be if they paid health care costs out of their own pockets. If the revenue now being lost to the health insurance exclusion were used instead to fund expanded health savings accounts—a sort of Individual Retirement Account from which health care costs can be paid—workers would benefit financially from reducing their own health care spending.

Unfortunately this sensible proposal got deep-sixed when Democrats initiated health care reform. Republicans concluded that their political fortunes would be maximized by opposing whatever the Democrats supported without putting forward any alternative of their own. Those few Republicans willing to say that this was misguided, that their party had a responsibility to put forward legislation that embodied their vision of health care reform, were ignored. One, David Frum, was fired by the Republican-leaning American Enterprise Institute for saying so publicly. Another, Sen. Robert

Bennett of Utah, was denied renomination by Republicans in his state because he cosponsored a health care reform bill with Sen. Ron Wyden, Democrat of Oregon.

Something similar is also happening with tax reform. Republicans claim they are for it, but they steadfastly refuse to name a single existing tax provision that is worth getting rid of. They are only for tax rate cuts, and that is the sum total of their contribution to the tax reform debate. Their rationale is that eliminating any tax loophole, no matter how egregious or unjustified, would constitute a tax increase, and they are against all tax increases, period.

Occasionally Republicans will proclaim a willingness to wipe the slate clean and abolish all tax preferences as part of some impossible-to-imagine tax reform. But by being vague about the details and failing to explain that people would be forced to give up the mortgage interest deduction, the charitable contributions deduction, the exclusion for health insurance, all tax-favored retirement savings accounts, and all the rest, they allow people to focus only on the rate cuts and to imagine that somehow or other the taxpayers themselves will pay no price.

The other factor in Republicans' thinking is just cynical politics. They are for the sugar of rate cuts, but it is the sole responsibility of Democrats to come up with the medicine of reform by proposing revenues to pay for the rate cuts. When I asked Norquist about coming up with offsets to pay for tax reform, he told me, "I recommend taking the corporate rate to 25 percent. The Dems can suggest tax hikes if they believe they need to 'make up' revenue. That is a bipartisan division of labor."

The political trap is obvious. Any reform that would increase revenue will be attacked by Republicans as a tax increase. They will send out fundraising letters to the affected group or industry requesting campaign donations to prevent the Democrats from increasing its taxes. They will not mention that the reforms would be coupled with tax rate reductions in a revenue-neutral manner that neither raises nor lowers net tax revenue in the aggregate. Unfortunately this strategy will doom any hope of tax reform.

I have questioned a number of Republican tax experts on whether they would name a single existing tax preference worth abandoning. None were forthcoming. The only reform any of them would name is cutting tax rates, although all proclaimed they were willing to replace the entire tax system with some comprehensive, idyllic reform with zero chance of enactment.

This was not always the Republicans' philosophy. Back in the 1980s they were willing to repeal specific tax preferences to pay for tax rate reductions. My old boss Rep. Jack Kemp (R-NY) teamed up with Sen. Bob Kasten (R-WI) on a tax reform plan that would have gotten rid of the Investment Tax Credit and most other tax credits, the deduction for state and local income and sales taxes, the deduction for consumer interest, and other politically popular provisions of the tax code at that time.

Subsequently Ronald Reagan endorsed many of the reforms in the Kemp-Kasten bill, as well as others, and sent a proposal to Congress in May 1985 that embodied both base-broadening reforms—tax increases, in other words—and tax rate cuts in a revenue-neutral package. Today's Republicans, it seems, don't have Reagan's wisdom, courage, or fortitude. They want only what's politically popular, especially with the Tea Party crowd.

TAX REFORM ENDGAME

One would think that an organization allegedly dedicated to tax reform, such as Americans for Tax Reform, would be vigilant about opposing the inclusion of new tax loopholes in the tax code. But ATR never opposes any tax reduction measure, no matter how narrowly focused the benefits are, no matter how thinly justified the measure is as a matter of policy, no matter how closely it resembles pure spending. When I asked ATR's Ryan Ellis if he could name one loophole that ATR had ever opposed, he could not.

Throughout 2011 Sen. Tom Coburn (R-OK), one of the most conservative members of Congress, tried to get Norquist and ATR to admit that tax subsidies for ethanol are no different from a direct subsidy for ethanol. But Norquist refused to bend. All tax cuts are good, even if they just subsidize one particular product, he said, and any effort to get rid of a tax subsidy, no matter how egregious, is a tax increase that violates the pledge. And members of the Tea Party stand ready to oppose in the primaries any Republican violating the pledge. The Club for Growth, a large political action committee dedicated to supporting all tax cuts and opposing all tax increases, will have an open checkbook for any challenger to a tax pledge violator. Coburn is immune from the usual political threats because he has already announced his retirement at the end of his current term.

But there is still the interesting question of how to handle the expiration of the Bush tax cuts. Norquist has said that doing nothing and allowing them to expire would not violate the pledge, as it doesn't involve a vote to raise taxes. Nor would a vote against legislation extending them be a violation of the pledge. However, Norquist personally and ATR as an organization support extending the Bush tax cuts forever, as they did at the end of 2010, warning that failure to do so will constitute the biggest tax increase in history. It is doubtful that members of the Tea Party will care that the pledge has not technically been violated if Norquist opposes any tax measure that looks like a tax increase.

It remains theoretically possible that in lieu of extending the Bush tax cuts, some substitute tax measure could be enacted that would pass muster with ATR, but it is hard to imagine Norquist supporting one that didn't cut taxes by an amount equal to the revenue cost of the Bush tax cuts. There is no reason for Republicans to support any actual tax reform measure and run the risk of being labeled tax increasers and pledge violators.

The success or failure of tax reform lies in the hands of Grover Norquist. If he relents and allows meaningful reforms that raise revenues to be discussed openly among Republicans as part of a package that also cuts rates—exactly as Reagan did in 1986—there is hope for success. But if he continues to hold the view that all tax reforms must come from the Democrats and that no Republican dare support a revenue raiser under threat of a primary challenge, the prospects for tax reform are bleak.

FURTHER READINGS

Barro, Robert J. "The Ricardian Approach to Budget Deficits." *Journal of Economic Perspectives* (Spring 1989): 37–54.

Bartlett, Bruce. "'Starve the Beast': Origins and Development of a Budgetary Metaphor." *Independent Review* (Summer 2007): 5–26.

Brown, Carrie Budoff. "Norquist, Coburn Duel over Tax Hikes." *Politico* (Mar. 8, 2011).

Congressional Research Service. "The Impact of Major Legislation on Budget Deficits: 2001 to 2009." Report No. R41134 (Mar. 23, 2010).

Gale, William G., and Brennan Kelly. "The 'No New Taxes' Pledge." *Tax Notes* (July 12, 2004): 197–209.

Gerson, Michael. "A Pledge Too Costly?" *Washington Post* (June 10, 2011).

Hohmann, James. "Daniels Open to VAT, Oil Tax Hike." *Politico* (Oct. 15, 2010).

Hohmann, James. "VAT Remarks Double the Trouble for Daniels." *Politico* (Oct. 16, 2010).

Horowitz, Jason. "Taxes Hold'em." *Washington Post* (July 13, 2011).

Judge, Clark. "10 Tips for the GOP in 2010." *Wall Street Journal* (Jan. 10, 2010).

Kumhof, Michael, Douglas Laxton, and Daniel Leigh. "To Starve or Not to Starve the Beast?" International Monetary Fund Working Paper WP/10/199 (Sept. 2010).

Montgomery, Lori. "For GOP, Anti-Tax Orthodoxy Goes Deep." *Washington Post* (June 6, 2011).

Niskanen, William A. "Limiting Government: The Failure of 'Starve the Beast.'" *Cato Journal* (Fall 2006): 553–58.

Norquist, Grover G. "Read My Lips: No New Taxes." *New York Times* (July 22, 2011).

Rojas, Warren. "Norquist Sees Antitax Crusade as Cornerstone of GOP Dominance." *Tax Notes* (Jan. 19, 2004): 307–17.

Romer, Christina D., and David H. Romer. "Do Tax Cuts Starve the Beast? The Effect of Tax Changes on Government Spending." *Brookings Papers on Economic Activity* (Spring 2009): 139–200.

Wolf, Frank R. "Standing Up to the Anti-Tax Bully." *Washington Post* (May 13, 2011).

Conclusion

What is so far lacking in the tax reform effort is a compelling reason to enact any actual reforms, as opposed to cutting taxes again or just extending the Bush tax cuts for another year or two. Unfortunately political tactics are also a barrier to a deal. With 2012 being a presidential election year, both parties would like to be on the winning side of the tax issue. But what is the winning side?

In principle, everyone favors tax reform—as long as it doesn't take away a person's own favorite deduction or credit or raise his or her taxes in any way. In principle, everyone favors tax simplification, base broadening, and lower rates. And in principle, everyone favors reducing the deficit, and a solid majority even support increasing taxes—as long as it's not their own taxes. Action before the election is unlikely because both parties will want to campaign on tax reform, hoping that the election results will strengthen their hand.

That means 2012 will probably be a year like 1984, when tax reform was a topic of discussion, and important progress was made in narrowing the issues and finding common ground. But legislative action probably won't happen until 2013 or 2014. Remember, it took two full years for final congressional action on the Tax Reform Act of 1986 after the Treasury had already done a thorough analysis and put forward a detailed proposal.

Citizens can help move the process forward by becoming educated about the nature of the tax system and forcing their elected representatives to give them detailed responses that go beyond opposition to any and all tax increases and support for any and all tax cuts. Tax reform involves trade-offs. Those who aren't willing to commit to any trade-off except in a vague, general way don't deserve to be taken seriously.

It might be that economic and political circumstances need to change to make meaningful tax reform possible. Tax reform efforts in the 1960s and 1970s were driven by revulsion for rich people who gamed the system and didn't pay their fair share. Such revulsion is not evident at this time. Even Democrats are fearful of being accused of class warfare and often have their hands out for campaign contributions from the nation's wealthy.

In the 1980s tax reform was driven by a willingness of Republicans to accept that the deficit prevented further tax cuts. This understanding imposed a hard revenue-neutrality requirement on the tax reform process that forced them to accept genuine reforms—higher taxes—in return for lower rates. It does not appear that Republicans have reached that point this time around. They still believe that the deficit problem can be dealt with on the spending side. To the extent that they are willing to even talk about higher revenues, it is only by way of some Laffer Curve miracle that will result from slashing tax rates. I see no evidence of a serious willingness to consider revenue offsets or challenge the no-tax-increase-ever orthodoxy imposed by Grover Norquist, the Tea Party, and the Club for Growth.

THE POLITICAL PRECONDITIONS FOR REFORM

I think it is possible that a Republican president and a Democratic Congress will be necessary before meaningful tax reform can be enacted. In the postwar era, every serious tax reform—in 1969, 1976, and 1986—took place when there was a Republican president and a Democratic Congress. The Tax Reform Act of 1986 is only a slight exception; there was a Republican president and Republicans controlled the Senate, but Democrats held the House of Representatives, as they had continuously since 1954. Democrats knew they had veto power and would not get rolled, so they were comfortable negotiating with Republicans. Without genuine compromise between the two parties, nothing would have happened.

The particular mix of a Republican president and a Democratic Congress may also be necessary to the ultimate resolution of the deficit problem. The reason, as Republicans will discover eventually, is that spending cannot be cut enough to get the deficit under control. The elderly will block any significant cut in entitlement programs, defense spending cannot be cut too much as long as Americans are fighting shooting wars abroad, veterans' programs are sacrosanct, and we are rapidly approaching the point where there is no domestic discretionary spending left to cut. Higher revenues will have to be a major part of a long-term deficit solution.

Democrats know this but lack the political courage or where-withal to allow a passive tax increase to take effect by refusing to extend the Bush tax cuts. They are too afraid of being attacked by Republicans as tax increasers. And it goes without saying that Republicans in Congress will never support a tax increase. Therefore it will require a Republican president—perhaps with his back against the wall in some future crisis—to support a tax increase, give cover to the Democrats, and prevent his own party from throwing up insurmountable obstacles, as was the case in 1990 when George W. Bush supported a tax increase with little support from Republicans in Congress.

However long tax reform takes, the problems of the tax code are not going away. They will only get worse over time, like a garden overrun by weeds. The longer we wait, the harder reform gets, but the more it is needed and the more beneficial the effort. Hopefully citizen action will hasten the day when substance triumphs over sound bites, when concern for the national interest takes precedence over partisanship, compromise stops being a dirty word, and standing for principle is no longer an all-purpose excuse for refusing to bargain in good faith.

Additional Readings

Below are some important works in the fields of tax policy, history, and reform that I didn't reference in the chapter readings. One should not be concerned that some of these publications appear dated. I have learned over the years that there are few ideas in the tax field that are really new, and most have been around for ages. Also, many aspects of current tax policy are built on a foundation of law and analysis that is just as relevant today as it was decades ago. I would especially recommend the works of the economists Henry Simons, Irving Fisher, and Joseph A. Pechman and the legal scholar Stanley Surrey as still worth reading for those wanting to understand the first principles of taxation.

Aaron, Henry J., and Michael J. Boskin. *The Economics of Taxation.* Brookings Institution, 1980.

Aaron, Henry J., and William G. Gale. *Economic Effects of Fundamental Tax Reform.* Brookings Institution, 1996.

Aaron, Henry J., and Joseph A. Pechman. *How Taxes Affect Economic Behavior.* Brookings Institution, 1981.

American Bar Association. *A Comprehensive Analysis of Current Consumption Tax Proposals: A Report of the ABA Section of Taxation Tax Systems Task Force.* 1997.

American Institute of Certified Public Accountants. *Flat Taxes and Consumption Taxes: A Guide to the Debate.* Dec. 1995.

Auerbach, Alan J., and Kevin A. Hassett. *Toward Fundamental Tax Reform.* American Enterprise Institute, 2005.

Auerbach, Alan J., Laurence J. Kotlikoff, and Jonathan Skinner. "The Efficiency Gains from Dynamic Tax Reform." *International Economic Review* (Feb. 1983): 81–100.

Auerbach, Alan J., and Joel Slemrod. "The Economic Effects of the Tax Reform Act of 1986." *Journal of Economic Literature* (June 1997): 589–632.

Ballard, Charles L., John B. Shoven, and John Whalley. "General Equilibrium Computations of the Marginal Welfare Costs of Taxes in the United States." *American Economic Review* (Mar. 1985): 128–38.

Ballard, Charles L., John B. Shoven, and John Whalley. "The Total Welfare Cost of the United States Tax System: A General Equilibrium Approach." *National Tax Journal* (June 1985): 125–40.

Bank, Steven A. *From Sword to Shield: The Transformation of the Corporate Income Tax, 1861 to Present.* Oxford University Press, 2010.

Bankman, Joseph, and David A. Weisbach. "The Superiority of an Ideal Consumption Tax over an Ideal Income Tax." *Stanford Law Review* (Mar. 2006): 1413–56.

Bittker, Boris I. "Tax Reform and Tax Simplification." *University of Miami Law Review* (Fall 1974): 1–20.

Blakey, Roy G. "Simplification of the Federal Income Tax." *American Economic Review* (Mar. 1928): 107–19.

Browning, Edgar K. "On the Marginal Welfare Cost of Taxation." *American Economic Review* (Mar. 1987): 11–23.

Buchanan, James M. "Tax Reform as Political Choice." *Journal of Economic Perspectives* (Summer 1987): 29–35.

Congressional Budget Office. *The Economic Effects of Comprehensive Tax Reform.* 1997.

Congressional Budget Office. *Revising the Corporate Income Tax.* May 1985.

Congressional Budget Office. *Revising the Individual Income Tax.* July 1983.

Congressional Research Service. "Consumption Taxes and the Level and Composition of Saving." Report No. RL30351 (Jan. 11, 2001).

Cordes, Joseph J., Robert D. Ebel, and Jane G. Gravelle. *The Encyclopedia of Taxation and Tax Policy.* Urban Institute, 1999.

Council of Economic Advisers. "Options for Tax Reform." *Economic Report of the President, 2005.*

Council of Economic Advisers. "Reforming the Tax Structure." *Economic Report of the President, 1954.*

Council of Economic Advisers. "Tax Policy for a Growing Economy." *Economic Report of the President, 2003.*

Cuccia, Andrew D., and Gregory A. Carnes. "Simplifying the Personal Income Tax." *Tax Notes* (June 29, 1992): 1917–25.

Dalsgaard, Thomas. "U.S. Tax Reform: An Overview of the Current Debate and Policy Options." International Monetary Fund Working Paper No. WP/05/138 (July 2005).

Diamond, John W., and George R. Zodrow. *Fundamental Tax Reform: Issues, Choices, and Implications.* MIT Press, 2008.

Eisenstein, Louis. *The Ideologies of Taxation*. Ronald Press, 1961.

Fairchild, Fred R., et al. *Tax Program for a Solvent America*. Ronald Press, 1945.

Federal Reserve Bank of Boston. *Economic Consequences of Tax Simplification*. Conference Series No. 29 (1985).

Feldstein, Martin. "On the Theory of Tax Reform." *Journal of Public Economics* (July–Aug. 1976): 77–104.

Fisher, Irving. "Income in Theory and Income Taxation in Practice." *Econometrica* (Jan. 1937): 1–55.

Fisher, Irving, and Herbert W. Fisher. *Constructive Income Taxation*. Harper, 1942.

Fox, John O. *If Americans Really Understood the Income Tax*. Westview Press, 2001.

Fried, Barbara H. "Fairness and the Consumption Tax." *Stanford Law Review* (May 1992): 961–1017.

Fullerton, Don, John B. Shoven, and John Whalley. "Replacing the U.S. Income Tax with a Progressive Consumption Tax." *Journal of Public Economics* (Feb. 1983): 3–23.

Gale, William G. "Tax Simplification: Issues and Options." *Tax Notes* (Sept. 10, 2001): 1463–83.

Goode, Richard. *The Corporation Income Tax*. John Wiley, 1951.

Goode, Richard. *The Individual Income Tax*. Brookings Institution, 1976.

Graetz, Michael J. "Implementing a Progressive Consumption Tax." *Harvard Law Review* (June 1979): 1575–661.

Graetz, Michael J. "Tax Reform Unraveling." *Journal of Economic Perspectives* (Winter 2007): 69–90.

Gravelle, Jane G. "Practical Tax Reform for a More Efficient Income Tax." *Virginia Tax Review* (Fall 2010): 389–406.

Hines, James R., Jr. "Taxing Consumption and Other Sins." *Journal of Economic Perspectives* (Winter 2007): 49–68.

Isenbergh, Joseph. "The End of Income Taxation." *Tax Law Review* (Spring 1990): 283–361.

Jensen, Erik M. "The Taxing Power, the Sixteenth Amendment, and the Meaning of 'Incomes.'" *Arizona State Law Journal* (Winter 2001): 1057–158.

Joint Committee on Taxation. "Factors Affecting the International Competitiveness of the United States." Report No. JCS-6-91 (May 30, 1991).

Jorgenson, Dale W. "The Agenda for U.S. Tax Reform." *Canadian Journal of Economics* (Apr. 1996): S649—S657.

Jorgenson, Dale W. "Efficient Taxation of Income." *Harvard Magazine* (Mar.–Apr. 2003): 31–33.

Jorgenson, Dale W., and Peter J. Wilcoxen. "The Long-Run Dynamics of Fundamental Tax Reform." *American Economic Review* (May 1997): 126–32.

Jorgenson, Dale W., and Kun-Young Yun. "Tax Reform and U.S. Economic Growth." *Journal of Political Economy* (Oct. 1990): S151—S193.

Kaldor, Nicholas. *An Expenditure Tax*. George Allen & Unwin, 1955.

Kelman, Mark. "Time Preference and Tax Equity." *Stanford Law Review* (Apr. 1983): 649–80.

Knoll, Michael S., and Thomas D. Griffith. "Taxing Sunny Days: Adjusting Taxes for Regional Living Costs and Amenities." *Harvard Law Review* (Feb. 2003): 987–1023.

Magill, Roswell. *The Impact of Federal Taxes*. Columbia University Press, 1943.

McCaffery, Edward J. "The Missing Links in Tax Reform." *Chapman Law Review* (Spring 1999): 233–52.

McCaffery, Edward J. "A New Understanding of Tax." *Michigan Law Review* (Mar. 2005): 807–938.

McCaffery, Edward J. "Tax Policy under a Hybrid Income-Consumption Tax." *Texas Law Review* (Apr. 1992): 1145–218.

McCaffery, Edward J., and James R. Hines Jr. "The Last Best Hope for Progressivity in Tax." *Southern California Law Review* (July 2010): 1031–98.

McLure, Charles E., Jr. "The Budget Process and Tax Simplification/Complication." *Tax Law Review* (Fall 1989): 25–95.

McMahon, Martin J., Jr. "Individual Tax Reform for Fairness and Simplicity: Let Economic Growth Fend for Itself." *Washington and Lee Law Review* (Spring 1993): 459–94.

New York State Bar Association Tax Section. "Simplification of the Internal Revenue Code." *Tax Notes* (Apr. 22, 2002): 575–85.

Paul, Deborah L. "The Sources of Tax Complexity: How Much Simplicity Can Fundamental Tax Reform Achieve?" *North Carolina Law Review* (Nov. 1997): 151–221.

Paul, Randolph E. *Taxation in the United States*. Little, Brown, 1954.

Pechman, Joseph A. *Comprehensive Income Taxation*. Brookings Institution, 1977.

Pechman, Joseph A. *Federal Tax Policy*, 5th ed. Brookings Institution, 1987.

Pechman, Joseph A. "The Future of the Income Tax." *American Economic Review* (Mar. 1990): 1–20.

Pechman, Joseph A. *Options for Tax Reform*. Brookings Institution, 1984.

Pechman, Joseph A. *Tax Reform and the U.S. Economy*. Brookings Institution, 1987.

Pechman, Joseph A. "Tax Reform: Theory and Practice." *Journal of Economic Perspectives* (Summer 1987): 11–28.

Pechman, Joseph A. *What Should Be Taxed: Income or Expenditure?* Brookings Institution, 1980.

Pollock, Sheldon D. *The Failure of U.S. Tax Policy.* Pennsylvania State University Press, 1996.

Rees, Thomas J. *The Politics of Taxation.* Quorum, 1980.

Roberts, Sidney I., et al. "A Report on Complexity and the Income Tax." *Tax Law Review* (1972): 325–76.

Schenk, Alan. "Radical Tax Reform for the 21st Century: The Role for a Consumption Tax." *Chapman Law Review* (Spring 1999): 133–56.

Seligman, Edwin R. A. *The Income Tax.* Macmillan, 1921.

Shaviro, Daniel. "Beyond the Pro-Consumption Tax Consensus." *Stanford Law Review* (Dec. 2007): 745–88.

Shaviro, Daniel. "Replacing the Income Tax with a Progressive Consumption Tax." *Tax Notes* (Apr. 5, 2004): 91–113.

Simons, Henry C. *Federal Tax Reform.* University of Chicago Press, 1950.

Simons, Henry C. *Personal Income Taxation.* University of Chicago Press, 1938.

Slemrod, Joel. *Do Taxes Matter? The Impact of the Tax Reform Act of 1986.* MIT Press, 1990.

Slemrod, Joel. *Does Atlas Shrug? The Economic Consequences of Taxing the Rich.* Harvard University Press, 2000.

Slemrod, Joel, and Jon Bakija. *Taxing Ourselves: A Citizen's Guide to the Great Debate over Tax Reform,* 4th ed. MIT Press, 2008.

Steuerle, C. Eugene. *Contemporary U.S. Tax Policy,* 2nd ed. Urban Institute, 2008.

Strnad, Jeff. "Taxation of Income from Capital: A Theoretical Reappraisal." *Stanford Law Review* (Apr. 1985): 1023–107.

Stuart, Charles. "Welfare Costs per Dollar of Additional Tax Revenue in the United States." *American Economic Review* (June 1984): 352–62.

U.S. Government Accountability Office. "Potential Impact of Alternative Taxes on Taxpayers and Administrators." Report No. GAO/GGD-98–37 (Jan. 1998).

U.S. Government Accountability Office. "Understanding the Tax Reform Debate: Background, Criteria, and Questions." Report No. GAO-05–1009SP (Sept. 2005).

Vickrey, William. *Agenda for Progressive Taxation.* Ronald Press, 1947.

Warren, Alvin. "The Case for an Income Tax." *University of Chicago Law Review* (Winter 1979): 370–400.

Warren Alvin. "Would a Consumption Tax Be Fairer Than an Income Tax?" *Yale Law Journal* (May 1980): 1081–124.

West, Philip R. "Across the Great Divide: A Centrist Tax Reform Proposal." *Tax Notes* (Feb. 28, 2011): 1025–51.

Wildasin, David. "R. M. Haig: Pioneer Advocate of Expenditure Taxation?" *Journal of Economic Literature* (June 1990): 649–54.

Zelenak, Lawrence. "The Theory and Practice of Tax Reform." *Michigan Law Review* (Apr. 2007): 1133–49.

Zodrow, George R., and Peter Mieszkowski. *United States Tax Reform in the 21st Century.* Cambridge University Press, 2002.

Appendix I

Federal Revenues and Outlays as a Share of GDP

Year	Revenues	Outlays	Surplus (+)/Deficit (−)	Year	Revenues	Outlays	Surplus (+)/Deficit (−)
1930	4.2	3.4	+0.8	1961	17.8	18.4	−0.6
1931	3.7	4.3	−0.6	1962	17.6	18.8	−1.3
1932	2.8	6.9	−4.0	1963	17.8	18.6	−0.8
1933	3.5	8.0	−4.5	1964	17.6	18.5	−0.9
1934	4.8	10.7	−5.9	1965	17.0	17.2	−0.2
1935	5.2	9.2	−4.0	1966	17.3	17.8	−0.5
1936	5.0	10.5	−5.5	1967	18.4	19.4	−1.1
1937	6.1	8.6	−2.5	1968	17.6	20.5	−2.9
1938	7.6	7.7	−0.1	1969	19.7	19.4	+0.3
1939	7.1	10.3	−3.2	1970	19.0	19.3	−0.3
1940	6.8	9.8	−3.0	1971	17.3	19.5	−2.1
1941	7.6	12.0	−4.3	1972	17.6	19.6	−2.0
1942	10.1	24.3	−14.2	1973	17.6	18.7	−1.1
1943	13.3	43.6	−30.3	1974	18.3	18.7	−0.4
1944	20.9	43.6	−22.7	1975	17.9	21.3	−3.4
1945	20.4	41.9	−21.5	1976	17.1	21.4	−4.2
1946	17.7	24.8	−7.2	TQ*	17.7	20.9	−3.2
1947	16.5	14.8	+1.7	1977	18.0	20.7	−2.7
1948	16.2	11.6	+4.6	1978	18.0	20.7	−2.7
1949	14.5	14.3	+0.2	1979	18.5	20.1	−1.6
1950	14.4	15.6	−1.1	1980	19.0	21.7	−2.7
1951	16.1	14.2	+1.9	1981	19.6	22.2	−2.6
1952	19.0	19.4	−0.4	1982	19.2	23.1	−4.0
1953	18.7	20.4	−1.7	1983	17.5	23.5	−6.0
1954	18.5	18.8	−0.3	1984	17.3	22.2	−4.8
1955	16.5	17.3	−0.8	1985	17.7	22.8	−5.1
1956	17.5	16.5	+0.9	1986	17.5	22.5	−5.0
1957	17.7	17.0	+0.8	1987	18.4	21.6	−3.2
1958	17.3	17.9	−0.6	1988	18.2	21.3	−3.1
1959	16.2	18.8	−2.6	1989	18.4	21.2	−2.8
1960	17.8	17.8	+0.1	1990	18.0	21.9	−3.9

Appendix I

Year	Revenues	Outlays	Surplus (+)/Deficit (–)	Year	Revenues	Outlays	Surplus (+)/Deficit (–)
1991	17.9	22.3	–4.5	2002	17.6	19.1	–1.5
1992	17.5	22.1	–4.7	2003	16.2	19.7	–3.4
1993	17.5	21.4	–3.9	2004	16.1	19.6	–3.5
1994	18.0	21.0	–2.9	2005	17.3	19.9	–2.6
1995	18.4	20.6	–2.2	2006	18.2	20.1	–1.9
1996	18.8	20.2	–1.4	2007	18.5	19.6	–1.2
1997	19.2	19.5	–0.3	2008	17.5	20.7	–3.2
1998	19.9	19.1	+0.8	2009	14.9	25.0	–10.0
1999	19.8	18.5	+1.4	2010	15.1	24.1	–9.0
2000	20.6	18.2	+2.4	2011e	15.5	24.3	–8.8
2001	19.5	18.2	+1.3	2012e	17.1	23.4	–6.1

*Historically, the federal fiscal year ran from July 1 to June 30. But in 1974 Congress changed it to run from Oct. 1 to Sept. 30, thus requiring a transition quarter between fiscal years 1976 and 1977.

Source: Office of Management and Budget.

Appendix II

Lowest and Highest Federal Income Tax Rates

Year	Lowest Bracket			Highest Bracket		
		Taxable Income Below			Taxable Income Over	
	Tax Rate	Nominal $	2010 $	Tax Rate	Nominal $	2010 $
1913	1.0	20,000	440,500	7.0	500,000	11,000,000
1914	1.0	20,000	436,100	7.0	500,000	10,900,000
1915	1.0	20,000	431,800	7.0	500,000	10,800,000
1916	2.0	20,000	400,100	15.0	2,000,000	40,000,000
1917	2.0	2,000	34,100	67.0	2,000,000	34,000,000
1918	6.0	4,000	57,800	77.0	1,000,000	14,400,000
1919	4.0	4,000	50,400	73.0	1,000,000	12,600,000
1920	4.0	4,000	43,600	73.0	1,000,000	10,900,000
1921	4.0	4,000	48,700	73.0	1,000,000	12,200,000
1922	4.0	4,000	51,900	58.0	200,000	2,600,000
1923	3.0	4,000	51,000	43.5	200,000	2,600,000
1924	1.5	4,000	51,000	46.0	500,000	6,400,000
1925	1.125	4,000	49,800	25.0	100,000	1,200,000
1926	1.125	4,000	49,300	25.0	100,000	1,200,000
1927	1.125	4,000	50,100	25.0	100,000	1,300,000
1928	1.125	4,000	51,000	25.0	100,000	1,300,000
1929	0.375	4,000	51,000	24.0	100,000	1,300,000
1930	1.125	4,000	52,200	25.0	100,000	1,300,000
1931	1.125	4,000	57,400	25.0	100,000	1,400,000
1932	4.0	4,000	63,700	63.0	1,000,000	15,900,000
1933	4.0	4,000	67,100	63.0	1,000,000	16,800,000
1934	4.0	4,000	65,100	63.0	1,000,000	16,300,000
1935	4.0	4,000	63,700	63.0	1,000,000	15,900,000
1936	4.0	4,000	62,700	79.0	5,000,000	78,400,000
1937	4.0	4,000	60,600	79.0	5,000,000	75,700,000
1938	4.0	4,000	61,900	79.0	5,000,000	77,300,000
1939	4.0	4,000	62,700	79.0	5,000,000	78,400,000
1940	4.4	4,000	62,300	81.1	5,000,000	77,900,000
1941	10.0	2,000	29,700	81.0	5,000,000	74,200,000
1942	19.0	2,000	26,800	88.0	200,000	2,700,000
1943	19.0	2,000	25,200	88.0	200,000	2,500,000
1944	23.0	2,000	24,800	94.0	200,000	2,500,000
1945	23.0	2,000	24,200	94.0	200,000	2,400,000

	Lowest Bracket			Highest Bracket		
		Taxable Income Below			Taxable Income Over	
Year	Tax Rate	Nominal $	2010 $	Tax Rate	Nominal $	2010 $
1946	19.0	2,000	22,400	86.45	200,000	2,200,000
1947	19.0	2,000	19,600	86.45	200,000	2,000,000
1948	16.6	4,000	36,200	82.13	400,000	3,600,000
1949	16.6	4,000	36,600	82.13	400,000	3,700,000
1950	17.4	4,000	36,200	84.36	400,000	3,600,000
1951	20.4	4,000	33,500	91.0	400,000	3,400,000
1952	22.2	4,000	32,900	92.0	400,000	3,300,000
1953	22.2	4,000	32,700	92.0	400,000	3,300,000
1954	20.0	4,000	32,400	91.0	400,000	3,200,000
1955	20.0	4,000	32,500	91.0	400,000	3,300,000
1956	20.0	4,000	32,100	91.0	400,000	3,200,000
1957	20.0	4,000	31,000	91.0	400,000	3,100,000
1958	20.0	4,000	30,200	91.0	400,000	3,000,000
1959	20.0	4,000	30,000	91.0	400,000	3,000,000
1960	20.0	4,000	29,500	91.0	400,000	2,900,000
1961	20.0	4,000	29,200	91.0	400,000	2,900,000
1962	20.0	4,000	28,900	91.0	400,000	2,900,000
1963	20.0	4,000	28,500	91.0	400,000	2,800,000
1964	16.0	1,000	7,000	77.0	400,000	2,800,000
1965	14.0	1,000	6,900	70.0	200,000	1,400,000
1966	14.0	1,000	6,700	70.0	200,000	1,300,000
1967	14.0	1,000	6,500	70.0	200,000	1,300,000
1968	14.0	1,000	6,300	75.25	200,000	1,300,000
1969	14.0	1,000	5,900	77.0	200,000	1,200,000
1970	14.0	1,000	5,600	71.75	200,000	1,100,000
1971	14.0	1,000	5,400	70.0	200,000	1,100,000
1972	14.0	1,000	5,200	70.0	200,000	1,000,000
1973	14.0	1,000	4,900	70.0	200,000	1,000,000
1974	14.0	1,000	4,400	70.0	200,000	885,000
1975	14.0	1,000	4,100	70.0	200,000	811,000
1976	14.0	1,000	3,800	70.0	200,000	766,000
1977	14.0	3,200	11,500	70.0	203,200	731,000
1978	14.0	3,200	10,700	70.0	203,200	680,000
1979	14.0	3,400	10,200	70.0	215,400	647,000
1980	14.0	3,400	9,000	70.0	215,400	570,000
1981	14.0	3,400	8,200	69.125	215,400	517,000
1982	12.0	3,400	7,700	50.0	85,600	193,000
1983	11.0	3,400	7,400	50.0	109,400	240,000
1984	11.0	3,400	7,100	50.0	162,400	341,000
1985	11.0	3,540	7,200	50.0	169,020	343,000
1986	11.0	3,670	7,300	50.0	175,250	349,000
1987	11.0	3,000	5,800	38.5	90,000	173,000
1988	15.0	29,750	54,800	28.0	29,750	54,800
1989	15.0	30,950	54,400	28.0	30,950	54,400
1990	15.0	32,450	54,100	28.0	32,450	54,100

Year	Lowest Bracket			Highest Bracket		
	Tax Rate	Taxable Income Below		Tax Rate	Taxable Income Over	
		Nominal $	2010 $		Nominal $	2010 $
1991	15.0	34,000	54,400	31.0	82,150	131,500
1992	15.0	35,800	55,600	31.0	86,500	134,500
1993	15.0	36,900	55,700	39.6	250,000	377,300
1994	15.0	38,000	55,900	39.6	250,000	367,800
1995	15.0	39,000	55,800	39.6	256,500	367,000
1996	15.0	40,100	55,700	39.6	263,750	366,600
1997	15.0	41,200	56,000	39.6	271,050	368,200
1998	15.0	42,350	56,700	39.6	278,450	372,500
1999	15.0	43,050	56,300	39.6	283,150	371,000
2000	15.0	43,850	55,500	39.6	288,350	365,100
2001	10.0	6,000	7,400	39.1	297,350	366,100
2002	10.0	12,000	14,500	38.6	307,050	372,200
2003	10.0	14,000	16,600	35.0	311,950	369,700
2004	10.0	14,300	16,500	35.0	319,100	368,400
2005	10.0	14,600	16,300	35.0	326,450	364,500
2006	10.0	15,100	16,300	35.0	336,550	364,000
2007	10.0	15,650	16,500	35.0	349,700	367,800
2008	10.0	16,050	16,300	35.0	357,700	362,300
2009	10.0	16,700	17,000	35.0	372,950	372,950
2010	10.0	16,750	16,750	35.0	373,650	373,650

Source: Tax Policy Center, Bureau of Labor Statistics.

Appendix III

The Personal Exemption

	Single		Married		Dependents	
Year	Nominal $	2010 $	Nominal $	2010 $	Nominal $	2010 $
1913	3,000	66,000	4,000	88,100	N/A	N/A
1914	3,000	65,400	4,000	87,200	N/A	N/A
1915	3,000	64,800	4,000	86,350	N/A	N/A
1916	3,000	60,000	4,000	80,000	N/A	N/A
1917	1,000	17,000	2,000	34,100	200	3,400
1918	1,000	14,400	2,000	28,900	200	2,900
1919	1,000	12,600	2,000	25,200	200	2,500
1920	1,000	10,900	2,000	21,800	200	2,200
1921	1,000	12,200	2,500	30,500	400	4,900
1922	1,000	13,000	2,500	32,450	400	5,200
1923	1,000	12,750	2,500	31,900	400	5,100
1924	1,000	12,750	2,500	31,900	400	5,100
1925	1,500	18,700	3,500	43,600	400	5,000
1926	1,500	18,500	3,500	43,100	400	4,900
1927	1,500	18,800	3,500	43,900	400	5,000
1928	1,500	19,100	3,500	44,600	400	5,100
1929	1,500	19,100	3,500	44,600	400	5,100
1930	1,500	19,600	3,500	45,700	400	5,200
1931	1,500	21,500	3,500	50,200	400	5,700
1932	1,000	15,900	2,500	39,800	400	6,350
1933	1,000	16,800	2,500	41,900	400	6,700
1934	1,000	16,300	2,500	40,700	400	6,500
1935	1,000	15,900	2,500	39,800	400	6,350
1936	1,000	15,700	2,500	39,200	400	6,300
1937	1,000	15,100	2,500	37,850	400	6,000
1938	1,000	15,500	2,500	38,650	400	6,200
1939	1,000	15,700	2,500	39,200	400	6,300
1940	800	12,500	2,000	31,150	400	6,200
1941	750	11,100	1,500	22,250	400	5,900
1942	500	6,700	1,200	16,050	350	4,700
1943	500	6,300	1,200	15,100	350	4,400
1944	500	6,200	1,000	12,400	500	6,200
1945	500	6,000	1,000	12,100	500	6,000
1946	500	5,600	1,000	11,200	500	5,600
1947	500	4,900	1,000	9,800	500	4,900
1948	600	5,400	1,200	10,850	600	5,400
1949	600	5,500	1,200	11,000	600	5,500
1950	600	5,400	1,200	10,850	600	5,400
1951	600	5,000	1,200	10,050	600	5,000

Year	Single		Married		Dependents	
	Nominal $	2010 $	Nominal $	2010 $	Nominal $	2010 $
1952	600	4,900	1,200	9,900	600	4,900
1953	600	4,900	1,200	9,800	600	4,900
1954	600	4,900	1,200	9,700	600	4,900
1955	600	4,900	1,200	9750	600	4,900
1956	600	4,800	1,200	9,600	600	4,800
1957	600	4,650	1,200	9,300	600	4,650
1958	600	4,500	1,200	9,050	600	4,500
1959	600	4,500	1,200	9,000	600	4,500
1960	600	4,400	1,200	8,850	600	4,400
1961	600	4,400	1.200	8,750	600	4,400
1962	600	4,300	1,200	8,650	600	4,300
1963	600	4,300	1,200	8,550	600	4,300
1964	600	4,200	1,200	8,450	600	4,200
1965	600	4,150	1,200	8,300	600	4,150
1966	600	4,000	1,200	8,100	600	4,000
1967	600	3,900	1,200	7,850	600	3,900
1968	600	3,750	1,200	7,500	600	3,750
1969	600	3,550	1,200	7,100	600	3,550
1970	625	3,500	1,250	7,000	625	3,500
1971	675	3,600	1,350	7,300	675	3,600
1972	750	3,900	1,500	7,800	750	3,900
1973	750	3,700	1,500	7,400	750	3,700
1974	750	3,300	1,500	6,650	750	3,300
1975	750	3,000	1,500	6,100	750	3,000
1976	750	2,900	1,500	5,750	750	2,900
1977	750	2,700	1,500	5,400	750	2,700
1978	750	2,500	1,500	5,000	750	2,500
1979	1,000	3,000	2,000	6,000	1,000	3,000
1980	1,000	2,650	2,000	5,300	1,000	2,650
1981	1,000	2,400	2,000	4,800	1,000	2,400
1982	1,000	2,250	2,000	4,500	1,000	2,250
1983	1,000	2,200	2,000	4,400	1,000	2,200
1984	1,000	2,100	2,000	4,200	1,000	2,100
1985	1,040	2,100	2,080	4,200	1,040	2,100
1986	1,080	2,150	2,160	4,300	1,080	2,150
1987	1,900	3,650	3,800	7,300	1,900	3,650
1988	1,950	3,600	3,900	7,200	1,950	3,600
1989	2,000	3,500	4,000	7,000	2,000	3,500
1990	2,050	3,400	4,100	6,850	2,050	3,400
1991	2,150	3,450	4,300	6,900	2,150	3,400
1992	2,300	3,600	4,600	7,150	2,300	3,600
1993	2,350	3,550	4,700	7,100	2,350	3,550
1994	2,450	3,600	4,900	7,200	2,450	3,600
1995	2,500	3,600	5,000	7,150	2,500	3,600
1996	2,550	3,550	5,100	7,100	2,550	3,550
1997	2,650	3,600	5,300	7,200	2,650	3,600
1998	2,700	3,600	5,400	7,200	2,700	3,600
1999	2,750	3,600	5,500	7,200	2,750	3,600
2000	2,800	3,550	5,600	7,100	2,800	3,550
2001	2,900	3,550	5,800	7,100	2,900	3,550
2002	3,000	3,600	6,000	7,300	3,000	3,600
2003	3,050	3,600	6,100	7,200	3,050	3,600

Year	Single		Married		Dependents	
	Nominal $	2010 $	Nominal $	2010 $	Nominal $	2010 $
2004	3,100	3,600	6,200	7,200	3,100	3,600
2005	3,200	3,600	6,400	7,150	3,200	3,600
2006	3,300	3,600	6,600	7,150	3,300	3,600
2007	3,400	3,600	6,800	7,150	3,400	3,600
2008	3,500	3,550	7,000	7,100	3,500	3,550
2009	3,650	3,700	7,300	7,400	3,650	3,700
2010	3,650	3,650	7,300	7,300	3,650	3,650

Source: Tax Policy Center, Bureau of Labor Statistics.

Appendix IV

Average and Marginal Federal Income Tax Rates for Four-Person Families at the Same Relative Position in the Income Distribution

Year	Median Income	Half Median Income		Median Income		Twice Median Income	
		Average	Marginal	Average	Marginal	Average	Marginal
1955	4,919	0.00	0.00	5.64	20.00	10.76	22.00
1956	5,319	0.00	0.00	6.38	20.00	11.22	22.00
1957	5,488	0.00	0.00	6.65	20.00	11.40	22.00
1958	5,685	0.00	0.00	6.96	20.00	11.59	22.00
1959	6,070	0.00	0.00	7.49	20.00	11.93	22.00
1960	6,295	0.15	20.00	7.77	20.00	12.11	22.00
1961	6,437	0.40	20.00	7.94	20.00	12.22	22.00
1962	6,756	1.19	20.00	8.30	20.00	12.44	26.00
1963	7,138	1.95	20.00	8.68	20.00	12.85	26.00
1964	7,488	2.06	16.00	7.56	18.00	11.66	23.50
1965	7,800	2.16	14.00	7.09	17.00	11.12	22.00
1966	8,341	2.72	14.00	7.48	19.00	11.50	22.00
1967	8,994	3.32	15.00	8.00	19.00	11.89	22.00
1968	9,834	4.03	15.00	9.21	20.42	13.37	26.88
1969	10,623	4.58	15.00	9.92	20.90	14.24	27.50
1970	11,165	4.65	15.00	9.35	19.48	13.47	25.62
1971	12,176	4.73	15.00	9.27	19.00	13.45	28.00
1972	12,808	4.37	15.00	9.09	19.00	13.52	28.00
1973	13,710	4.88	16.00	9.45	19.00	14.05	28.00
1974	14,969	4.17	16.00	8.99	22.00	14.35	33.00
1975	15,848	4.12	27.00	9.62	22.00	14.86	32.00
1976	17,315	4.68	17.00	9.89	22.00	15.51	32.00
1977	18,723	3.61	17.00	10.42	22.00	16.40	36.00
1978	20,428	4.73	19.00	11.07	25.00	17.38	39.00
1979	22,512	5.11	16.00	10.84	24.00	17.20	37.00
1980	24,332	6.02	18.00	11.42	24.00	18.25	43.00
1981	26,274	6.82	17.78	11.79	23.70	19.11	42.46
1982	27,619	6.51	16.00	11.06	25.00	18.01	39.00

Appendix IV

Year	Median Income	Half Median Income		Median Income		Twice Median Income	
		Average	Marginal	Average	Marginal	Average	Marginal
1983	29,181	6.53	15.00	10.38	23.00	16.83	35.00
1984	31,097	6.50	14.00	10.25	22.00	16.62	38.00
1985	32,777	6.56	14.00	10.34	22.00	16.78	38.00
1986	34,716	6.64	14.00	10.48	22.00	17.04	38.00
1987	37,086	5.16	15.00	8.90	15.00	15.80	35.00
1988	39,051	5.17	15.00	9.30	15.00	15.21	28.00
1989	40,763	5.29	15.00	9.36	15.00	15.28	28.00
1990	41,451	5.12	15.00	9.33	15.00	15.10	28.00
1991	43,052	5.04	15.00	9.30	15.00	15.03	28.00
1992	44,251	4.55	28.14	9.18	15.00	14.79	28.00
1993	45,161	4.35	28.93	9.18	15.00	14.73	28.00
1994	47,012	3.35	32.68	9.17	15.00	14.79	28.00
1995	49,687	3.52	35.22	9.28	15.00	15.04	28.00
1996	51,518	2.92	36.06	9.33	15.00	15.13	28.00
1997	53,350	3.09	36.06	9.32	15.00	15.16	28.00
1998	56,061	1.02	36.06	7.98	15.00	14.69	33.00
1999	59,981	2.15	36.06	7.88	15.00	15.27	33.00
2000	62,670	2.93	15.00	8.02	15.00	15.68	33.00
2001	63,278	−0.11	36.06	6.71	15.00	14.94	33.00
2002	62,372	−2.23	21.06	6.53	15.00	14.16	32.00
2003	65,093	−4.20	21.06	5.34	15.00	12.46	30.00
2004	66,111	−4.27	31.06	5.38	15.00	12.51	30.00
2005	70,312	−3.44	31.06	5.69	15.00	13.11	30.00
2006	73,415	−2.79	31.06	5.85	15.00	13.42	30.00
2007	75,675	−2.79	31.06	5.93	15.00	13.53	25.00
2008	76,470	−8.33	31.06	3.54	15.00	12.35	30.00
2009	74,406	−9.10	31.06	4.47	15.00	12.35	30.00
2010	76,502	−8.04	31.06	4.68	15.00	12.64	27.00

Note: The median is the exact middle of the income distribution, with half of families above and half below. Minus sign indicates a negative tax liability, that is, a zero income tax liability plus a government refund due to refundable tax credits. High marginal tax rates on those with half the median income in the 1990s and 2000s reflect the phaseout of the Earned Income Tax Credit. The median income for four-person families is higher than the median for the population as a whole.

Source: Tax Policy Center.

Appendix V

Capital Gains and Taxes Paid on Capital Gains (millions of dollars)

Year	Total Realized Capital Gains	Taxes Paid on Capital Gains	Average Effective Tax Rate	Realized Gains as a Percent of GDP	Maximum Tax Rate on Long-Term Gains
1954*	7,157	1,010	14.1	1.88	25.00
1955	9,881	1,465	14.8	2.38	25.00
1956	9,683	1,402	14.5	2.21	25.00
1957*	8,110	1,115	13.7	1.76	25.00
1958*	9,440	1,309	13.9	2.02	25.00
1959	13,137	1,920	14.6	2.59	25.00
1960*	11,747	1,687	14.4	2.23	25.00
1961*	16,001	2,481	15.5	2.94	25.00
1962	13,451	1,954	14.5	2.30	25.00
1963	14,579	2,143	14.7	2.36	25.00
1964	17,431	2,482	14.2	2.63	25.00
1965	21,484	3,003	14.0	2.99	25.00
1966	21,348	2,905	13.6	2.71	25.00
1967	27,535	4,112	14.9	3.31	25.00
1968	35,607	5,943	16.7	3.91	26.90
1969*	31,439	5,275	16.8	3.19	27.50
1970*	20,848	3,161	15.2	2.01	32.21
1971	28,341	4,350	15.3	2.52	34.25
1972	35,869	5,708	15.9	2.90	36.50
1973*	35,757	5,366	15.0	2.59	36.50
1974*	30,217	4,253	14.1	2.02	36.50
1975*	30,903	4,534	14.7	1.89	35.50
1976	39,492	6,621	16.8	2.16	39.875
1977	45,338	8,232	18.2	2.23	39.875
1978	50,526	9,104	18.0	2.20	39.875/33.85

Year	Total Realized Capital Gains	Taxes Paid on Capital Gains	Average Effective Tax Rate	Realized Gains as a Percent of GDP	Maximum Tax Rate on Long-Term Gains
1979	73,443	11,753	16.0	2.87	28.00
1980*	74,132	12,459	16.8	2.66	28.00
1981*	80,938	12,852	15.9	2.59	28.00/20.00
1982*	90,153	12,900	14.3	2.77	20.00
1983	122,773	18,700	15.2	3.47	20.00
1984	140,500	21,453	15.3	3.57	20.00
1985	171,985	26,460	15.4	4.08	20.00
1986	327,725	52,914	16.1	7.35	20.00
1987	148,449	33,714	22.7	3.13	28.00
1988	162,592	38,866	23.9	3.19	28.00
1989	154,040	35,258	22.9	2.81	28.00
1990*	123,783	27,829	22.5	2.13	28.00
1991*	111,592	24,903	22.3	1.86	28.93
1992	126,692	28,983	22.9	2.00	28.93
1993	152,259	36,112	23.7	2.28	29.19
1994	152,727	36,243	23.7	2.16	29.19
1995	180,130	44,254	24.6	2.43	29.19
1996	260,696	66,396	25.5	3.33	29.19
1997	364,829	79,305	21.7	4.38	29.19/21.19
1998	455,223	89,069	19.6	5.18	21.19
1999	552,608	111,821	20.2	5.91	21.19
2000	644,285	127,297	19.8	6.47	21.19
2001*	349,441	65,668	18.8	3.40	21.17
2002	268,615	49,122	18.3	2.52	21.16
2003	323,306	51,340	15.9	2.90	21.05/16.05
2004	499,154	73,213	14.7	4.21	16.05
2005	690,152	102,174	14.8	5.46	16.05
2006	798,214	117,793	14.8	5.96	15.70
2007*	861,220	121,933	14.2	6.12	15.70

*Recession years.

Note: The maximum effective tax rate is affected by the Alternative Minimum Tax and other tax provisions.

Sources: Treasury Department; National Bureau of Economic Research.

Index

NOTE: Bold page numbers refer to tables.

adjusted gross income (AGI), 35, 40, 127, 157, **157**, 168
administration, tax, 155–63, 179–80, 203. *See also* collection, tax
Affordable Care Act, 92, 97, 102
"agency problem," 143
Alesina, Alberto, 76
Alternative Minimum Tax (AMT), **36**, 119, 120, 181, 203
American Action Forum, 220
American Enterprise Institute, 230
American Recovery and Reinvestment Act (2009), **220**
American Rights Litigators, 158
Americans for Tax Reform, 225, 232, 233
amnesty, tax, 159–60
Anderson, Martin, 45
Andrews, William D., 169
Archer, Bill, 172
audits, tax, 156, 160
Auerbach, Alan, 68
Australia, 77, 79, **93**, 110, **150**, 201, 210, **211**
Austria, **79**, **93**, 128, **150**, **211**
average tax rate. *See* effective tax rate
avoidance, tax, 62–63, 158, 160

Bachmann, Michele, 49
Bank Bailout Bill (2008), **216**
Barr, Joseph W., 168
Barrasso, John, 229
Barro, Robert, 229
behavioral economics, 41–44, 45, 71
Belgium, 75, **93**, **150**, **211**
Bennett, Robert, 230–31
Blinder, Alan, 69
"Blueprints" study, Treasury Department's, 168–69
Blumenthal, Michael, 136, 169
bonds, 34, 115, 119–21, 191
Boskin, Michael, 216
Bowles, Erskine, 181
Bradford, David, 94, 168

Bradley, Bill, 171–72
Brookings Institution, 179
Buckley, William F., 170
budget: balanced, 90, 120, 170, 189; Bush tax cuts and, 216, 217–18; discretionary, 185, 186; history of tax reform and, 170; long-term forecasts about, 185; mandatory spending and, 185; need for more revenue and, 189; and revenue as negative spending, 87; semantics about, 94–95; surplus, 180, 216, 217–18, 220, **220**, 228; and tax expenditures budget, 167–69; tax loopholes and, 90; tax reform proposals and, 180. *See also* deficit, budget
Budget Committee, U.S. Senate, 46, 218
Burman, Len, 40
Bush, George H.W., 9, 91, 137, 152, 217, 227, 237
Bush, George W.: and budget surplus as dangerous, 10; business cycles and, 69–70; capital gains and, 138; corporate taxes and, 149; elections of 2000 and, 10, 217, 218; history of tax reform and, 172; and impact of federal taxes on state and local government, 118; refundable tax credits and, 91; Social Security and, 181; tax cuts of, 10, 44, 45–46, 55, 186, 187, 215–24, **216**, **219**, 227, 233, 235, 237; tax legislative process and, 17; tax rebates and, 69–70; tax reform commission of, 180–81
business cycles, 67–74
businesses: Bush tax cuts and, **219**, 221; and business cycle, 67–74; deductions for, 177; FairTax and, 179; flat tax and, 176, 178; foreign taxes and, 80; forms of, 146; interest deductions and, 108; need for more revenue and, 191; progressive taxation and, 62; savings by, 51; spending by, 70; tax administration and, 159; tax rebates and, 70; tax reform proposals and, 181–82; and time period over which to tax people, 25; VAT and, 177, 203. *See also* corporations

Cailleteau, Pierre, 187

Cain, Herman, 181–82

California: Proposition 13 in, 169, 170

Canada, 77, **93**, 110, **150**, 151, 156, 201, 203, 210, **211**

capital consumption allowances, 148

capital gains: business cycles and, 72; Clinton administration and, 227–28; corporate taxes and, 144; death and, 133, 140; definition of income and, 22, 23, 24; distribution by income of, **139**; economic growth and, 51, 53–54; fairness and, 134, 137, 140; flat tax and, 176; foreign taxes and, 77, 80; GDP and, 136, 137, 138; on home sales, 107; horizontal equity and, 88; as income, 133–34; inflation and, 133, 135–36; in 1940s and 1950s, 54; Norquist role in tax reform and, 227, 228; on owner-occupied housing, 111–12; problem of taxing, 133–42; progressive taxation and, 61; as regular income, 137–39; revenue and, 72, 134, 136–38, 139; tax cuts and, 136–38, 219, 227; tax history of, 134–36; tax rates and, 35, 54, 134, 135, 136, 137–38, 139, 140, 169; tax reform and, 138, 139–40, 168, 169, 170; unrealized, 133

capital losses, 51, 88, 134, 135

"carried interest," 140

Carroll, Robert, 46

Carter, Jimmy, 13, 136, 169

"cascading," 179, 198, 199, 200

Chambliss, Saxby, 226

charitable contributions, 35, 123–31, 177, 217, 231

cheating, tax, 156

Cheney, Dick, 90, 214

child tax credit, **36**, 91, 217, 218

citizens: role in tax reform of, 235

citizenship, 63, 81

Civil War, 4, **5**, 22, 133, 147

class warfare: future of tax reform and, 236

Clinton, Bill, 9–10, 91, 137, 217, 227–28

Club for Growth, 232–33, 236

Coburn, Tom, 226, 232, 233

Cogan, John, 216

collection, tax, 155–57, 178, 179, 198, 199, 203

compliance, tax, 157–58, 159–61, 199

conference committees, 16–17

Congress, U.S.: attendance at hearings before, 15–16; Bush tax cuts and, 217, 218; business cycles and, 68, 70, 72; capital gains and, 134–35, 136, 137, 138, 139, 140; charitable contributions and, 128; corporate taxes and, 145, 148, 149, 208; debt limit and, 189; deductions and, 111; definition of income and, 24, 26, 27; distribution tables and, 26, 27; elections of 1994 and, 227–28; future of tax reform and, 236–37; health care and, 100–101, 102, 103; history of tax reform and, 167, 168, 169, 171, 172; housing and, 107, 111–12; ITC and, 68; mandatory spending and, 185; need for more revenue and, 185, 187, 190, 193; R&D investments and, 55; revenue estimating and, 40–41; revenue volatility and, 72; Social Security taxes and, 102; spending and, 190; tax administration and, 157; tax experts staff of, 14; tax legislation process and, 13–18; tax rebates and, 70; tax subsidies enacted by, 54; taxing powers of, 207–8; VAT and, 209, 210; witnesses before, 15–16. *See also* House of Representatives, U.S.; Senate, U.S.; *specific person or committee*

Congressional Budget and Impoundment Control Act (1974), 168

Congressional Budget Office (CBO): budget surplus projections of, **220**; and Bush (George H.W.) tax increases, 227; Bush (George W.) tax cuts and, 187, 220, 221; business cycle and, 71; health care and, 102–3; inflation estimates of, 188; long-term budget forecasts of, 185–86; and relationship of tax rates and revenue, 40–41, 42, 43, 46; revenue estimations of, 40–41, 42, 43, 46; tax rebates and, 71; tax reform proposals and, 181; VAT and, 203

Congressional Research Service, 102, 134, 138, 221

conservatives: capital gains and, 138, 139; and "compassionate conservatism," 217; corporate taxes and, 150, 151, 152; and economic growth in foreign countries versus U.S., 78; health care and, 100, 101; history of federal income taxation and, 9, 10; history of tax reform and, 167, 168–69, 170–72; and impact of taxes on economic growth, 49, 51; and need for more revenue, 189–93; Norquist role in tax reform and, 226, 229, 232;

progressivity and, 59, 62, 63, 64; and relationship between tax rates and tax revenues, 39, 41, 45; spending and, 81, 94; tax administration and, 156; tax credits and, 92; tax reform proposals and, 182; VAT and, 197, 200, 201–2, 210, 213; and welfare states, 81. *See also specific person*

Consolidated Omnibus Budget Reconciliation Act (1985), **45**

Constitution, U.S., 3, 5, 13, 76. *See also specific amendment*

consumer spending, 32, 67, 69, 118

consumption-based tax system, 168–69, 170, 178, 182. *See also* flat tax; value-added tax

consumption/consumption tax: conspicuous, 64; corporate taxes and, 152; definition of income and, 23, 24, 27–28; economic growth and, 54; FairTax and, 180; foreign taxes and, 78, **78**, 79, 81; of health care, 99–100; history of tax reform and, 168–69, 170, 171; home equity loans and, 109; income over lifetime and, 213; Norquist role in tax reform and, 225; progressive taxation and, 64; revenue volatility and, 72; savings as forgoing, 50; Sixteenth Amendment and, 208; tax rebates and, 69; tax reform and, 180, 181. *See also specific tax*

Continuing Resolution (1987), **45**

Continuing Resolution (1988), **45**

Coolidge, Calvin, 6, 10

corporations: beginning of taxing of, 147–49; broadening of tax base for, 152; Bush tax cuts and, 219; buybacks by, 144, 219; "C," 143, 146; capital gains and, 53–54; compensation in, 62, 143; debt of, 162; deductions for, 143; depreciation and, 147–49; double taxation and, 143, 144–46, 150, 208; economic growth and, 53–54; flat tax and, 176, 208; foreign taxes and, 78, 150, **150**, 151; inflation and, 148; investments and, 144, 145, **145**, 148–49; Norquist views about, 231; Norquist's role in tax reform and, 226; "privatization" of taxes on, 152; progressive taxation and, 61, 62; revenue and, 146, 151–52; S–, 146; shareholders and, 143, 144, 150; takeovers and mergers by, 144; tax administration and, 160; tax holidays for, 151; tax loopholes

and, 151; tax rates for, 53–54, 143, 144–45, **145**, 150, 151, 226, 231; tax reform and, 145–46, 149, 151–52, 160, 168, 169, 170, 181; unresolved issues concerning, 143–54; VAT and, 200, 203, 226; where to tax, 149–51

Council of Economic Advisors, President's, 41, 43–44, 45–46, 70, 229

Crapo, Mike, 226

credits, tax: business cycle and, 71; charitable contributions and, 127; definition of income and, 26, 27; distribution tables and, 26, 27, 91; first-time home buyer, 112; flat tax and, 176, 177; foreign taxes and, 76–77; health care and, 99–100, 103; housing and, 111; Norquist role in tax reform and, 225, 232; problems with, 91–92; R&D, 55; refundable, 90–92, 94, 99–100, 103; and relationship of tax rates and revenue, 42; spending and, 88, 90–92; tax rates and, 35; tax rebates versus, 71; tax reform and, 91–92, 170, 176, 177, 235; VAT and, 199, 200. *See also specific credit*

Cuomo, Mario, 118

cuts, tax: budget semantics and, 95; Bush, 10, 44, 45–46, 55, 186, 187, 215–24, **216**, **219**, 227, 233, 235, 237; business cycles and, 69, 71, 72, 73; capital gains and, 136–38; definition of income and, 27; distribution tables and, 27; economic growth and, 49, 55; flat tax and, 175, 177; impact of federal taxes on state and local government and, 120; impact of taxes on economic growth and, 49; Kennedy, 8–9; Norquist and, 225–30, 231, 232–33; Reagan, 9–10, 44–45, 215, 232, 233; relationship of tax rates and revenue and, 41–46; revenue and, 39, 72, 73; spending and, 8, 49, 52, 91, 217, 220, 221; tax credits and, 68, 91; tax loopholes and, 90; tax rebates and, 69, 71; tax reform and, 39, 167, 169–70, 171, 172, 175, 177, 180, 225–30, 231, 232–33, 235, 236, 237; Truman, 215. *See also specific legislation*

Czech Republic, **93**, 210, **211**

Daniels, Mitch, 226

day care, 79

deadweight cost: VAT and, 197–98, 202, 203, 210

debt, corporate, 144, 162

debt, national: Bush tax cuts and, 217, 220, 221; business cycles and, 72; default on, 189, 191, 193; "financial repression" and, 191; GDP and, 186–87; history of federal income taxes and, 7–8; inflation and, 188–89; interest on, 185, 186–87; mandatory spending and, 185, 186; maturity of, 188; need for more revenue and, 185–90, 191, 193; in 1940s, 7–8; Norquist role in tax reform and, 229; ownership of, 188–89; raising of limit on, 189; revenue volatility and, 72; risk, 186–87; sustainability of, 186–87; VAT and, 203

debt, personal, 70

debt, sovereign, 186

"declining marginal utility" principle, 61–62

deductions: alternative minimum tax and, 119; capital gains and, 135; corporate taxes and, 143; flat tax and, 110, 176, 177–78; health care and, 97, 100–101, 103; horizontal equity and, 88; and impact of revenue on tax reform, 40; itemizing of, 35, 40, 100, 108, 119, 123, **124**, 127; Norquist organization and, 225; progressive taxation and, 60; refundable tax credits and, 91; standard, 108, 181; tax rates and, 35; tax reform and, 167, 170, 181, 235. *See also type of deduction*

defense, 79, 185, 236

Defense Department, U.S., 62, 94

deficit, budget: Bush tax cuts and, 10, 220, 222; business cycles and, 69, 72; CBO projections about, **220**; Clinton administration and, 10; economic growth and, 49, 52; history of federal income taxes and, 8, 9, 10; Kennedy tax cut and, 8; Keynesian economics and, 9; need for more revenue and, 190, 191, 192, **192–93**; Norquist role in tax reform and, 226–29; public opinion about, 192, **192–93**, 229; relationship of tax rates and revenue and, 41; revenue as negative spending and, 87; revenue volatility and, 72; tax loopholes and, 90; tax rebates and, 69; tax reform and, 170, 171, 172, 181, 235, 236–37; VAT and, 201, 207, 210, 213, 214

Deficit Reduction Act (1984), **45**

Democrats: AMT and, 119; Bush tax cuts and, 217, 218; capital gains and, 136, 137; future of tax reform and, 235–37;

health care and, 92; history of federal income taxation and, 4, 5, 10; history of tax reform and, 169, 172; need for compromise between Republicans and, 236–37; and need for more revenue, 185; Norquist role in tax reform and, 226, 227, 230, 231, 233; tax credits and, 91. *See also specific person*

Denmark, 75, 77, 81, 93, **93**, **150**, **211**

depreciation, 52, 147–49, 168, 176, 178

distribution tables, 25–28, 91

dividends: Bush tax cuts and, 219; corporate taxes and, 143, 144, 145, 208; definition of income and, 23; flat tax and, 176; foreign taxes and, 77, 80; progressive taxation and, 61, 62; tax rates and, 35, 145, **150**

Dole, Bob, 180

Domenici, Pete, 180

Dorgan, Byron, 201

double taxation, 143, 144–46, 150, 169, 208

drafting errors, 16

dual income tax, 80

"dynamic" effects. *See* "feedback" effects

dynamic scoring, 42–44

Earned Income Tax Credit (EITC), 26, 35, 36, **36**, 90–91, 158, 160, 212

economic growth: basic government functions necessary for, 49–50; Bush tax cuts and, 55, 216, 218, 219, 221, 222; business cycles and, 68, 69, 71; capital gains and, 51, 53–54, 134, 138; debt/GDP ratio and, 186; foreign taxes and, 78–79, **79**; housing deductions and, 109; impact of revenue on tax reform and, 39; impact of taxes on, 49–57; investments and, 50–53, 54, 55, 68; labor supply and, 50, 53; lack of permanence in tax code and, 55; long-term interest rates and, 186; mandatory spending and, 186; need for more revenue and, 186, 191, 193; progressive taxation and, 64; savings and, 50–53; spending and, 49, 52; subsidies and, 54; tax increases and, 49, 52; tax rebates and, 69, 71; VAT and, 201

Economic Growth and Tax Relief Reconciliation Act (2001), **216**, **220**

Economic Recovery Tax Act (1981), 170

Economic Stimulus Act (2008), **216**, **220**

economy: impact of Bush tax cuts on, 219–20; impact of government on, 87,

94, 95; impact of taxes on, 67. *See also* economic growth

education, 50, 118, 123, 124

effective tax rate: calculation of, 32; capital gains and, 137; corporate taxes and, 144–45, **145**, 150, 151; flat tax and, 176; foreign taxes and, 76, 77; importance of, 32–33; labor supply and, 36–38; overestimation of, 33; progressive taxation and, 61; tax reform and, 38, 95, 167; taxable income and, 36; variation in, 89–90, **90**; wealthy and, 33–34, **34**

Eisenhower, Dwight D., 8

elderly, 79, 111–12, 190, 236

elections of 1994, 227–28

elections of 1996, 172, 217

elections of 2000, 10, 217, 218

elections of 2008, 99, 172, 207

elections of 2012, 10, 235

Ellis, Ryan, 232

employment-based health care, 24, 35, 92, 97–100, 103, 176, 230

employment/unemployment, 37, 109, 191, 216, 218, 219, **219**

energy, 13, 54, 81, 232

Energy Department, U.S., 41

entitlements, 226. *See also* Medicare; Social Security

environmental taxes, 80–81

estate taxes, 61, 217, 218

ethanol tax subsidies, 232

European Union, 200, 203

evasion, tax, 63, 156–57, 158, 159–60, 161, 178, 198, 209

excise taxes, 6, 103, 197, 212

exclusions: flat tax and, 176; on gains on home sales, 111–12; health care, 97–99, 103; history of tax reform and, 167; progressive taxation and, 60; spending and, 88. *See also specific exclusion*

exemptions: FairTax and, 179; flat tax and, 177; hidden American welfare state and, 92; history of tax reform and, 170; personal, 35, 60, 61, 64, 119, 171, 176, 177, 180, 181; progressive taxation and, 60; refundable tax credits and, 91; spending and, 88, 92; VAT and, 202, 209

expenditures. *See* expenditures, tax; spending

expenditures, tax, 88, 94–95, 102, 167–69

fairness: Bush tax cuts and, 217; capital gains and, 134, 137, 140; cascading and, 198; charitable contributions and, 123,

127, 128; definition of income and, 24; foreign taxes and, 81; health care and, 100; history of federal income taxes and, 6–7; horizontal equity and, 88; housing and, 111; means testing and, 102; mortgage interest and, 108–9; regressive tax systems and, 81; Roosevelt's proposal concerning, 6–7; Social Security and, 102; tax expenditures and, 88; tax loopholes and, 89, 90; tax reform and, 172, 236; tax unit and, 24; and time period over which to tax people, 25

FairTax, 172, 178–80, 182

federal government: business cycle and, 67; economic growth and, 51–53; functions of, 185; impact on economy of, 87, 94, 95; impact on taxes of, 87; investment by, 51–53; savings by, 51–53; size of, 95, 200; wealthy as benefiting from, 62. *See also specific topic*

Federal Reserve, U.S., 9, 67, 71, 109, 158, 188

"feedback" effects, 42, 45

Feldstein, Martin, 101, 136, 216

Fifth Amendment, 158

Finance Committee, U.S. Senate, 13, 14, 15, 17, 94, 167, 171

financial repression, 191, 193

financial sector, 51, 178, 188, 191

financial transactions tax, 71–72

Finland, 79, **93**, 110, 128, 210, **211**

First Amendment, 125, 158

Fisher, Irving, 23

501(c)(3) organizations, 127–28

flat tax: as consumption-based tax system, 182; on corporations, 208; deductions and, 110, 112; foreign taxes and, 78, 80; Hall-Rabushka plan for, 175–78; history of federal income taxation and, 4–5; history of tax reform and, 170–72; and impact of federal taxes on state and local government, 116, 118; mortgage interest deduction and, 110, 112; personal allowance, 176, 177; progressive taxation and, 60, 61; pros and cons of, 175–78; for Social Security financing, 7; support for, 171–72; tax base and, 175; tax credits and, 91–92; tax rates, 175–76; value-added tax and, 177

"flow-through" entities, 146

Forbes, Steve, 118, 172, 217

Ford, Gerald, 91, 168

forecasting, economic, 40–44

foreign countries: charities in, 128; citizenship and, 63; complexity of taxes and, 160; corporate taxes in, 78, 150, **150**, 151; economic growth in, 78–79, **79**; government services in, 75–77; health care in, 92, 93; marginal income tax rates in, 77; mortgage interest in, 110; ownership of U.S. debt by, 188–89; progressive taxation and, 63; tax administration and, 158, 159, 160; tax/GDP ratios in, 78–79; tax ideas from, 80–82; VAT and, 201, 202, 203, 210. *See also specific nation*

foreign exchange rates, 53, 72, 188, 189

401(k) plans, 23, 51, 93, 158, 169

France, 75, **77**, **93**, **150**, 151, 156, 203, 210, **211**

fraud, tax, 91

free riders, 50

Frum, David, 230

"full integration," 145

Gephardt, Dick, 172

Germany, **77**, **93**, 110, **150**, 151, 156, 203, **211**

Gingrich, Newt, 180

Giuliani, Rudolph, 118

giveaways, 17

Glaeser, Edward, 76

gold standard, 67

Goolsbee, Austan, 68

government. *See* federal government; local government; states

Government Accountability Office, U.S., 185

Graetz, Michael, 159, 203

Great Britain, 110, 134, 156. *See also* United Kingdom

Great Depression, 6, 67

Great Recession, 109

Greece, 201, **211**

Green Book (Treasury), 14

Greenspan, Alan, 217, 218

Gregg, Judd, 181

gross domestic product (GDP): Bush tax cuts and, 215, 216, 218, 219, **219**, 221; business cycles and, 68, 71; capital gains and, 136, 137, 138, 228; Clinton administration and, 228; economic growth and, 50; FairTax and, 179; foreign taxes and, 75, 76, 78–79, **79**, 81; health care and, 93; hidden American welfare state and, 93; and impact of government on economy, 87;

Medicare and, 186; national debt and, 186–87; need for more revenue and, 185, 186–87, 191; Norquist role in tax reform and, 227; revenue as share of, 4, 9, 10, 45, 197; Social Security and, 185; spending and, 92, 93, **93**, 95, 185, 190; tax rates and, 32; tax rebates and, 71; tax reform proposals and, 181; VAT and, 197, 203

gross income, 21, 26

Gruber, Jonathan, 100

Haig, Robert M., 23

Haig-Simons tax system, 24, 26, 182

Hale, David, 171

Hall-Rabushka plan, 175–78

Hall, Robert, 171, 175–76

Halperin, Daniel, 128

Hamilton, Alexander, 3, 22, 198

Harding, Warren, 6

Hatch, Orrin, 94–95, 229

Hayek, F. A., 64

health care, 97–105; charitable contributions and, 123, 124; deductions for, 97, 100–101; employment-based, 24, 35, 92, 97–100, 103, 176, 230; excessive, 99–100; exclusions for, 97–99; flat tax and, 177; in foreign countries, 92, 93; GDP and, 93; hidden American welfare state and, 92, 93; increase in coverage for, 98–99; national, 92, 93; Norquist and, 230–31; reform of, 102–3, 230–31; savings account for, 97, 100–101, 103, 230; spending and, 91, 92, 93, 97–99; tax credits and, 91, 99–100; tax rates and, 98, 100; tax reform and, 97; taxes in foreign countries and, 76, 79; wealthy and, 100, 101. *See also* Medicare

Hearst, William Randolph, 6–7

hedge funds, 140

Heritage Action for America, 126

Heritage Foundation, 44, 126, 171, 218

Highway Revenue Act (1982), **45**

Hobbes, Thomas, 168, 197–98

Holtz-Eakin, Doug, 43, 220–21

home equity, 39–40, 88–89, 109

homeland security, 185

homes. *See* housing/homes

Hoover, Herbert, 6

horizontal equity, 88–89, 95

House of Representatives, U.S., 13, 15–16. *See also* Congress, U.S.; *specific person or committee* housing/homes: bubble in, 54, 112; buying of, 191; capital gains and, 107, 111–12; downturn in prices of, 109, 110; fairness and, 111; hidden American welfare state and, 92–93; horizontal equity and, 88–89, 95; need for more revenue and, 191; ownership of, 88–89, 91, 109–11; refundable tax credits and, 91; sales of, 92, 107; spending and, 88, 92–93; tax credits and, 111; tax reform and, 107–13. *See also* mortgage interest; property taxes

Howard, John, 201

Hubbard, Glenn, 69–70

Huckabee, Mike, 172, 178

Iceland, **93, 211**

income: capital gains as, 133–34, 137–39; corporate taxes and, 151; definition of, 21–29, 61, 80, 182, 208; disposable, 32; distribution of, 64; equality in, 79; exclusion of, 34–35, 40, 51; flat tax and, 177; foreign-source, 158; foreign taxes and, 80; inequality of, 63–64; redistribution of, 63; tax rates and, 32; tax reform proposals and, 182; taxable, 34–36; transfers of, 37–38, 79, 101. *See also type of income*

"income effect," 36–37

income taxes, federal: business cycles and, 72; Civil War, 4, 5, 22, 133, 147; constitutional basis for, 3, 5; constraints on levying of, 3; dual, 80; filers paying no, **27**, 91–92, 168, 202, 212, 213, **213**; history of, 3–12, 22; 1913 Act for, 4, 5, 22, 108, 133; resistance to, 3; underreporting of, 160; VAT as way to abolish, 203. *See also specific topic*

income taxes, local, 115, 232

income taxes, state, 115, 116, 179–80, 232

increases, tax: Bush tax cuts and, 215; Clinton administration and, 227–28; economic growth and, 49, 52; flat tax and, 175, 177; and impact of federal taxes on state and local government, 120–21; need for more revenue and, 189, 190, 191, 192, **192–93**, 193; between 1982–1988, **45**; Norquist role in tax reform and, 225, 227, 228, 229–30, 231, 233; public opinion concerning, 187, 192, **192–93**, 229; of Reagan, 44, **45**, 215, 227, 232; relationship of tax rates and revenue and, 41–44; tax credits and, 92; tax reform and, 175, 177, 181, 235, 236,

237; of Truman, 215; VAT and, 201, 210, 214. *See also specific legislation*

Individual Retirement Accounts, 23, 51, 60, 93, 158

inflation: business cycles and, 68, 69; capital gains and, 133, 135–36, 139; corporate taxes and, 148; debt and, 188–89; definition of income and, 22, 24; health care and, 99, 100; history of federal income taxes and, 6, 7–9; history of tax reform and, 168, 170; Kennedy tax cut and, 8–9; need for more revenue and, 188–89, 190, 191, 193; progressive taxation and, 60; tax rates and, 35; tax rebates and, 69; VAT and, 201, 209, 210–11, 213; in World War II, 98

infrastructure, public, 79

inheritances: capital gains and, 133

interest: business cycles and, 72; caps on, 191; corporate taxes and, 152; creation of 1913 income tax and, 108; debt ratings and, 186; definition of income and, 22–23; economic growth and, 53; flat tax and, 176, 178; foreign taxes and, 80; horizontal equity and, 88, 89; and impact of revenue on tax reform, 39–40; inflation and, 188; mandatory spending and, 186; on national debt, 186–87, 188, 190, 191; need for more revenue and, 186–87, 188, 190, 191, 193; Norquist role in tax reform and, 232; progressive taxation and, 63; revenue volatility and, 72; tax rates and, 32, 35; VAT and, 201, 213. *See also type of interest*

Internal Revenue Service, U.S. (IRS): abolition of, 178; capital gains and, 133–34; corporate taxes and, 147–48, 152; data about wealthy of, 33; definition of income and, 21, 24, 26; distribution tables and, 26; FairTax and, 178; health care and, 98, 102; image of, 160; resources of, 160–61; state government and, 115; tax administration and, 155, 156, 157–58, 160–61; tax legislation process and, 14; tax rates and, 33; VAT and, 203

International Monetary Fund (IMF), 72, 187

Investment Tax Credit (ITC), 68, 148, 232

investments: Bush tax cuts and, **219**; business cycles and, 68; capital gains and, 138, 140; of charities, 128; corporate taxes and, 144, 145, **145**, 148–49; economic growth and, 50–53, 54, 55; excessive, 144; foreign, 53; foreign taxes and, 80; housing deductions and, 109;

investments (con't):
need for more revenue and, 191; portfolio, 53; progressive taxation and, 63, 64; purpose of, 50; in research and development, 50, 55; rewards for, 50–51; risk and, 50–51; tax reform proposals and, 182
Ireland, **79**, **93**, 128, **150**, 210, **211**
Italy, 75, 77, **93**, 128, 156, 203, **211**

Japan, 77, 79, **93**, 110, **150**, 201, **211**
Jefferson, Thomas, 4
Job Creation and Worker Assistance Act (2002), **216**
jobs. *See* employment/unemployment
Jobs and Growth Tax Relief Reconciliation Act (2002), **220**
Jobs and Growth Tax Relief Reconciliation Act (2003), **216**
Johnson, Calvin, 160
Johnson, David, 70
Johnson, Lyndon B., 8–9, 168
Johnson, Simon, 187
Joint Committee on Taxation, U.S. Congress, 14, 25, 40, 41, 42, 100, 117, 134, 168, 171, 179
Jorgenson, Dale, 220
Judge, Clark, 228

Kaplow, Louis, 100
Kasten, Bob, 171–72, 232
Kemp, Jack, 9, 13, 169–70, 171–72, 180, 232
Kennedy, John F., 8–9, 64, 68, 167
Keogh plans, 93
Keynes, John Maynard, 71, 168
Keynesian economics, 8–9, 210, 218
Klein, Ezra, 227, 228
Kleinbard, Edward, 182
Korea, **93**, **150**, 210, **211**
Korean War, 8, 98
Kosciuszko, Thaddeus, 4
Kuznets, Simon, 64

labor: Bush tax cuts and, **219**; corporate taxes and, 145; economic growth and, 50, 53; FairTax and, 179; foreign taxes and, 79, 80; homeownership and, 109; immobility of, 109; supply of, 36–38, 50, 53, 79; tax rates and, 36–38, 53; in World War II, 98
Laffer, Arthur, 228
Laffer Curve, 228, 236
Lazear, Edward, 46

legislative process, tax, 13–18
Levenstam, David, 207–8
liberals: Bush tax cuts and, 217; capital gains and, 137, 138; corporate taxes and, 146, 151, 152; history of federal income taxation and, 10; tax reform and, 167, 168, 169, 172, 182; and unfairness of regressive tax systems, 81; VAT and, 201, 202, 212. *See also specific person*
lifetime learning credit, **36**
Lindsey, Lawrence, 45, 216
lobbyists, 15–17, 55
local government/taxes, 33, 35, 52, 111, 115–22, 179
loopholes, tax, 38, 39, 40, 89–90, 137, 151, 161, 167–68, 181, 209, 231, 232
Luxembourg, 76, **93**, **211**

macroeconomic effects: tax changes and, 41–44, 45
Making Work Pay Credit, 71, 91
Mankiw, Greg, 43–44
manufacturing, 4, 5
Marès, Arnaud, 186–87
marginal tax rates: Americans for Tax Reform and, 225; charitable contributions and, 123, 127; corporate taxes and, **145**; distribution (2011) of, 32, **32**, 33; effects on selected tax provisions of (2010) of, **36**; foreign taxes and, 77–78, **77**; importance of, 32; labor supply and, 36–38, 53; in 1970s, 9; phaseouts and, 35, **35**; tax-exempt bonds and, 120; tax reform and, 38; wealthy and, 33
mark–up sessions, 16, 17
Marx, Karl, 59
McCain, John, 99–100, 217, 230
McConnell, Mitch, 44, 189
McCulloch, J. R., 59
Medicare, 87, 97, 100, 101–2, 185, 186, 190, 201, 212, 227
Mexico, **93**, **211**
Mill, John Stuart, 23
Mills, Ogden, 170
Mills, Wilbur, 8
Modigliani, Franco, 69
monetary policy, 191
Moody's, 186, 187
mortgage interest: capping of, 110; as deduction, 107–9, **108**, 112; expenditures and, 98, 107, 112; fairness and, 108–9; flat tax and, 176, 177;

in foreign countries, 81, 110; hidden American welfare state and, 92; horizontal equity and, 88; Norquist and, 231; poor and, **108**; progressive taxation and, 60; revenue and, 39–40, 98; spending and, 92, 107, 112; tax loopholes and, 89; tax rates and, 35, 39–40, 107, 110; and time period over which to tax people, 25; wealthy and, 108

Moscovitch, Edward, 116

Mulligan, Casey, 209

Mulroney, Brian, 201

Murdoch, Rupert, 144

mutual funds, 140

Nakasone, Yasuhiro, 201

National Association of Home Builders, 107

National Association of Realtors, 107

national highway system, 50

Netherlands, 80, 81, **93**, **150**, 210, **211**

News Corporation, 144

9-9-9 plan, 181–82

Niskanen, Bill, 45, 229

Nixon, Richard M., 168, 200

Norquist, Grover, 225–34, 236

Norway, **79**, **93**, **150**, **211**

Nunn, Sam, 180

Obama, Barack, 10, 17, 71, 138, 149, 215

Office of Legislative Affairs, U.S. Treasury, 14

Office of Management and Budget, U.S., 41, 188

Office of Tax Analysis, U.S. Congress, 40

Office of Tax Policy, U.S. Treasury, 14

"offsetting receipts/collections," 87

oil production tax, 41

Omnibus Budget Reconciliation Act (1986), **45**

Omnibus Budget Reconciliation Act (1987), **45**

O'Neill, Paul, 69

Organization for Economic Cooperation and Development (OECD), 75, 76, 77, **78**, 81, **93**, **93**, **150**, 156, 210, **211**

Parker, Jonathan, 70

partnerships, 143, 145, 146

"pass-through" entities, 146

Pawlenty, Tim, 44

PAYGO (pay-as-you-go) requirement, 41

payroll taxes: EITC and, 212; FairTax and, 178; flat tax and, 176; foreign taxes and, 77, **78**; health care and, 97–98, 103, 212; Social Security and, 7; tax credits and, 90, 91; tax rates and, 33; tax reform proposals and, 176, 178, 180; VAT and, 202, 212

"Pease," 119

pensions, 35, 52, 93, 99, 102

personal exemptions, 60, 61, 64, 119, 171, 176, 177, 180, 181

phaseouts, 35–36, **35**, 111, 119

Philo, 155–56

Poland, **93**, 210, **211**

political contributions, 55, 125–26, 236

politics: Bush tax cuts and, 217; future of tax reform and, 235–37; national debt and, 189; need for more revenue and, 192–93; think-tank corruption and, 126–27; VAT and, 201–2, 203, 209

poor/poverty: capital gains and, 139, **139**; definition of income and, 26; distribution tables and, 26; FairTax and, 178; foreign taxes and, 79; income tax liability of, **213**; mortgage interest and, **108**; progressive taxation and, 59, 60, 64; refundable tax credits and, 90–91; tax administration and, 160; tax reform proposals and, 180; VAT and, 202, 212–13

Portugal, **93**, 201, 210, **211**

Posner, Richard, 192

presidency: future of tax reform and, 236–37; tax legislation process and, 14

productivity, 50, 52, **219**

progressive movement, 5

progressive taxation: businesses/corporations and, 61, 62; citizenship and, 63; de facto, 60–61; foreign taxes and, 77–78, 80; justification/intention for, 59, 61, 63–64; personal exemptions and, 60, 61, 64; poor and, 59, 60; as practical necessity, 63–64; tariff as form of, 4, 21; tax rates and, 60, 63, 64; tax reform proposals and, 181; tax unit and, 24; wealthy and, 59, 60, 61–63, 64

property taxes: business cycles and, 72; and community property laws, 24; as deduction, 107, 111, 115; definition of income and, 21; economic growth and, 54; foreign taxes and, 78; hidden American welfare state and, 93; horizontal equity and, 88; impact of federal taxes on state and local government and, 117; revenue volatility and, 72; and time period over which to tax people, 25

proportionate taxation, 59
Proposition 13 (California), 169, 170

Rabushka, Alvin, 171, 175–76
Railroad Retirement Revenue Act (1983), 45
railroads, 147
Rand, Ayn, 62
Reagan, Ronald: capital gains and, 137; EITC and, 91; history of tax reform and, 170, 171, 172; and impact of federal taxes on state and local government, 117; Norquist comments about, 227; tax cuts of, 9–10, 44–45, 215, 232, 233; tax increases of, 44, **45**, 215, 227, 232; tax reform and, 232; VAT and, 200
rebates, tax, 69–71, 200, 202, 218, 221
recession: Bush tax cuts and, 216, 218; business cycles and, 68, 69, 70, 72; capital gains and, 136; of 1937–38, 7; of 1969, 9; of 1973–75, 69, 70; progressive taxation and, 64; revenue volatility and, 72; tax rebates and, 69, 70; of 2001, 70; of 2008, 70
Recovery Act (2009), 121
refunds, tax, 156
regressive taxes, 78, 81, 202, 212–13
rent, 23, 80, 88, 108–9, 111, 176
Republicans: Bush tax cuts and, 217–20; capital gains and, 137, 138; "deficits don't matter" views of, 90; future of tax reform and, 225–32, 235–37; history of federal income taxation and, 10; and how tax legislation is made, 16; and impact of taxes on economic growth, 49; need for compromise between Democrats and, 236–37; and need for more revenue, 189; Norquist role in tax reform and, 225–32; and relationship between tax rates and tax revenues, 43, 44; tax administration and, 157; tax credits and, 91; and tax cuts as means to achieving economic growth, 71; tax reform and, 168, 169, 170, 171–72, 180–82, 225–32; VAT and, 207. *See also specific person*
research and development, 50, 55
retail sales taxes. *See* sales taxes
retirement, 35, 93, 190, 231
return-free system, 159
revenue: Bush tax cuts and, 215, 216, **216**, 219, 220, 221, 222; business cycle and, 71; capital gains and, 134, 136–38,

139; charitable contributions and, 123, 127; Clinton administration and, 228; corporate taxes and, 146, 151–52; dynamic scoring and, 42–44; FairTax and, 179; flat tax and, 177; forecasts about, 40–41, 185–86; GDP and, 4, 9, 10, 45, 197; and government impact on economy, 87; health care and, 97–99; history of federal income taxes and, 4, 9, 10; and impact of federal taxes on state and local government, 120–21; inflation and, 188–89; mandatory spending and, 185–86; mortgage interest deduction and, 112; need for more, 185–95; as negative spending, 87; Norquist role in tax reform and, 228, 233; politics and, 192–93; progressive taxation and, 63; relationship between tax rates and, 39–48; tariff as primary source of, 4; tax rebates and, 71; tax reform and, 39, 46, 167–68, 171, 181, 236, 237; VAT and, 197, 200, 202–3, 207, 210; volatility of, 72–73, 120–21
"Ricardian equivalence" theory, 229
rich. *See* wealthy
risk, 50–51, 186–87, 189
Roberts, Paul Craig, 64
Rockefeller, John D. Jr., 7
Romer, Christina, 191
Roosevelt, Franklin D., 6–7
Roth, Bill, 9, 169–70
Ryan, Paul, 181

sales taxes: as consumption tax, 197; FairTax and, 172, 178, 179; and impact of federal taxes on state and local government, 115; Norquist role in tax reform and, 232; rates for, 198; tax reform and, 111, 172, 181; VAT and, 200, 203, 209, 213
savings: Bush tax cuts and, **219**, 221; business cycles and, 69, 70, 71; by businesses, 51; capital gains and, 138; definition of income and, 22–23, 24; economic growth and, 50–53; foreign taxes and, 80; by government, 51–52; home equity as, 89; motives for, 51; need for more revenue and, 191; negative, 52; Norquist role in tax reform and, 226; personal/private, 51, 52; tax rebates and, 69, 70, 71; tax reform proposals and, 180, 182; VAT and, 197–98, 201; yield on, 50–51
savings account, health care, 97, 100–101, 103, 230

Schiff, Irwin, 158
Schumer, Charles, 118
Scott, Maurice, 149
securities tax, 71–72
self-employed, 35, 93, 97, 103, 160
semantics, budget, 94–95
Senate, U.S.: tax legislation process and, 13, 15–16. *See also specific person or committee*
services, government: in foreign countries, 75–77
Shapiro, Matthew, 70
shareholders, 143, 144, 150. *See also* dividends
shelters, tax, 62, 167
Simon, William, 168
Simons, Henry C., 23
simplification of tax code, 155, 159, 161, 172, 175, 235
Simpson, Alan, 181
Simpson-Bowles plan, 181
Sixteenth Amendment, 5–6, 158, 207–8
Slemrod, Joel, 70
Slovak Republic, **93**, 210, **211**
Snipes, Wesley, 158
Social Security, 7, **36**, **45**, 102, 181, 185, 190, 201, 212
sole proprietorships, 143, 146
Souleles, Nicholas, 70
Spain, **79**, **93**, **211**
spending: age-related, 190; Americans for Tax Reform and, 225; budget semantics and, 94–95; Clinton administration and, 10, 228; cuts in, 189–91, **192–93**, 207, 229; discretionary, 237; distribution tables for, 27; economic growth and, 49, 52; foreign taxes and, 76–77, 79; GDP and, 92, 190; government impact on economy and, 87; history of federal income taxes and, 8, 10; and impact of federal taxes on state and local government, 117–18, 120–21; mandatory, 185–86, 189–90, 220; need for more revenue and, 185–86, 189–91, 192, **192–93**, 193; negative, 87; Norquist role in tax reform and, 226, 227, 229; public opinion about, 192, **192–93**; relationship of tax rates and revenue and, 41, 42; revenue volatility and, 72; and tax expenditures budget, 167–69; tax reform and, 167–69, 179, 182, 236–37; tax visibility and, 209; through the tax code, 87–96. *See also type of spending or specific topic*

Stabilization Act (1942), 98
Standard and Poor's, 186, 189, 190
starve-the-beast theory, 170, 226–29
state taxes: complexity of taxes and, 160; deduction for, 111, 115–22; FairTax and, 179–80; foreign taxes and, 77; Norquist and, 232; tax base for, 115; tax rates for, 33, 35, 115
states: economic growth and, 52; FairTax and, 178, 179; impact of federal taxes on, 115–22; IRS relationship with, 115; tax administration and, 160; tax units and, 24; VAT and, 213. *See also* state taxes
Steindel, Charles, 69
stimulus, 138, 186, 201, 216
stock market, 219, 228
Stockman, David, 171, 192
subsidies, 54, 232
"substitution effect," 37–38
Summers, Larry, 68, 202
Superfund Amendments and Reauthorization Act (1986), **45**
Supreme Court, U.S., rulings of: about capital gains, 133, 134; about corporate taxes, 208; about definition of income, 21, 22; about elections of 2000, 218; about flat tax (1895), 5; about tax exemptions on state and local bonds, 120; about tax legislation process, 13; about tax unit, 24; about taxing powers of Congress, 207–8
Surrey, Stanley, 167–68
surtax, 8–9, 190
Suskind, Ron, 69–70
Sweden, 75, 77, **93**, 128, **150**, **211**
Switzerland, 128, 151, 156, **211**

Taft, William Howard, 5
tariffs, 4–5, 21
Tax Act (2010), **220**
tax base: Americans for Tax Reform and, 225; broadening of, 38, 39, 107, 152, 225, 232, 235; definition of, 175; flat tax and, 175, 177; state, 115; tax reform and, 38, 39, 171, 175, 177, 181, 182, 235; VAT and, 177, 202, 203, 213
tax code: anomalies in, 36; complexity of, 26, 155, 159–60, 175; distribution tables and, 26, 27; interaction of provisions in, 39–40; investments and, 54; need for changes in, 237; progressive taxation and, 63; and relationship of tax rates and revenue, 39–40, 42; sav-

ings incentives in, 51; simplification of, 155, 159, 161, 172, 175, 235; spending through the, 87–96; tax legislation process and, 18

Tax Equity and Fiscal Responsibility Act (TEFRA) (1982), 13, **45**, 171

tax holidays, 151

Tax Increase Prevention and Reconciliation Act (2005), **216**

tax policies: assumptions concerning, 43; incoherent, 17–18; lobbyists' role in determining, 15–17; tax legislation process and, 13–18

Tax Policy Center, 61, 89, 181

tax rates: Bush tax cuts and, 217, 218, 219; capital gains and, 35, 54, 134, 135, 136, 137–38, 139, 140, 169; for corporations, 53–54, 143, 144–45, **145**, 150, 151; definition of income and, 26; distribution tables and, 26; dividends and, **150**; FairTax and, 178–79; federal income (2011), **31**; flat tax and, 175–76, 177; foreign taxes and, 77–78, 80; future of tax reform and, 235, 236; GDP and, 32; health care and, 98, 100; history of federal income taxes and, 5–6, 7–8, 9–10; history of tax reform and, 167, 169–70, 172; how to understand, 31–38; and impact of federal taxes on state and local government, 116, 117–18; individual, **31**, 146; Kennedy tax cut and, 8; labor supply and, 36–38, 53; mortgage interest and, 107, 110; need for more revenue and, 193; negative, 26; between 1913 and mid-1930s, 5–6; between 1940 and 1990s, 7–10, 98; Norquist and, 225, 228, 231, 232; perceptions and reality of, 33, **33**; progressive taxation and, 60, 63, 64; Reagan tax cut and, 9–10; relationship of revenue and, 39–48; sales, 198; state, 115; tax loopholes and, 89; tax reform proposals and, 178–79, 180, 181; taxable income and, 34–36; variety of, 31; VAT and, 202–3, 207, 208–9, 210, 211, 212, 213; for wealthy, 33–34, **34**, 64, 89–90, **90**, 100; and which rate matters, 32–33. *See also* tax cuts; tax increases

tax reform: agreement in views about, 235; Bush commission for, 180–81; Bush tax cuts and, 222; citizens' role in, 235; complexity of, 18; corporate taxes and, 145–46, 149, 151–52, 160; definition of income and, 27–28; distribution tables and, 27–28; essence of, 38; fairness and, 172, 236; foreign taxes and, 81; goals of, 27–28, 39, 95, 155, 193, 230; history of, 167–74; and impact of federal taxes on states, 115–22; need for compelling reason to enact, 235; of 1980s, 236; and Norquist's role/views, 225–34; politics and, 235–37; popular proposals for, 175–84; principles for guiding, 180; tax legislation process and, 18; trade-offs for, 235; of 2012, 215. *See also specific proposal or topic*

Tax Reform Act (1969), 18, 136, 168, 169

Tax Reform Act (1976), 18, 168, 169

Tax Reform Act (1986), 9, 18, 111, 146, 152, 172, 180, 225, 235, 236

tax software, 156

tax units, 24, **27**

taxes: as levied on taxes, 198; as painful, 178, 190, 197, 201–2, 210; public's tolerance for, 187; and time period over which to tax people, 25; visibility of, 209. *See also specific topic*

"taxpayer protection pledge," Norquist, 225

Taylor, John, 216

Tea Party, **33**, 225, 232, 233, 236

technical corrections bill, 16

technology, 50, 98, 138, 228

Tennessee Valley Authority (TVA), 87

think tanks, 125–27, 168

Thirteenth Amendment, 158

Thompson, Earl, 62

Tobin, James, 72

transactions tax, 140

transfers, income, 37–38

Treasury Department, U.S.: "Blueprints" study of, 168–69; Bush tax cuts and, 215, 216; business cycles and, 72; capital gains and, 136–37, 228; charitable contributions and, 123; corporate taxes and, 145, 152; definition of income and, 25, 26; distribution tables and, 25, 26; FairTax and, 179; history of tax reform and, 167–69, 172; and impact of federal taxes on state and local government, 115, 117, 118; marginal tax rates and, 9; and relationship of tax rates and revenue, 42–44; revenue estimating by, 40, 41; revenue volatility and, 72; role in tax reform of, 18; tax administration and, 156, 159, 161; tax credits and, 91; tax cuts and, 136–37; tax legislation process and, 14, 17, 18; Tax Reform Act of 1986 and, 235

Treasury securities, 188, 189, 191

Truman, Harry S., 215

Ture, Norman, 200

two-earner couples, 24

Ullman, Al, 201

unearned income: flat tax and, 176, 177. *See also* capital gains; dividends; interest; rent

unemployment compensation, 37

United Kingdom, 21–22, **77**, **79**, **93**, 150, 203, **211**

Urban Institute, 101

USA Tax, 180

value-added tax (VAT): businesses/corporations and, 177, 200, 203; case against, 207–14; case for, 197–205; as complicated, 209; as consumption tax, 197, 207, 226; credit-invoice style, 177; deadweight cost and, 197–98, 202, 203, 210; exemptions and, 209; FairTax and, 180; flat tax and, 177; in foreign countries, 201, 202, 203, 210; GDP and, 197, 203; as hidden tax, 208–9; history of, 199–200; and how it works, 199; implementation of, 203; inflation and, 201, 209, 210–11; as money machine, 200, 202, 210–12; Norquist and, 225–26; politics of, 201–2, 203; poor and, 212; as regressive tax, 212–13; revenue and, 197, 200, 202–3; savings and, 197–98, 226; Sixteenth Amendment and, 207–8; spending and, 200, 207, 210, 214; "subtraction method," 177, 182; tax base and, 177, 202, 203, 213; tax cuts and, 226; tax rates and, 202–3, 207, 210, 211, 212, 213; tax reform and, 159, 181, 182, 203, 212

Viard, Alan, 45–46

wages, 77, 80, 91, 98, 99, 109, 145, 176, 177, 179, 182

"Wagner's Law," 75

Ways and Means Committee, U.S. House, 14, 15, 17, 167, 172

wealthy: AMT and, 119; as benefiting from government, 62; Bush tax cuts and, 221; capital gains and, 138, **139**, 140; charitable contributions and, 123, 124–25; corporate taxes and, 146; definition of income and, 26, 27; distribution tables and, 26, 27; economic growth and, 53; foreign taxes and, 80; health care and, 100, 101; history of federal income taxes and, 6–8; and impact of federal taxes on state and local government, 118; income tax liability of, **213**; labor supply and, 53; mortgage interest and, 108; phaseout of personal exemptions for, 119; political contributions of, 236; progressive taxation and, 59, 60, 61–63, 64; property taxes and, 111; Reagan tax cut and, 9; Roosevelt proposal concerning, 6–7; Social Security and, 102; tax administration and, 159; tax credits and, 91; tax loopholes and, 89; tax rates and, 33–34, **34**, 64, 89–90, **90**, 100, 146, 172; tax reform and, 167, 172, 180, 182, 235–36; VAT and, 202

Weidenbaum, Murray, 200

welfare, 26, 90, 91, 92–93, **93**

welfare state, 76, 81

Will, George, 192, 200, 207

Williamson, Kevin, 226

Wilson, Woodrow, 5

windfall profits tax, 41, 55

withholding taxes, 156, 159

Working Families Tax Relief Act (2004), **216**, **220**

working poor. *See* poor/poverty

World War I, 5, 22, 134, 170, 199

World War II, 4, 7–8, 67, 76, 98, 188

Wyden, Ron, 181, 231

About the Author

Bruce Bartlett is a columnist for the Economix blog of the *New York Times*; for the *Fiscal Times,* an online newspaper covering the economy, business, and personal finance; and for *Tax Notes,* a weekly magazine for tax policymakers and practitioners. He also contributes regularly to the *Financial Times.* Bartlett's work is informed by many years in government, including service on the staffs of Congressman Ron Paul, Congressman Jack Kemp, and Senator Roger Jepsen and as staff director of the Joint Economic Committee of Congress, senior policy analyst in the Reagan White House, and deputy assistant secretary for economic policy at the Treasury Department during the George H. W. Bush administration. He lives in Virginia.